Half a Job

Bad and Good Part-Time Jobs
in a Changing Labor Market

Half a Job

Bad and Good Part-Time Jobs in a Changing Labor Market

CHRIS TILLY

Temple University Press **T** Philadelphia

To Marie and Amanda

Temple University Press, Philadelphia 19122
Copyright © 1996 by Temple University
All rights reserved
Published 1996
Printed in the United States of America

♾ The paper used in this publication meets the requirements
of the American National Standard for Information Sciences—
Permanence of Paper for Printed Library Materials,
ANSI Z39.48-1984

Text design by Arlene Putterman

Library of Congress Cataloging-in-Publication Data

Tilly, Chris.
    Half a job : bad and good part-time jobs in a changing
labor market / Chris Tilly.
        p.   cm.
    Includes bibliographical references and index.
    ISBN 1-56639-381-7 (cloth). — ISBN 1-56639-382-5
(paper)
    1. Part-time employment—United States. I. Title.
HD5110.2.U5T548   1996
331.25′72—dc20   95-20654

CONTENTS

TABLES AND FIGURES

ACKNOWLEDGMENTS

■ IT IS TRADITIONAL TO WAIT UNTIL THE END OF THE acknowledgments for a nod to the patient spouse and family, but let me instead begin by thanking my wife, Marie Kennedy, and my stepdaughter, Amanda Kennedy. The two of them provided me with every conceivable form of support as I wrote the dissertation out of which this book developed: emotional, financial, intellectual. Amanda even served as an able research assistant for data entry tasks. By the time I began to turn the dissertation into a book, Amanda had left home to pursue her own part-time jobs, but Marie continued to provide warmth, wisdom, and the occasional hard question. I dedicate this book to them.

There are many other people I want to thank for their assistance on this project. First and foremost, I owe a debt of gratitude to my dissertation committee in the departments of Economics and Urban Studies and Planning at the Massachusetts Institute of Technology: Ben Harrison, Michael Piore, and Lester Thurow. Their guidance, patience, and support made this research an enjoyable and enriching experience. Their secretaries, Meg Gross, Linda Woodbury, and Mary Lane, also helped make the process a pleasure, not least by facilitating communication with these sometimes elusive professors. For the book phase of the project, I thank Charlie Derber for spurring me to turn this work into a book, Eileen Appelbaum for offering a very helpful review of the manuscript, and Michael Ames, my editor at Temple University Press, for providing clear and useful advice.

Others at MIT also offered their help along the way. Bob McKersie set up my initial company interviews, thereby boosting my confidence and giving me a flying start. And my "shadow" dissertation committee of Katharine Abraham, Hank Farber, Tom Kochan, Lisa Lynch, Paul Osterman, and Bob Thomas faithfully read and commented on early drafts, giving me essential feedback even though they were not serving on my official committee.

Many people took the time to discuss ideas and research techniques with me. I had helpful discussions with Teresa Amott, Eileen Appelbaum, Rick Belous, Barry Bluestone, Françoise Carré, Joel Cutcher-Gershenfeld, the *Dollars and Sense* editorial collective, Virginia duRivage, Jeff Faux, Roz Feldberg, Lucy Gorham, Judy Gregory, Chuck Heckscher, Steve Herzenberg, Sarah Kuhn, Gary Loveman, Larry Mishel, Thierry Noyelle, Jim Rebitzer, Bert Spector, Miren Uriarte, Kirsten Wever, and many others, including seminar audiences at MIT, Wellesley College, the University of Massachusetts at Lowell, the Harvard Trade Union Program, and the Allied Social Sciences Association annual meetings.

Still other people generously provided specific types of information. I am particularly grateful to Tom Nardone of the U.S. Bureau of Labor Statistics, Ellen Newton of the United Food and Commercial Workers, and Jean Ross of the Service Employees International Union for offering assistance with data above and beyond the call of duty. Laura Carcia and Marian McKenzie, reference librarians extraordinaire, made using the MIT Dewey Library's Industrial Relations Collection a breeze. I also wish to single out Barbara Baran, Kathleen Christensen, Thierry Noyelle, Paul Osterman, and Jim Rebitzer, who made available unpublished and hard-to-find research. For information on the retail industry, I thank Leslie Nulty of the United Food and Commercial Workers. For information about insurance, I thank Sharon Danaan of Nine to Five, Alan Janger of the Conference Board, Johanan Lew, and Pat Reeve. Matt Bralis and Don Hopey of the *Pittsburgh Press,* Denise DiPasquale, Steve Garber, John Miller, and Ed Montgomery oriented me to the unfamiliar city of Pittsburgh. Jennifer Coplon, Michael Lettau of the U.S. Census Bureau, Edie Rasell of the Economic Policy Institute, Jim Sauber of the National Association of Letter Carriers, Kathy Schoen of the Service Employees International Union, and Phil Tabbita of the American Postal Workers Union also provided vital information.

In addition to the people I can name, there are the dozens of interviewees who must remain anonymous. To my amazement, every interviewee was cheerful and eager to help, even when I caught them in the middle of crises at work. I particularly thank the informants at the Boston-area companies I have dubbed EZ Mart, SuperValu, Healthco, and Eternal Life, who submitted to repeated interviews, dug up data, and prevailed upon their colleagues, their employees, and sometimes even their bosses to be interviewed.

The staffs of MIT's Information Processing Services and of Mercury Manuscripts gave excellent assistance with data processing and tape transcription, respectively. At a later phase of the project, the computer support staff of the University of Massachusetts at Boston, and particularly the unflappable Gourish Hosangady, helped me with additional analysis; my colleague Randy Albelda generously allowed me to conduct this analysis on her computer account.

Partial funding for this research was provided by the National Graduate Fellowship/Jacob Javits Fellowship Program, the National Association of Letter Carriers and the American Postal Workers Union, the Cuddahy Foundation, the Economic Policy Institute, and the MIT Department of Economics.

Portions of this book are based on my earlier published work. Chapter 2 draws in part on "Reasons for the Continuing Growth of Part-Time Employment," *Monthly Labor Review*, Vol. 114, No 3 (March 1991), pp. 10–18. Some elements of Chapters 4 and 5 build on "Dualism in Part-Time Employment," *Industrial Relations*, Vol. 31, No. 2 (Spring 1992), pp. 330–47; and on "Two Faces of Part-Time Work" in Barbara Warmé, Katherina Lundy, and Larry Lundy, eds., *Working Part-Time: Risks and Opportunities* (New York: Praeger, 1992), pp. 227–38. I advanced my general argument, in rough form, in *Short Hours, Short Shrift: The Causes and Consequences of Growing Part-Time Work,* a report issued by the Economic Policy Institute in Washington, D.C., in 1990, which later was published, in revised form, as a chapter in Virginia duRivage, ed., *New Policies for the Part-Time and Contingent Workforce* (Armonk, NY: M. E. Sharpe, 1992), pp. 15–44. I owe very special thanks to Karin Aguilar San Juan, at that time an editor of *Dollars and Sense* magazine, who dreamed up the title "Half a Job" for my article for that magazine: "Working Half a Job: Part-Timers Fill Employers' Need for Disposable Workers," No. 130 (October 1987), pp. 20–22.

Chapter 8, the concluding policy chapter, is less an individual product than the other seven chapters. Its central ideas are the product of my long and fruitful collaboration with Françoise Carré of the University of Massachusetts at Boston and Virginia duRivage of the Communication Workers of America. This association has resulted in three papers: "Representing the Part-Time and Contingent Workforce: Challenges for Unions and Public Policy," in Sheldon Friedman, Richard W. Hurd, Rudolph A. Oswald, and Ronald L. Seeber, eds., *Restoring the Promise of American Labor Law* (Ithaca, NY: ILR Press, 1994), pp. 314–23, "Piecing Together the Fragmented Workplace: Unions and Public Policy on Part-Time and Temporary Employment," in Lawrence Flood, ed., *Unions and Public Policy* (Westport, CT: Greenwood Press, 1995); and

"Making Labor Law Work for Part-Time and Contingent workers," in Kathleen Barker and Kathleen Christensen, eds.; *Contingent Workers: From Entitlement to Privilege* (chapter and book titles are working titles; manuscript currently under consideration). In Chapter 8, I have drawn extensively on these papers.

Half a Job Is Not Enough

1

■ AMERICA IS WORRIED ABOUT THE GROWTH OF PART-TIME and temporary employment. *Time* magazine, in a 1993 cover story, bemoaned "The Temping of America" (Castro 1993). A 1994 *Fortune* cover story trumpeted "The Contingency Work Force" (Fierman 1994). The new prominence of part-time and temporary jobs brings with it fears of widening instability and insecurity in the workforce. "If there was a national fear index," Richard Belous, chief economist for the National Planning Association, told *Time*'s reporter, "it would be directly related to the growth of contingent work" (quoted in Castro 1993, 44).

But how much do we actually know about these growing forms of employment? Start with a key fact: out of the 25 percent of the U.S. workforce usually identified as contingent, roughly four fifths—the large majority—is accounted for by part-time workers.[1] In addition, 40 percent of temporary workers work part-time hours (Plewes 1988). Part-time work is by far the most common form of nonstandard employment.

Moreover, part-time work is not new. In 1957, 13 percent of the workforce toiled part-time. The part-time legions have grown gradually over the last 40 years, unlike the temporary workforce, which exploded fifteen-fold between 1968 and 1992 (while the labor force as a whole did not even double).

What *is* new, or at least newer, is the long-term expansion of the *involuntary* part-time workforce—part-time workers who would prefer full-time work.[2] Between the 1950s and the early 1970s, only voluntary part-time employment outgrew the workforce as a whole, while involuntary part-time work simply kept pace with workforce growth. Beginning in the early 1970s, these positions were reversed, and the ranks of involuntary part-timers swelled faster than overall workforce expansion.

The result—a growing percentage of the working population who are trapped in part-time jobs against their will—is cause for serious concern.

But despite the large size and long standing of the part-time workforce, and despite the warning flag raised by widening involuntary part-time employment, many questions about part-time work remain unanswered. Three major issues stand out, which this book shall address. Why is part-time employment growing? Since it is the involuntary part-time workforce that has grown in relative terms, it must be the choices of employers, not workers, that are driving the process. Why, then, are employers creating more part-time jobs? Second, what are the different types of part-time employment that serve distinct purposes for employers? And third, exactly how do businesses use and make decisions about their part-time workers?

Should We Be Worried?

Before digging more deeply into the questions, it is useful to return to the note on which this chapter opened: should we worry about the growth of part-time employment? Is it fair to disparage a part-time job as only "half a job"?

No consensus reigns on this issue. In a variety of forums, experts argue whether part-time and contingent work represents the "innovation and flexibility" that are "the keys to successful work patterns of the future" (Randolph Hale of the National Association of Manufacturers, quoted in Bureau of National Affairs 1986, 91) or the basis of "a new sub-class of workers" (John Zalusky of the AFL-CIO, quoted in ibid., 99). Among Fortune 500 CEOs, 48 percent say the trend toward using more part-time and contingent workers is "good for the U.S." (Fierman 1994, 32). But Deb Donaldson, a part-time retail clerk in Moline, Illinois, responds, "We understand it's just business, but it's still awfully demeaning" (quoted in Castro 1993, 46).

In an optimistic view, part-time job growth could be seen as responsive to the needs of both businesses and employees. Potential workers—students, housewives, retirees—want jobs on nonstandard schedules and perhaps are willing to accept somewhat lower compensation in return for this flexibility. Employers are looking for workers to staff peak times or odd hours. Part-time employment brings the two groups together in a felicitous match. The gradual growth of part-time employment reflects the increase of both sets of needs. If this were the explanation for part-time expansion, it would seem to be a fairly benign one.

But this explanation is wrong. The expansion in the U.S. part-time labor market actually gives us a great deal of worry. Most importantly, virtually all of the increase in the rate of part-time employment in the United States during the last two decades is due to the expansion of *involuntary* part-time employment. An involuntary part-time job *is* only half a job in the sense that it is only half the job that the employee wants. And about one-quarter of the part-time workers in the United States are working part-time involuntarily—most of them because they are unable to find a full-time job. At the same time, millions of full-time workers would prefer part-time hours but are unable to obtain them, while millions of others remain jobless as they search for a part-time job.

Throughout 1993, an average of 6.1 million Americans, or 5.5 percent of those at work,[3] were working part-time involuntarily—a number comparable to the annual average of 6.5 million who were unemployed (U.S. Bureau of Labor Statistics, *Employment and Earnings,* January 1994). Although the rate of involuntary part-time employment (the percentage of the workforce who are involuntary part-timers) usually drops during economic expansions, this rate has risen over the last 20 years (Ichniowski and Preston 1985; Ehrenberg, Rosenberg, and Li 1988). Furthermore, in the current "jobless recovery," involuntary part-time employment actually grew as the economy expanded—the only time this has happened in the post–World War II period (Mishel and Bernstein 1993).

If involuntary part-time jobs were transitory, or if they involved only a few hours less than full-time jobs, there would be less cause for concern. But neither is true. Involuntary part-time employment is in many cases a prolonged predicament. Of persons with involuntary part-time employment during 1985 (the last year these particular data were published), 38 percent experienced the problem for 15 weeks or more, including 19 percent who were involuntarily working part-time for over 26 weeks (U.S. Bureau of Labor Statistics 1987). The average number of hours worked by involuntary part-timers in 1993 was 22.3 hours per week, about half of the full-time hours they sought.

In addition to the roughly one-quarter of part-time workers who would prefer full-time jobs, many others would like to have more hours. Economist Susan Shank (1986) of the Bureau of Labor Statistics reported that 45 percent of those between the ages of 25 and 54 who were working 1 to 14 hours a week would prefer to be working more hours (and earning more money). As the hours of work increase, the percentage of workers who would prefer more hours declines.

Furthermore, many people counted by the official statistics as voluntary part-time workers are in fact trapped in part-time hours by the unavailability of satisfactory child care or elder care. Nearly 35 percent of women who are working part-time or looking for part-time work say they would work more hours if good child care were available (Presser and Baldwin 1980). These constraints bind most severely among the one-quarter of U.S. families with children that are headed by a mother only. Half of these women who worked part-time in 1983 said they would rather have worked full-time but were constrained by the high costs and unavailability of quality child care (U.S. House of Representatives 1989).

In addition to the involuntary part-time workers, many people who want part-time jobs are unable to find them. As many as 3 million people—7 percent of the full-timers in nonagricultural industries—are involuntary full-time workers who would prefer to work fewer hours and earn less money (Shank 1986). Another 1.6 million are unemployed workers seeking part-time jobs.[4] The inability to find a part-time job forces both groups to make an unpleasant choice between giving up income or sacrificing other needs, such as time spent on family or school responsibilities.

Both involuntary part-time and involuntary full-time employment are likely to be underreported due to the psychological phenomenon of cognitive dissonance (Akerlof and Dickens 1982), whereby people who find themselves in a situation that goes against their previous preferences will in many cases change their preferences. In other words, people will rationalize their situation *post hoc;* for example, some involuntary part-time workers will convince themselves that they actually prefer part-time hours.

The fact that workers are unable to obtain the hours of work they would prefer represents the most serious problem raised by part-time work. But the part-time surge raises other concerns as well. In terms of wages and benefits, the average part-time job can—once more—accurately be described as half a job. Part-timers—with median hourly wages 40 percent below those of full-time workers, fewer hours of work per week than full-timers, and on average fewer weeks of work per year than full-timers—are a growing group with low hourly wages and *very* low annual wages. Although not all part-time jobs are poor jobs, many are: part-time workers make up two-thirds of all people working at or below the minimum wage (Mellor and Haugen 1986).

Furthermore, families of part-time workers, and particularly of involuntary part-timers, tend to be at economic risk. In 1991 voluntary part-time workers had a median total family income approximately $1,600 less than full-timers, while involuntary part-timers in turn had a median family income $17,000 below that of voluntary part-timers. About 1 in 6 part-time workers—and 1 in 5 involuntary part-time workers—has a family income below the poverty line, compared to 1 in 37 year-round, full-time workers (Levitan and Conway 1988). And in half a million two-earner families, a spouse's part-time job is the slim margin keeping the family out of poverty (ibid.). In short, questions about what regulates the creation and compensation level of part-time jobs have major implications for understanding income distribution.

Taking a step back, the expanding part-time employment may be seen as part of a broader pattern of growing inequality and deteriorating employment opportunities. Observers ranging from liberal Paul Krugman (1990) to conservative Kevin Phillips (1990) have remarked on the widening gap between rich and poor during the 1970s and 1980s (for one recent review, see Tilly 1991c). In 1973 the richest one-fifth of U.S. households garnered 9.8 times as much income as the poorest fifth; by 1992 this ratio had risen to 11.7. Over the same period, the share of the wealthiest 5 percent rose from 4.0 to 4.9 times as much as that of the bottom fifth (U.S. Census Bureau 1993). The rising part-time employment helped feed this surge in inequality. Chris Tilly, Barry Bluestone, and Bennett Harrison (1986) discovered that some 42 percent of the growth of inequality in annual wages and salaries between 1978 and 1984 could be accounted for by the growth of part-time employment and the increased disparity in the earnings of part-time and full-time workers.[5]

Closely related to the concern about income distribution is the debate over the quality of jobs being created in the United States. This debate starts from the fact that the United States generated 32 million new jobs between 1973 and 1989, a period during which employment growth in Europe was essentially zero. It is common to attribute the difference to the greater "flexibility" of employment arrangements in the United States. But observers have questioned the advantage of such flexibility. For example, a participant at an Organization for Economic Cooperation and Development conference on "The Mechanisms of Employment Creation" expressed skepticism as "he returned to the familiar question of the flexibility of American workers, but pointed out that it [has] major drawbacks. Flexibility [is] associated with low wages, precarious jobs, poor social protection and poverty" (OECD Observer 1988, 12).[6]

The claim (made by Bluestone and Harrison 1986, among others) that U.S. employment growth has been fueled by low-paid, dead-end jobs provoked a flurry of research and polemic (Loveman and Tilly 1988; Burtless 1990). And on the surface, there is considerable evidence to support this contention. For example, between 1973 and 1993 real hourly wages for nonsupervisory workers fell by 14 percent, reversing the steady upward trend of the post—World War II years.

Again, part-time employment figures prominently in this debate. The vast majority of jobs with low annual wages—89 percent in 1985—are part-time or part-year jobs (Norwood 1987).[7] The AFL-CIO's Industrial Union Department (1986) calls the growth of involuntary part-time employment in particular an important reason "to be concerned not only with job creation but also with the *quality* of the jobs created" (p. 19).

Why Has Part-Time Employment
Continued to Grow?

Now we return to the three questions posed earlier: Why has part-time employment grown? What kinds of part-time jobs can be identified? How do employers use and manage these differing types of part-time employment? These queries frame the remainder of the book.

Chapter 2 takes on the challenge of explaining the long-term increase in part-time employment and starts by dismissing several possible explanations. Neither demographic trends, such as women's expanded participation in the labor force, nor higher unemployment (which generally brings involuntary part-time employment), nor a widening part-time/full-time wage and fringe benefit differential (which would make part-time workers cheaper and thus more attractive to employers) can account for the upward trend.

Instead, the rising part-time tide follows from two major changes. First, the industry mix in the United States has tilted toward trade and services, which have long depended on large numbers of part-timers. These industries have organized much of their workforce in a secondary labor market—a pool of low-wage, low-skill, high-turnover workers. Frequently, they have built this secondary labor market around part-time employment. Second, businesses within virtually every industry have switched from full-time to part-time work, once more expanding the secondary labor market.

Chapter 2 continues with an overview of the data and case studies used in this volume. This book combines two types of data. The first is survey data gathered by the U.S. Census Bureau and related agencies. The second, and more important, type comes from the 82 semistructured, face-to-face interviews that I conducted with employers, workers, unions, and other labor organizations during 1987 and 1988. Surprisingly few studies have utilized this method to obtain data. Given the size and complexity of the part-time workforce, I chose to focus on two industries—retail and insurance—which use high part-time and low part-time employment, respectively. I interviewed employers in these industries in two metropolitan areas; Boston and Pittsburgh, then experiencing a labor shortage and a labor surplus, respectively. Chapter 2 concludes by placing these industry-, city-, and time-specific case studies in context, comparing the broad patterns of part-time work in retail and insurance, and in Boston and Pittsburgh, with nationwide patterns.

To understand why the rate of part-time work has climbed within so many industries, we must turn to the questions of what kinds of part-time work businesses create and how they use them. Before attempting to answer these questions, I briefly consider in Chapter 3 what theory to use in scrutinizing part-time employment, a discussion that readers eager to examine the more empirical results may hurdle if they wish. In my theoretical explorations, I compare the reigning neoclassical economic approach with institutionalism, a mode of analysis that, despite its equally long pedigree, has fallen into disrepute in recent decades. I shall combine elements from both perspectives but draw particularly heavily on institutionalist thought. The story of part-time employment is driven by strategic behavior of employers, and features labor markets with persistent labor surpluses and sharp distinctions among the various categories of workers and jobs. While neoclassical theory cannot readily explain these phenomena, institutionalist thinking can offer important insights.

A key institutionalist concept for understanding part-time work is the internal labor market, which is a set of jobs within a firm linked by such common features as breadth of job definition, level of skill and responsibility, connection with job ladders, amount of compensation, and expected tenure. For this book, the critical distinction is between the secondary labor market—low-wage, low-skill jobs with little or no job ladder and high turnover—and all other labor markets, which do not share these features, although they differ among themselves in other ways. Internal labor markets other than the secondary one are collectively referred to as primary labor markets.

What Kinds of Part-Time Work Exist?

Chapters 4 and 5 consider the kinds of part-time work that are being created. Most writing treats part-time work as an undifferentiated mass. But part-time employment in the retail and insurance industries is not homogeneous but rather appears in two major types: secondary and retention.[8] In effect, they are "bad" and "good" part-time jobs, respectively.[9]

Secondary part-time employment is the form that part-time jobs take in secondary labor markets. A secondary part-time job is truly half a job. It is marked by low skill, low pay and fringe benefits, low productivity, and high turnover. Managers cite low compensation and scheduling flexibility as its key advantages. Secondary part-time work is founded upon the distinction between breadwinners and secondary workers, and is explicitly designed for the latter.

Secondary part-time workers include a substantial contingent of involuntary part-timers, who are not those faced with temporary reductions in hours but rather persons unable to find full-time jobs. Some of this involuntary part-time employment is frictional, meaning that workers take part-time jobs while looking for full-time work, which is available. But in many cases the full-time jobs do not exist, and workers remain in part-time positions. Persistent, involuntary part-time employment results from rigid part-time/full-time differentials in pay and benefits. When labor supply and demand are out of balance, the economy adjusts by shifting workers between part-time and full-time categories rather than altering the relative prices of part-time and full-time labor. Macroeconomic slack—the persistent excess supply of labor—removes the pressure to squeeze the resulting job "mismatches" out of the economy.

Retention part-time jobs are created to retain (or in some cases to attract) valued employees whose life circumstances prevent them from working full-time, particularly women with young children. Retention part-time jobs are found in primary labor markets and tend to be relatively skilled. Contrary to secondary part-time employment, retention part-time employment involves high compensation, high productivity, and low turnover. Rather than gaining schedule flexibility as an advantage, managers must flex around the worker's schedule. The "half a job" label does not fit these part-time jobs; they may involve half-schedules, but they are full jobs in every other way.

Because there are queues for retention part-time jobs, firms with retention part-timers in general tend to have some involuntary full-timers. Involuntary full-time employment exists for the same reasons as involuntary part-time employment: labor market friction, rigid compensation differentials, and macroeconomic slack. Some involuntary full-time employment is also due to the force of tradition and managers' beliefs about the appropriateness of part-time employment rather than any economic calculus by employers.

How Do Employers Use and Manage Part-Time Workers?

The difference between secondary and retention part-time employment, coupled with the notion that firms choose their own internal labor markets, helps to explain the striking variations in the amount of part-time employment used in different industries, discussed in Chapter 6. Retail and insurance workers sampled in the Current Population Survey in March 1992 had rates of part-time employment of 37 percent and 8 percent, respectively, while the retail and insurance companies I surveyed had even more divergent average part-time rates of 60 percent and 5 percent, respectively.

This difference between retail and insurance, although partly the result of different time patterns of product demand in the two industries, is due in large part to the fact that insurers and retailers have chosen very different labor markets. Insurers have chosen to arrange most of their labor force in a particular type of primary labor market that MIT economist Paul Osterman (1988) calls a salaried labor market, which is characterized by job designs entailing significant responsibility and broad job definitions—hence, continuity—as well as substantial training ladders. To secure a stable workforce to fill these jobs, insurers aim for primary earners. All of these features make it difficult for the salaried labor market to accommodate part-time work. To the extent that a company using this labor market employs part-timers, it will create retention part-time jobs. But retention part-time employment is by its nature an exception—a particular arrangement granted to a valued employee in exceptional circumstances—so few such jobs are created.

Retailers, on the other hand, have chosen to place most of their jobs in a secondary labor market, which means that jobs are broken down into units involving little skill or responsibility. Their workforce need not be especially stable or committed, but it must be cheap. Secondary part-time employment is consistent with this labor market. In fact, creating part-time jobs is a way to attract a secondary workforce and to legitimize a lower standard of pay. Whereas retention part-time jobs are created one at a time, secondary part-time jobs are created in whole classes of jobs at a time. To put it another way, the creation of retention part-time jobs is opportunistic, whereas the creation of secondary part-time jobs is often strategic.

One consequence of the compatibility of part-time employment with secondary labor markets is that secondary part-time jobs outnumber retention part-time jobs. In fact, although there are other varieties of part-time employment in addition to secondary and retention, secondary part-time jobs make up the majority of part-time employment.

To some extent, firms' choices of internal labor markets are constrained by the shape of their product markets. But there is an element of employer discretion in these labor market arrangements that is highlighted by the exceptions to the rule: companies that have altered the boundaries between primary and secondary labor markets that usually exist within their industry. For example, some insurance companies run many of their clerical functions as a secondary labor market, staffed with part-timers, whereas some retailers organize their workforce in a primary labor market and use many fewer part-timers than is the industry standard.

How do employers make these choices? As chapter 6 illustrates, the particular distribution of part-time and full-time jobs at a firm is the result of the interaction and at times contention among a large and varied cast of economic characters, including different levels and sections of management, unions (if any), unorganized workers, and the state. In retail, for example, secondary part-time employment is an integral part of a strategic labor market choice laid down and enforced by top operations management, over the resistance of unions and in some cases store-level management. On the other hand, in insurance, retention part-time employment is generally negotiated by department managers with individual employees, as a creative extension of a salaried labor market.

Finally, Chapter 7 closes the circle by returning to the unfinished issue of explaining changes in the rate of part-time employment over time. Overlaying the long-term growth trend are the contracyclical fluctuations in involuntary part-time employment, which increases during recessions and drops during expansions, although the most recent recovery has departed somewhat from this pattern. Part of this cyclical pattern can be explained by the cyclical incidence of temporary reductions in hours in full-time jobs and by changes in the industry composition of employment over the business cycle (since services are more recession-proof and use more part-timers than goods-producing industries). But there remains the baffling problem of explaining the cyclical movements of the rate of part-time employment within noncyclical industries. The explanation I offer is that switching from full-time to part-time employment serves to reduce average compensation, since part-timers receive lower compensation than full-timers. When unemployment rises, workers are more willing to accept part-time jobs. More precisely, the turnover of involuntary part-time employees falls, making the average part-time employee less costly. Then firms hire more part-timers, leading to a reduction in average compensation. When unemployment falls, the reverse takes place.

In industries such as insurance, where involuntary full-timers are numerous, this cyclical model works in reverse, leading to the procyclical movement of voluntary part-time employment (increasing during expansions, decreasing during contractions). In these industries, involuntary full-time employment presumably rises in recessions and falls during expansions (although it is not measured in standard statistical sources). In the economy as a whole, the procyclical pattern of voluntary part-time employment is swamped by the more common contracyclical pattern of involuntary part-time employment.

The difference in the utilization of part-time employment between Boston and Pittsburgh in the late 1980s points to the importance of cyclical effects as well as to the limits of these effects. Pittsburgh's higher rate of part-time employment in retail and lower rate in insurance resulted in part from the cyclical model outlined above. But despite the quantitative differences, there was no qualitative difference in the way part-time employment was used in the two cities.

In the second half of Chapter 7, a closer look at how supermarkets and health insurance companies decided to make more jobs part-time illuminates how part-time employment grew within specific industries over the long term. These firms moved the boundary between primary and secondary labor markets within their workforces, thereby expanding the secondary labor market to include more of their workers. In the examples studied, it was not just that "one day the light bulb went on," as a union representative said. The companies developed a new mix of internal labor markets in response to changing competitive and technological conditions. Specific scheduling issues—such as the extension of store hours and the adoption of video display terminal technology, for which peak productivity is achieved with short shifts—led the companies to focus on part-time workers rather than some other secondary workforce. And the receptiveness of a given firm to a new type of labor market, as well as the speed with which it made the change (if any), depended on a variety of its institutional features. For example, all of the companies converted full-time jobs to part-time jobs on the basis of attrition, thus slowing the transition.

When employers expand the secondary labor market, they get low productivity along with low labor costs. Indeed, in retail food productivity growth was actually negative in the 1970s and early 1980s. Unfortunately, in the product markets in question, this "low road" approach was an effective competitive strategy: savings on compensation outpaced losses in productivity. Once a critical mass of employers in a given product market shifted to a secondary labor market using part-time workers, competitive pressures tended to compel other employers to follow suit.

Policy Consequences

In the book's final chapter, I make the case for new policies to regulate part-time employment. The growth of part-time employment has most certainly contributed to the polarization of the earnings distribution. The rapidly growing segment of part-time jobs is made up of low-paid, secondary part-time jobs. Because employer creation of such "bad" part-time jobs has outrun the desire for these jobs in the workforce, on the margin involuntary part-time jobs are being created (although it is important to keep in mind that on average, about three-quarters of part-time jobs are voluntary). Part-time employment can take the form of well-compensated, "good" retention part-time jobs, but their internal labor market context makes them the exception.

Less clear is the effect of increasing part-time employment on the distribution of family income. Secondary part-time jobs are held mainly by secondary earners—persons who are not the sole support of a family. The growth of part-time work appears to be part of a more general movement away from the traditional (although never universal) model of a family supported by one breadwinner. The distributional consequences of this change are not obvious and await further research.

In addition to the distributional effects of the spread of secondary part-time employment, the findings in this book raise three related issues. First, the problem with secondary part-time jobs is not just low compensation, but also low productivity and slow (or even negative) productivity growth. Second, involuntary part-time and full-time employment pose equity and efficiency problems in their own right. And third, part-time employment often impedes worker representation and voice as exercised through unions.

Current policies on part-time employment are scattered, incoherent, and incomplete. Existing and proposed governmental policies include some that favor part-time employment (such as the overtime wage premium) and some that discourage it (such as proposals to require employers to offer health insurance to part-timers). Few policies in either category were designed with part-time employment itself in mind. U.S. unions are debating whether to focus on preventing the creation of secondary part-time jobs, equalizing the compensation of part-time and full-time employees, winning the right of a worker to move to retention part-time status, or supplementing employer-provided benefits with government- or union-provided ones.

Once existing labor market and collective bargaining policies are acknowledged as a de facto policy on part-time employment, steps can be taken to integrate them into an effective set of policy instruments and then to fill in the gaps in this set. To limit the spread of low-compensation secondary part-time employment, it is appropriate to use policies designed to discourage secondary labor markets in general. These policies include labor law reforms that give unions a larger workplace presence and direct controls on compensation differentials. Policies to reduce involuntary part-time and full-time employment would range from promoting the role of women and older workers—who tend to be the main advocates for retention part-time jobs—in labor and management to taking involuntariness into account explicitly when setting macroeconomic targets. More broadly, the spread of more flexible and transitory forms of employment, including part-time work, requires the construction of a new system establishing some basic level of security for workers by linking employer-provided benefits and guarantees with government-provided ones. Taken together, all of these policies would help to upgrade secondary part-time jobs where they exist, limit their further growth, and foster the increase in of retention part-time jobs so that the flexibility of part-time work can be combined with choice and security for the workforce.

Why Has Part-Time Employment Continued to Grow?

2

■ PART-TIME EMPLOYMENT IS BIG AND GETTING BIGGER. Almost 21 million people, or 19 percent, of the U.S. nonagricultural workforce worked part-time in 1993. A full 83 percent of these part-timers reported that they usually worked part-time. Close to one-third of the part-time workers—over 6 million people—were involuntary part-time workers who would have preferred a full-time job.[1] These figures represent averages over 12 months; about twice as many people had worked part-time at some time during the year (Terry 1981).

Since the 1950s, the proportion of part-timers in the workforce has grown gradually, climbing from 13 percent in 1957 to 19 percent in 1993 (Figure 2.1). This upward trend was noted early: for example, U.S. Bureau of Labor Statistics analyst Jane Meredith commented in 1963 that "the growth of the part-time work force represents one of the major labor market developments of the post-World War II period" (Meredith 1963, iii). In the short run, the rate of part-time employment has climbed during economic recessions and dipped during expansions (see Figure 2.1). But over the long run, increases have exceeded decreases, with an average increase of roughly .16 percentage points per year since the 1950s; the growth was most rapid during the 1970s.

The expansion of part-time employment would appear even more rapid if U.S. statistics counted the number of part-time jobs rather than the number of persons whose total hours worked fall below the full-time threshold. Workers holding multiple jobs climbed from 4.9 percent of the workforce in 1979 to a record high of 6.2 percent in 1989, and have remained at about that level. Since 85 percent of multiple-job holders work 24 hours or less a week on their second job, although most work more than 35 hours per week in all, this marks an increase in part-time jobs

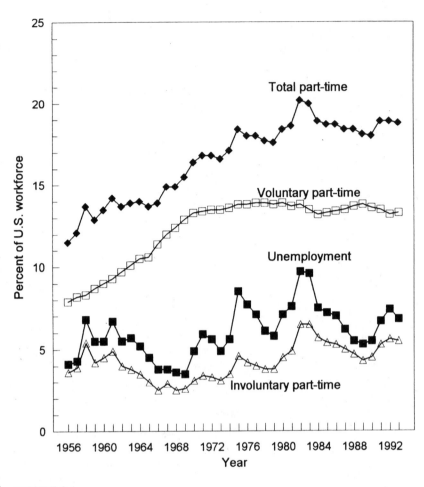

FIGURE 2.1
Unemployment Rates and Rates of Part-Time Employment, 1956–93

Source: Unemployment rate from U.S. Council of Economic Advisors (1994). Part-time employment rates from U.S. Bureau of Labor Statistics (1988b), with additional data from the U.S. Bureau of Labor Statistics, based on the Current Population Survey.

without a corresponding increase in the number of persons counted as working part-time (Stinson 1986; U.S. Bureau of Labor Statistics 1989, 1994).

Until about 1970, the part-time growth trend was driven by expanding voluntary part-time employment, as women and young people desiring part-time hours streamed into the workforce. But since that time, the rate of voluntary part-time employment has stagnated, and the growing rate of *involuntary* part-time work has propelled the upward trend. Of the 3.3 percent increase in the rate of part-time employment between 1969 and 1993, 3 percent is accounted for by the growth in involuntary part-time work. In other words, companies are creating part-time jobs even though workers do not want them. Why are they doing this?

The Beginning of an Explanation: Demographic Shifts

In searching for explanations of the growth in part-time employment, it is helpful to separate the last 25 years into three periods, 1969–79, 1979–89, and 1989–93. The first two periods are chosen not only because they are ten years long, but also because 1969, 1979, and 1989 represented business cycle peaks, which means that their labor markets can appropriately be compared. The last period examines change from a business cycle peak to an early recovery year and thus yields a less informative comparison, pending the unfolding of the current recovery.

Between 1969 and 1979, the rate of part-time employment grew relatively rapidly—climbing 2.1 percentage points—and about half of the increase was due to higher involuntary part-time employment. Between 1979 and 1989, total growth was slower—only .5 percent—but involuntary part-time work accounted for the entire increase. Finally, after 1989 the pace of part-time expansion picked up again, increasing .7 percent. Again widening involuntary part-time employment explains the entire rise—and more, since it offsets a drop in the rate of increase in voluntary part-time work.

One possible explanation for growing part-time employment lies with recent demographic shifts in the workforce. Part-time workers in the United States are primarily female, young, or old. Almost two-thirds are women, and another 15 percent are men aged 16 to 21 or 65 and over.

Slicing up the workforce by family relationships, most part-time employees—54 percent—are wives and "others" (mostly children) in married-couple families (Table 2.1). Another 9 percent are "other" members of single-parent families. Thus part-timers are most often supplying a second or third income to a family.

Reinforcing these observations, companies interviewed by Nollen, Eddy, and Martin (1978) and by Levine (1987) almost always responded that substantial numbers of their part-time employees are students and housewives (see Table 2.2). Many companies also use moonlighters and retired persons.

Because women with home responsibilities, students, and people of retirement age might be expected to prefer part-time schedules in many cases, one might try to explain the growth of part-time work by the influx of these groups—especially women—into the workforce. William

TABLE 2.1
Part-Time Employees' Family Position, Percent, 1985*

Family Position	Percent of Part-Timers by Family Position		
	Involuntary	Voluntary	Total
Husbands	26.2	9.6	16.2
Wives	21.9	39.2	32.3
Others in married-couple families	15.8	26.5	22.2
Women who maintain families	7.0	3.8	5.1
Others in families maintained by women	7.9	6.7	7.2
Men who maintain families	1.7	0.6	1.1
Others in families maintained by men	1.9	1.4	1.6
All other men	9.9	5.3	7.1
All other women	7.6	6.9	7.2
Total	100.0	100.0	100.0

*Part-time employees are here defined as persons who worked part-time at least one week during the year.
Source: Data from U.S. Bureau of Labor Statistics (1987), Table 6. These data were not published for later years.

TABLE 2.2
Major Life Roles of Part-Time Workers, 1978 and 1987

Role	Percent of Companies Surveyed*	
	1978	1987
Student	90	66
Housewife	87	88
Moonlighter	39	8
Retired	23	40
Handicapped	8	18
Other	5	11

*Total percent exceeds 100 because of multiple responses. 1978 sample is 39 companies, 1987 sample is 73.
Source: Data from Stanley D. Nollen, Brenda Broz Eddy, and Virginia H. Martin, Permanent Part-Time Employment: The Manager's Perspective (New York: Praeger, 1978), p. 139; and Hermine Zagat Levine, "Alternative Work Schedules: Do They Meet Workforce Needs? Part 1," *Personnel,* February 1987, p. 61.

Deutermann and Scott Brown (1978) of the Bureau of Labor Statistics commented that between 1954 and 1977, "changes in the composition of the labor force, particularly the increasing proportions of women and school-age youth, have had a profound impact on the growth of part-time labor supply" (p. 3). But while the demographics may explain the rise of part-time employment during the 1950s and 1960s, it fails to do so for the 1970s and 1980s. Furthermore, such factors can only account for growing *voluntary* part-time employment. Thus demographic shifts would be expected to explain at most half of the increase in the rate of part-time employment in 1969–79 and none of the increase since 1979.

Numerical analysis confirms these expectations. The effect of demographic changes from 1969 to 1979 can be approximated by holding the rate of part-time work within each age-gender group in the workforce constant at 1969 levels but allowing the age-gender composition of the workforce to change as it actually did. Based on this approximation, demographic shifts can account for .9 percentage points of the 2.1 percent rise in part-time employment in 1969–79, or somewhat less than half (Table 2.3). For the periods 1979–89 and 1989–93, the demographics predict decreases in part-time employment rather than the increases that in fact took place. So, as expected, they explain none of the later growth.

In both later periods, most of the growth of part-time employment is due to increases in the rate of part-time work among youths (aged 16–21), prime-age men (aged 22–64), and elders (aged 65 and over). Interestingly, women's rate of part-time employment has remained essentially unchanged over this period. In fact, women in the main child-rearing years (22–44) have slightly *decreased* their rate of part-time employment; in their increasing attachment to the workforce, more women have shifted to full-time work. Meanwhile, the proportion of prime-age men working part-time has more than doubled. Northwestern University economist Rebecca Blank (1990) has confirmed this pattern, finding a slightly declining trend in part-time work among women (although their rate of involuntary part-time work has climbed, their rate of voluntary part-time status has fallen faster), but a growing trend among men.

More Unsatisfactory Explanations

Since demographic shifts account for only a part of the story, we must seek other explanations for the climbing rate of part-time employment. It turns out that two other possible causes for the ongoing growth can be eliminated: long-term growth in unemployment and a widening part-time/full-time wage differential.

Given that involuntary part-time employment rates climb in times of high unemployment (see Figure 2.1), one might suppose that long-term

TABLE 2.3
Rate of Part-Time Employment Employment by Age and Gender, 1969, 1979, 1989, and 1993*

	1969		1979		1989		1993	
Characteristic	Percent of Workforce	Percent Working Part-Time	Percent of Workforce	Percent Working Part-Time	Percent of Workforce	Percent Working Part-Time	Percent Workforce	Percent Working Part-Time
All, 16–21	12.8	40.6	14.0	41.7	10.3	46.3	8.8	50.4
Women, 22–44	17.3	22.7	23.1	22.5	27.7	21.9	27.7	22.5
Women, 45–64	13.2	22.5	11.3	24.4	11.6	23.8	12.8	22.1
Men, 22–64	53.2	3.7	48.9	4.8	47.8	6.7	48.0	8.1
All, 65+	3.5	41.0	2.7	52.9	2.6	52.4	2.6	53.5
Total	100.0	15.5	100.0	17.6	100.0	18.1	100.0	18.8
Total, holding within-group rates at 1969 levels				16.4		15.9		15.6
Total, holding within-group rates at 1979 levels						17.0		16.7
Total, holding within-group rates at 1989 levels								17.8

*Includes only nonagricultural workers at work.
Source: Data from U. S Bureau of Labor Statistics, Employment and Earnings, January of 1970, 1980, 1990, and 1994.

growth in unemployment rates has caused long-term growth in part-time employment. But once more, the evidence says no. A number of studies, including my own statistical analysis, confirm that for every percentage point rise in unemployment, involuntary part-time employment also rises by about one-half a point (Ichniowski and Preston 1985; Ehrenberg, Rosenberg, and Li 1988). This research also confirms that even after taking unemployment into account, the part-time employment rate kept trudging upward at an average of one-tenth of a point per year or more.

Researchers Bernard Ichniowski of Columbia University and Anne Preston of the State University of New York reported that as much as 90 percent of the climb in part-time employment remains even after controlling for changes in the unemployment rate. In fact, their estimates suggest that because of the underlying growth in involuntary part-time employment, even if the 1993 unemployment rate had been *zero,* involuntary part-time employment would still have been 2.9 percent—well above its 1969 level!

What about the possibility that full-time workers simply "became too expensive," causing employers to substitute part-timers wherever possible? The wage gap between part-time and full-time workers is indeed substantial: part-timers earned about 62 percent as much per hour as full-timers in 1993. But the overall full-time/part-time wage differential and the wage differential for men in particular have not grown significantly over the last 20 years (Figure 2.2). The one wage differential that *has* widened somewhat is the part-time/full-time wage gap for women, but the percentage of women working part-time has remained static over this period.

While widening wage differences cannot account for the part-time ascent, a more likely suspect for boosting full-time expenses is the cost of fringe benefits. According to the annual surveys published by the U.S. Chamber of Commerce in *Fringe Benefits,* these costs have climbed steadily from 28 percent of total compensation in 1969 to 40 percent in 1992. Since part-time workers are much less likely to receive fringe benefits than full-timers, employers may be hiring more part-timers to avoid growing benefit costs. If this is true, we would expect that whenever full-time/part-time differentials in wages or fringe benefits increase, employers would react by hiring more part-timers. But statistical analysis indicates that changes in the wage and benefit gap simply have not contributed to the recent growth of part-time employment. In fact, when all else is equal, wider gaps in compensation are associated with *less* utilization of part-time employment![2]

This finding does not rule out the possibility that the mere existence of a compensation gap leads employers to switch from full-time to part-time employees. Rather, what it does rule out is that the growth of that gap has led to increasing use of part-timers. The essential change is not a

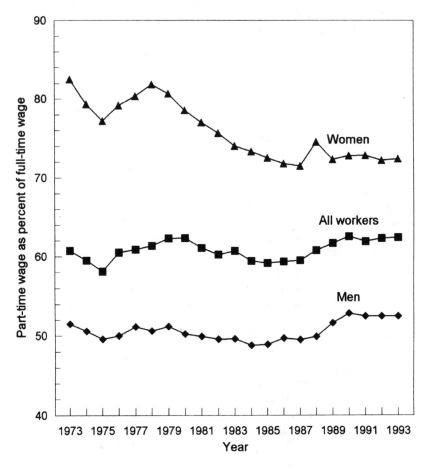

FIGURE 2.2
The Part-Time/Full-Time Hourly Wage Gap, 1973–93

Source: U.S. Bureau of Labor Statistics, unpublished Current Population Survey data, provided by Thomas Nardone.

growing part-time/full-time cost difference but changing needs and strategies of employers.

Growing Demand by Employers

If demographic movements, changes in unemployment, and a widening part-time/full-time wage gap can only account for a small part of the continuing climb of part-time jobs, where does the rest of the explanation lie? The answer is twofold. First, the industry composition of employment has shifted away from manufacturing and toward industries such as trade and services that employ larger numbers of part-timers. These industries use so many part-time workers because they are predominantly made up of firms that have adopted a low-wage, low-skill, high-turnover secondary labor market. Second, more jobs within almost every industry have been absorbed into this type of labor market. These changes have swelled the ranks of part-time workers even though the workforce's desire for part-time jobs has not kept pace, resulting in the growth of involuntary part-time employment.

Much of the recent long-term growth of part-time work can be explained by changes in the industry composition of employment. As Table 2.4 shows, if rates of part-time employment within each industry had remained at 1969 levels but each industry had followed its actual employment growth pattern from 1969 to 1979, part-time workers would have risen from 15.5 percent of the workforce to 16.2 percent rather than 17.1 percent, for a rate of increase that was somewhat less than half of the actual figure. (The Bureau of Labor Statistics publishes rates of part-time employment broken down by industry only for nonagricultural wage and salary workers at work, so these figures differ from those cited earlier in the chapter, which include all nonagricultural workers at work.) Between 1979 and 1989, industry shifts account for "more" than the total increase—1 percentage point compared to the actual 0.5 percent—indicating that this shift was offset by other factors, such as demographics. Finally, between 1989 and 1993, industry shifts account for "all" of the part-time jump. However, since we already know that over this final four-year period, demographic changes alone would have led to a decrease in part-time employment, some hidden factor must be supplementing the effect of the industry mix to yield the observed increase.

The evidence suggests that the industry composition effect represents the growth of "bad" part-time employment rooted in secondary labor markets. Essentially all of the increase in the part-time rate accounted for by changes in industry shares in both periods is explained by the growth of trade and services, where secondary labor markets are particularly prevalent. In fact, between 1969 and 1993, part-time workers in trade and services rose from 11 percent to 15 percent of all nonagricultural wage and salary workers.

The occupational slant of part-time job growth confirms this connection. Part-time employment grew fastest in less-skilled white- and pink-collar occupations: part-time workers in clerical, sales, and service occupations climbed from 9.5 percent to 11.7 percent of all nonfarm workers between 1969 and 1993.[3]

Employment in the trade and service industries has grown so rapidly

TABLE 2.4
Rate of Part-Time Employment by Industry Composition, 1969, 1979, 1989, and 1993*

Industry	1969		1979		1989		1993	
	Percent of Workforce	Percent Working Part-Time	Percent of Workforce	Percent Working Part-Time	Percent of Workforce	Percent Working Part-Time	Percent of Workforce	Percent Working Part-Time
Construction	6.4	8.6	6.0	10.5	5.9	10.5	5.3	11.9
Durable manufacturing	16.7	3.2	15.3	3.8	12.0	3.9	10.4	4.1
Nondurable manufacturing	11.4	7.8	9.9	8.6	8.3	8.1	7.6	8.1
Transportation, communication, utilities	7.2	7.8	7.0	9.0	7.3	8.7	7.5	8.6
Trade	20.6	26.3	20.7	30.0	21.4	29.7	21.5	30.3
Finance	5.8	10.5	6.2	11.9	7.1	11.5	6.9	11.0
Service	24.9	26.2	28.1	25.0	32.1	24.0	34.8	23.6
Public administration	6.2	6.2	5.9	6.6	5.3	5.8	5.4	5.9
Mining	0.8	5.0	1.0	4.0	0.6	4.8	0.6	3.5
All industries	100.0	15.5	100.0	17.1	100.0	17.6	100.0	18.1
All industries, holding within-industry rates at 1969 levels			16.2			17.2	17.8	
All industries, holding within-industry rates at 1979 levels					18.1		18.6	
All industries, holding within-industry rates at 1989 levels							18.1	

*Includes only nonagricultural wage and salary workers at work.

Source: U.S. Bureau of Labor Statistics, *Employment and Earnings*, January of 1970, 1980, 1990, and 1994. The percent working part-time in mining in 1969, which was not published separately, was computed from available information.

for several reasons. These industries have grown in relative terms because manufacturing has increasingly shifted to other countries. The absolute level of demand for the output of the trade and services industries has expanded in a number of areas. Final demand for consumer services has grown via the commoditization of goods formerly produced at home (for example, breakfast at McDonald's), in part because women entering the workforce provide fewer of these services through the family. Intermediate demand for producer services has boomed because of the growing importance of specialized business services such as legal advice, advertising, and accounting. Because productivity growth in the trades and services has been very slow (or even negative), increases in output have translated directly into increases in employment. And finally, the use of low-cost secondary labor markets has facilitated the growth in demand, enabling employers in these industries to keep prices relatively low despite lagging productivity growth (Waldstein 1989).

Although the employment growth of industries that use part-time work heavily is numerically important, the growth of part-time employment within industries is potentially more interesting, since it reflects not just changes in the composition of output but changes in firms' behavior and strategies. As Table 2.5 shows, between 1969 and 1993 the rate of part-time employment rose within every major industry except for services, public administration, and mining. Most of the increases were complete by 1979. But remember that after that point the demographics were pushing against part-time employment, so small increases—or even small decreases—in the use of part-timers must be explained in the face of strong demographic pressures to shift away from part-time work.

Behind the Corporate Door

The part-time employment growing within industries is *involuntary* part-time work. So we return to the question posed at the beginning of this chapter: why are companies creating part-time jobs if workers do not want them?

Statistical analysis of government-collected data cannot answer this question. Instead, we must step behind the corporate door to examine how employers make strategic decisions about their workforce and job structure. To understand why businesses continue to create part-time jobs, we need to see what kinds of part-time jobs they are creating, and how they are using part-time employment.

This is precisely what I set out to do several years ago. I knocked on corporate doors in the retail and insurance industries in the Boston and Pittsburgh areas. Before swinging the doors open for a look inside, however, it is necessary to set the scene by describing these two industries and two cities.

TABLE 2.5
Percent of Involuntary, Voluntary, and Total Part-Time Employment by Industry, 1969, 1979, 1989, and 1993[1]

Industry	Involuntary				Voluntary				Total			
	1969	1979	1989	1993	1969	1979	1989	1993	1969	1979	1989	1993
Construction	4.4	5.4	6.1	7.6	4.2	5.0	4.4	4.4	8.6	10.5	10.5	11.9
Durable manufacturing	1.4	1.5	1.6	1.8	1.8	2.3	2.3	2.2	3.2	3.8	3.9	4.1
Nondurable manufacturing	3.4	3.8	3.4	3.9	4.4	4.8	4.7	4.2	7.8	8.6	8.1	8.1
Transport, communication, utilities	1.8	2.6	2.7	3.2	6.0	6.4	6.0	5.4	7.8	9.0	8.7	8.6
Trade	2.9	5.4	6.3	8.4	23.4	24.5	23.4	21.9	26.3	30.0	29.7	30.3
Finance	1.0	1.7	1.8	2.3	9.5	10.2	9.6	8.7	10.5	11.9	11.5	11.0
Service	3.1	4.1	4.7	5.9	23.1	21.0	19.3	17.6	26.2	25.0	24.0	23.6
Public administration	0.8	1.3	0.9	1.3	5.4	5.3	4.9	4.6	6.2	6.6	5.8	5.9
Mining[2]	1.6	2.3	2.5	1.5	3.4	1.7	2.3	2.0	5.0	4.0	4.8	3.5
All industries	2.5	3.6	4.1	5.2	13.0	13.5	13.5	12.9	15.5	17.1	17.6	18.1

[1]Includes only nonagricultural wage and salary workers at work.
[2]The 1969 figure for mining is actually for 1976, because earlier figures are not available in published form.
Source: U.S. Bureau of Labor Statistics *Employment and Earnings,* January 1970, 1980, 1990, and 1994.

Two industries
The two industries chosen for examination, although similar in some ways, could hardly be more different in their use of part-time employment. Retail trade and insurance are both service industries with rapidly growing employment. But while retailers employ part-time workers in increasing abundance, insurers use part-timers only sparingly, as a diminishing fraction of their workforce. Comparison of the two industries can therefore tell us something about both the causes of interindustry variation in the rate of part-time employment and the reasons for changes over time.

Retail   The retail industry is a prodigious employer of part-time workers. A full 35 percent of all retail workers were part-time in 1993, almost double the rate in the nonagricultural economy as a whole. Retailers employed 6.3 million part-time workers, or one-third of all part-timers, far outstripping retail's 18 percent share of total employment.[4] Much of the research in this book focuses on grocery stores, whose rate of part-time employment in March 1992 matched the overall retail rate of 37 percent in that month.[5] *Progressive Grocer,* an industry publication that conducts its own survey, reports that supermarkets (defined as groceries, other than wholesale clubs, with $2 million or more in annual sales) used still more part-timers in 1992, racking up a 63 percent part-time ratio.

Part-time employment has grown rapidly in the retail sector, from 24 percent of total employment in 1962 to 35 percent in 1993 (see Figure 2.3). Essentially every section of retail underwent this increase, from gas stations to grocery stores. But more than any other type of retail business, eating and drinking places—which the Bureau of Labor Statistics counts as part of retail—drove the overall rise. They saw both an escalating part-time rate and a rapid growth in size, particularly after 1970.[6] By 1980, over half of the jobs in eating and drinking places were part-time, and these businesses accounted for more than one out of three retail jobs (U.S. Census Bureau 1980).

Although food stores' share of total retail employment has declined, their rate of part-time employment has most certainly increased—from 29 percent in 1960 to 36 percent in 1992. Within the supermarket sector of food stores, the rate of part-time employment shot up even more rapidly: from 35 percent of supermarket employees in 1962, part-timers climbed to 63 percent by 1992 (*Progressive Grocer* 1986, 1993).

Within the U.S. economy as a whole, the retail industry is a large employer, with about 20 million workers in 1993, or almost one in five U.S. workers, and is expanding apace. Retail employment surged by 68 percent between 1973 and 1993, while economywide employment grew by only 43 percent. Eating and drinking establishments accounted for not only most of the part-time growth in retail but also most of the overall growth—54 percent of the increase between 1973 and 1993.

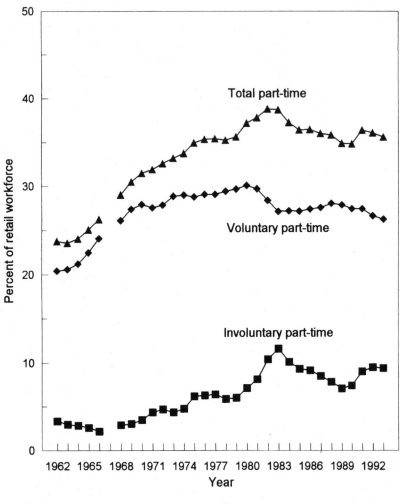

FIGURE 2.3
Rate of Part-Time Employment in Retail, 1962–93

Note: From 1968 on, figures include people with a job but temporarily away from work.
Source: U.S. Bureau of Labor Statistics, unpublished Current Population Survey data, provided by Thomas Nardone.

Although retail employment grew rapidly, productivity actually fell. From 1973 to 1993, overall retail productivity plummeted by 19 percent.[7] Grocery stores in particular saw a stunning productivity drop of 23 percent from 1973 to 1992.[8] In eating and drinking places and the broad category of food stores, productivity stumbled as well, but not as severely. Labor productivity in food stores fell by close to 12 percent between 1975 and 1990; eating and drinking places lost 7 percent (U.S. Census Bureau 1992). In other words, employment grew much more quickly than output throughout the retail industry.

Insurance   Only 8 percent of insurance employees worked part-time in March 1992, well below the U.S. economywide rate of 21 percent.[9] What's more, this rate has been declining since the early 1970s. Although the part-time ratio in insurance rose modestly—from 10 percent to 14 percent—during the 1960s (U.S. Census Bureau 1960, 1970), Figure 2.4 shows that it peaked in the early 1970s (although there also appears to be a strong up-and-down cyclical pattern in voluntary part-time employment in insurance).

Insurance is a small industry but has kept pace with the economy's overall employment growth, doubling from 1 to 2 million employees between 1960 and 1993. The number of insurance companies exploded in the postwar period, only to level off and even begin declining in the 1980s: for example, life insurance companies numbered 473 in 1945, 2,343 in 1988, and 2,105 in 1991 (American Council of Life Insurance 1992).

Insurance has shown lackluster productivity growth, but at least its productivity has increased, unlike that of retail. Productivity rose 0.6 percent annually between 1969 and 1986 in finance and insurance.[10]

The bulk of insurance employment—over two-thirds in 1991—is among insurance carriers rather than distributors (agents, brokers, service personnel) (U.S. Department of Commerce 1994). However, the distributor share of employment has grown over time. While some companies employ agents and sales personnel directly, others sell insurance through outside agents and brokers, who may be either exclusive (committed to one company) or independent.

Insurance companies sell three main products: life insurance, property and casualty insurance, and health insurance. In 1991 life insurance companies controlled 41 percent of insurance carrier employment; property and casualty companies, 37 percent; and health insurance companies, 10 percent (ibid.). Health insurance companies' employment share has grown substantially since 1960, when it stood at only 6 percent (American Council of Life Insurance 1985).

The Labor Market: Boston and Pittsburgh

My interviews of employers captured a snapshot of Boston and Pittsburgh, including their labor markets, during 1987 and 1988. I chose these two metropolitan areas in part because at that time their images were radically different: Boston, a high-tech and service boom town; Pittsburgh, a heavy manufacturing bust town. In actuality, the two economies

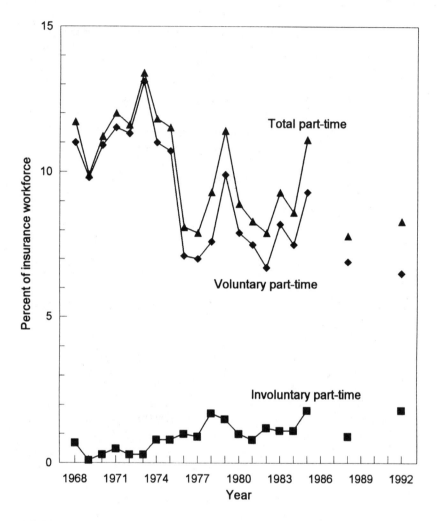

FIGURE 2.4
Rate of Part-Time Employment in Insurance, 1968–92

Note: Data based on the Current Population Survey for March of each year only, rather than annual averages. This is one reason for the observed volatility.
Source: Current Population Survey computer tapes.

were—and remain—more similar than the stereotypes would suggest, for Pittsburgh also has a large and thriving service sector. But the two areas did manifest striking differences in their rates of unemployment and of part-time employment, particularly involuntary part-time employment. Comparison of Boston and Pittsburgh thus assists us in distinguishing between cyclical and structural influences on part-time work.

First, consider in more detail the differences between the two areas. As of January 1988, in the middle of my interviews, unemployment rates in the Boston and Pittsburgh metropolitan areas differed significantly: 2.2 percent and 7.1 percent, respectively. (But during the early 1990s recession, the two cities actually traded places, with unemployment at 7.8 percent in Boston and 6.8 percent in Pittsburgh in 1992!) These large differences in overall unemployment carried over to unemployment in trade and in finance, insurance, and real estate. Unemployment in Pittsburgh's retail and wholesale trade sector was more than twice as high as in Boston in 1987 (7.5 percent versus 3.4 percent); unemployment in the Iron City's finance sector was more than seven times that in Boston (5.7 percent versus 0.8 percent) (U.S. Bureau of Labor Statistics 1988a, Table 26).

Pittsburgh had a higher rate of part-time employment than Boston in 1988; both areas had rates above the national average (Table 2.6). The major difference between the two in part-time employment is in the composition of that employment. In Boston, less than one-tenth of part-timers were involuntary in 1988; in Pittsburgh, about one-third were involuntary. This reflected Boston's taut labor market and Pittsburgh's drooping one.

In other ways, however, the two labor markets were, and are, quite similar. Both are medium-sized labor markets: 1987 employment in the Boston metropolitan area was 1.5 million; Pittsburgh had 1 million. The industry composition of employment in the two areas is comparable, although surprisingly Pittsburgh had (and still has) a smaller manufacturing share than Boston (Table 2.7). In fact, the industry mix of employment in both areas is quite similar to the U.S. averages.

Both Boston and Pittsburgh have undergone wrenching transformations from manufacturing to service economies. However, in Boston manufacturing declined much earlier, during the 1930s, and the service

TABLE 2.6
Percent of Involuntary, Voluntary, and Total Part-Time Employment in Boston, Pittsburgh, and the United States, 1988*

	Involuntary	Voluntary	Total
Boston	1.8	18.4	20.1
Pittsburgh	6.7	14.5	21.2
United States	4.7	13.7	18.4

*Includes only those at work. Boston and Pittsburgh rates are for March 1988 only. U.S. rates are 1988 annual averages.
Source: Boston and Pittsburgh figures computed from the March 1988 Current Population Survey computer tapes. U.S. figures are from U.S. Bureau of Labor Statistics *Employment and Earnings,* January 1989.

TABLE 2.7
*Industry Composition of Nonagricultural Employment in Boston, Pittsburgh,
and the United States, Percent, 1987**

Industry	Boston	Pittsburgh	United States
Construction	4	5	6
Mining	0	1	1
Durable manufacturing	14	12	12
Nondurable manufacturing	5	5	8
Transportation, communication, and utilities	5	6	6
Wholesale and retail trade	18	25	21
Finance, insurance, real estate	10	7	7
Service	30	27	22
Government	12	12	17
Total	100	100	100

*Includes only nonagricultural wage and salary workers.
Source: Data from U.S. Bureau of Labor Statistics (1988a).

resurgence began in earnest in the 1960s. Pittsburgh, on the other hand, still bears the scars of the "steel depression" of the late 1970s and early 1980s, and in the late 1980s those scars were quite fresh.

Knocking on the Door

To learn more about part-time employment in these settings, I knocked on the doors of businesses in the Boston and Pittsburgh areas. Between February 1987 and April 1988, I conducted 82 wide-ranging interviews covering 31 companies and 15 unions and other worker advocacy organizations. Due to confidentiality considerations, the names of the companies, unions, and individuals have been withheld. Most of the interviews (with 29 of the companies and 9 of the labor organizations) focused on the retail and insurance industries, although I also added a few informants from other industries to round out the picture. Within retail and insurance, quite a varied group of companies and unions were included (Table 2.8).

Within the businesses I pursued an elite interviewing strategy, most often conducting interviews with higher officials with an overview of the entire company. In fewer than one-third of the firms, interviews were conducted at a lower management level because of either a need for information about particular geographic labor markets or ease of access to

TABLE 2.8
Types of Retail and Insurance Organizations Interviewed

Retail	Insurance
BUSINESSES	BUSINESSES
4 supermarket chains	5 life insurance companies
3 supermarket independents	4 property and casualty insurance companies
7 convenience store chains	
2 department store chains	3 health insurance companies
1 fast food chain	
LABOR ORGANIZATIONS	LABOR ORGANIZATIONS
2 union locals representing retail workers	3 union locals representing or organizing insurance workers
2 union internationals representing retail workers	1 union international organizing insurance workers
	1 worker advocacy group organizing insurance workers

Source: Interviews by author.

respondents. In every firm the initial interviewee was someone chiefly responsible for personnel/human resources at his or her level of management, most typically the personnel director. Human resource officials, of course, are the staff members most intimately involved in hiring decisions and policy.

I built up more detailed case studies in four companies based in the Boston-area by repeated interviews of top managers plus interviews of lower-level managers. Part-time and full-time workers were also interviewed in two of these companies. Slightly different questions were asked of lower-level managers and workers than of higher officials. These four companies are identified by the pseudonyms "SuperValu" (a supermarket chain), "EZ Mart" (a convenience store chain), "Healthco" (a health insurer), and "Eternal Life" (a life insurance company).

The employment units range in size from a 20-employee independent supermarket to an 85,000-employee insurance company, with businesses of every size in between. The sample is skewed toward large enterprises but not necessarily toward large establishments; for example, the convenience store chains studied employ up to 1,500 people nationwide, but typically only have 7 to 10 employees per store.

Once I got in the door, I carried out what are known as semistructured interviews in which I asked a standard set of questions but encouraged respondents to speak freely based on their own experience and knowledge, and then followed up on interesting or surprising revelations that emerged during the interview. Most of these conversations lasted about an hour. The result is a rich, nuanced look at the experience and thinking of managers, representatives, and others on the front lines of the part-time revolution.

While nonrandom,[11] the sample is stratified by industry, subsector, and geographic location. Almost all of the organizations are based in, or specifically discussed their operations in, eastern Massachusetts (around Boston) and western Pennsylvania (around Pittsburgh). The exceptions are two insurers based in the New York City area, and two union organizations based in Rhode Island and upstate New York. Many of the companies, and a few of the union organizations, operate in larger regions, and a small number are nationwide. I asked informants to make comparisons between operations in different regions when relevant.

Should we believe what the company and union representatives told me? Of course, there is no way to be sure that their answers were honest and well informed. But I have a great deal of confidence in most of the information they provided. Respondents had little incentive to distort the truth, since they knew the interviews would remain confidential. Equally important, a face-to-face, semistructured interview generates a high level of rapport and trust between the two parties, eliciting more candid and full responses than more formal surveys.

I did, however, use several methods to evaluate the accuracy of statements made during interviews. The most important checks were the internal consistency of an informant's account, the amount of detail an informant was able to provide, and the informant's ability to know certain facts. On the last point, for example, I discounted a respondent's description of changes in company policies that had taken place years before that person had joined the company. Statements about a particular company made by different informants were weighed against each other. Seventeen of the 31 companies were discussed by more than one respondent, and in 11 of these cases more than one respondent provided an indepth discussion. Where possible, both union and management views of the same company were gathered.

Finally, I checked informants' statements against four forms of published or written documentation. First, and most commonly, interviewees volunteered or were asked to check written (or on-line) records during the interview; for example, some checked the precise number of part-time and full-time workers at their company. Second, a half-dozen companies and unions provided written documentation of company policy (typically the employee handbook) in addition to interviews. Third, other published accounts furnished specific information on three of the companies and illuminated other issues (such as the nature of laws affecting part-time employment) that were discussed by a number of informants. Fourth, I compared some of the major patterns respondents described with those present in large, national data sets such as the Census Bureau's Current Population Survey, a monthly survey of roughly 1 in 1,000 U.S. households.

This last point merits further discussion. Unfortunately, most U.S. economists confine their empirical research to formal, statistical tests of hypotheses. That is, they use numerical data sets to prove certain regularities or relationships in the economy, as I have used the Current Population Survey. While such testing is important, by itself it can only yield limited insight into how the economy works, because it is usually deductive (the theories tested are derived from a set of assumptions about the way economies are expected to work) and always quantitative. There is much to be learned instead from research that is inductive (looking at the economy directly and trying to discern the forces at work) and qualitative (asking the "what," "how," and "why" questions, rather than "how much"). Such methods can generate far richer, more complex hypotheses.

This book combines both approaches to research. The quantitative analysis of the growth of part-time employment presented earlier in this chapter raises one set of questions to which my interviews throw up a welter of answers and other ideas. In turn, I shall test some of the hypotheses that emerge from the interviews.

No matter how inductively one approaches theory, it is essential to begin from some theoretical base. I shall spell out my theoretical base in the next chapter.

Two Theoretical Frameworks

3

■ BEAUTY IS IN THE EYE OF THE BEHOLDER. ECONOMIST Paul Samuelson put on his neoclassically tinted glasses and looked out on the United States's market economy. He saw a well-oiled machine—rational, symmetrical, and supremely indifferent. Do employers exercise excessive power over their workers? No, scoffed Samuelson (1957), for "in a perfectly competitive market, it really doesn't matter who hires whom: so have labor hire 'capital'" (p. 894). Samuelson (1983) did acknowledge in passing that "often the economist takes as data certain traditionally noneconomic variables such as technology, tastes, social and institutional conditions, etc.; although to the students of other disciplines these are processes to be explained and analyzed, and are not merely history" (pp. 318–19). But he seemed untroubled by the admission; such details apparently matter little in comprehending the workings of the economy.

Yet when Thorstein Veblen donned his institutionalist specs and observed the very same economy (albeit several decades earlier), he saw a totally different picture. Where Samuelson approvingly noted rationality, Veblen critiqued myth and emulation. Samuelson's evenhanded market gave way, in Veblen's view, to an economy striated with inequities of power and privilege. And Veblen believed that, for better or worse, the market was buffeted by the "opaque," blind drift of history (Dente 1977; Dugger 1988).

There are plenty of other monumental debates about the economy. But the neoclassical-institutionalist confrontation casts a particularly long shadow on analysis of the labor market in general and of part-time employment in particular. The neoclassical and institutionalist approaches bring very different strengths to bear on the problem. Neoclas-

34

sical, or mainstream, economic theory offers simplicity, generality, and the clarity of mathematical expression; institutionalist theory offers institutional specificity and social and historical context.

I confess to eclecticism: I have sought to gain insight into questions about part-time employment through *both* approaches. But institutionalist theory serves as the guiding paradigm for most of my research. This chapter starts by explaining why the institutionalist approach appears particularly well equipped to address the puzzles about part-time work. Following that explanation, there is a brief discussion of neoclassical perspectives on the determination of hours of work and a more detailed exposition of institutionalist insights on the labor market, drawing particularly on a model of the labor market developed by Paul Osterman (1988). A final section summarizes the differences between the two approaches.

Why Emphasize Institutionalist Theory?

When it comes to understanding the demand side of part-time employment, institutionalist theory holds more promise than does neoclassical theory. There are three reasons for this. First, neoclassical theory builds on choices made along continuous spectra, whereas the choice between part-time and full-time employment is a discrete, yes/no choice for employers. Second, counter to neoclassical expectations, the labor market persistently fails to clear, that is, to equalize labor supply and demand. These two facts suggest that institutional features of the labor market prevent it from reaching a competitive equilibrium in the mixture of part-time and full-time jobs. The reality seems distant from Samuelson's "perfectly competitive market" in which buyers and sellers of labor adjust their wage offers to bid away any excess supply or demand. Third, this book addresses particular questions about qualitative distinctions and changes, which sit at the core of institutionalist theory, whereas neoclassical theory focuses on quantitative differences.

Employers make a choice between creating part-time or full-time jobs that is discrete in two senses. For one thing, with some exceptions, firms do not freely vary the hours of work of jobs. This is particularly true during a given employee's tenure in a job. There are also significant limits to employer alteration of job hours during vacancies. Since employers exercise limited choices over job hours, the distribution of hours worked in the United States is bimodal, with one mode at 40 hours and a second, smaller mode between 30 and 34 hours.

But the firm's choice between part-time and full-time jobs is also discrete in a second, even more important way. Part-time status is not simply one parameter of a job that firms can vary at will while leaving other aspects untouched. Rather, part-time status comes bundled with other job characteristics. This discontinuity is equally obvious from examining the personnel policies of individual firms—which typically specify different benefits, protections, and procedures for full-time and part-time employees—and from looking at aggregate statistics showing that part-time workers on average receive lower wages and benefits (see Chapter 4).

A fundamental tenet of institutionalist theory is the importance of discrete choices and particularly of bundles of job characteristics that tend to accompany each other. Certainly neoclassical theory can also accommodate such discrete choices, but the basic neoclassical model applies to decisions made in a continuous environment. Thus, neoclassical theory is not particularly suited to analyzing discontinuities.

The existence of persistent involuntary part-time and full-time employment also points to the usefulness of institutionalist theory. The biggest and best known failure of labor markets to clear is unemployment, but involuntary part-time and full-time work as well involve gaps between labor supply and demand. To be sure, neoclassical economics is not incapable of modeling outcomes in which qualified workers are constrained from obtaining the jobs or hours they desire. A spate of neoclassical "microfoundations" theories propose explanations for the analogous phenomenon of unemployment, but all of these theories turn on some institutional imperfection in the labor market. To determine what institutional features of equilibrium part-time and full-time employment are likely to prevent the labor market from clearing along the hours dimension, it makes sense to start with an institution-centered examination.

Finally, on the whole, institutionalist theory more naturally lends itself to explaining this book's central questions about part-time employment: to what extent firms create different types of part-time jobs with distinct qualities, why they make particular groups of jobs part-time, and why they change these decisions over time. The distinction between different types of part-time jobs is difficult to frame in terms of continuous parameters but easier to describe in terms of qualitative distinctions and choices. Explaining why employers make some jobs part-time and not others returns to the issue of the bundling of job characteristics. The long-term growth of part-time employment involves qualitative changes in employment practices in certain industries. A neoclassical model can, in principle, be designed to reproduce all of these twists—but only at the price of adding quite a bit of structure to a model whose chief advantage is its simplicity. Institutionalist theory, on the other hand, starts from the premise that lots of institutional structure overlays markets, so it is relatively well equipped to tackle these issues.

In fact, I shall implement both neoclassical and institutionalist frameworks in this book, but because of the particular advantages of the institutionalist concepts and arguments for confronting the questions at hand, they surface more frequently. The remainder of this chapter summarizes neoclassical and institutionalist views of the labor market and hours of work.

The Neoclassical Theory of the Labor Market and Hours of Work

Let's put on Paul Samuelson's glasses. There: all around us are economic actors rationally pursuing their self-interest. In a neoclassical world, firms maximize their profits and households maximize their utility (well-being) by combining the consumption of market goods, household-produced goods, and leisure. Within this framework, there are many possible ways to conceptualize the determination of hours of work. Here, three are briefly considered: one drastic simplification (the standard labor supply and demand model), a more subtle model (the compensating differentials model), and a set of extensions that explain how workers can be constrained in their choices of hours.

The Standard Labor Supply and Demand Model

In the standard model of the labor market, a person is presented with a wage and decides how to divide his or her time between hours of work and hours of "leisure" (defined, despite the work of housewives, home-repair buffs, students, and volunteers, as all time not spent working for pay). The "wage" should be considered in this discussion (and in all of these simplified models) to stand for total compensation, including fringe benefits as well as direct wages.

A rational person will work until the marginal utility of leisure (the added value of one more unit—say one more hour—of leisure) equals the marginal utility of the wage (the added value of goods and services that can be purchased with the hour's wage). This person would be foolish to take *more* leisure, since it is assumed that each additional hour of leisure is worth less (the first few hours of leisure in a 24-hour day are a matter of survival, but the twentieth hour is something of a luxury), so extending leisure beyond this critical point means giving up something that is worth more (an hour's wages) for something that is worth less (one more hour of leisure). Working more hours would likewise be irrational, since the value to the individual of goods purchased with each succeeding hour's wage also diminishes (again, the first few dollars go to necessities, whereas beyond a certain point they purchase luxuries).

This choice process yields an individual supply curve, showing for each possible wage how much this person would choose to work. Individual supply curves can then be aggregated to form a market supply curve.

The firm is also presented with a wage, since in a competitive economy any one business is too small to affect the wage and has no choice but to pay the going wage. The firm hires labor until that turning point where the value of marginal product (the value to the firm of the production that comes from adding one more unit—again, say one hour—of labor) fails to equal the wage. Neoclassical models assume that at this point, as with the value of leisure to the person, the payoff to the firm of each added hour of labor is less than the value of the one before, perhaps because the firm has fixed amounts of capital or limited management capacity. So a sensible business will hire neither more nor less labor than the turning point demands: hiring more would mean paying more out than the company gets in return; hiring less would mean saving one hour's wage but giving up production worth more than that wage. This choice process generates a demand curve showing for each wage level how many hours of labor this firm (or all firms) would choose to hire. Then, as all survivors of courses on the principles of economics know, the labor market reaches an equilibrium where the supply curve and the demand curve intersect—where both workers and employers choose the same total number of work hours given the going wage.

In the simplest version of this model, the wage is invariant with hours worked, and the value of marginal product is a function only of total hours of labor hired, not the number of hours put in by any individual worker. That is, the constraints, or budget set (the dollars-for-hours tradeoffs faced by workers and firms), are linear (always the same number of dollars for an hour of labor). Hours restrictions are accordingly seen as strictly supply driven, since employers do not care how many hours an individual worker works.

This simple model is appealing. As University of Chicago economist Sherwin Rosen (1986) points out, "the main advantage of the neoclassical framework is the linearity of the budget set, and the practical advantages of this are so great that they should not be given up lightly" (p. 683). Abandoning this simplification and adding refinements such as wages or productivity that vary with hours moves the model into a domain better dealt with by using compensating differentials.

The Compensating Differentials Model
In a compensating differentials model of the labor market, workers do not unilaterally set their hours of work subject to a wage. Instead, employers care about hours because both the marginal cost (added cost per hour) of employing a worker and the marginal product are functions of

hours. This covariance of cost and/or productivity with time worked may be due to any of a number of causes, including biology (workers tire out as hours increase); set-up, hiring, or training costs; or discontinuities such as the legally mandated pay differential for overtime.

Within this model, the determination of work hours is a joint decision by employer and employee. There is no reason to expect that a single wage will clear the labor market for all hours choices by all workers. Rather, different firms will offer different packages of wages and hours. In the market equilibrium, the wage will be a function of hours (Moffitt, 1984; Kahn and Lang, 1992). The market equilibrium is reached by matching workers who prefer longer (or shorter) hours with firms whose technology or product demand leads them to value long-hour (or short-hour) workers most highly.

Models with Constrained Worker Choices of Hours
When the neoclassical labor market model is extended by postulating that workers may be constrained for any of a number of reasons, it can yield explanations of involuntary part-time employment. By this point, of course, Samuelson's original vision has become somewhat blurred. There are two general approaches to extending the model: creating a microfoundation that explains why labor markets may generate constraints, or simply placing the labor market in a macroeconomic context where insufficient aggregate demand is a fact of life.

Much recent research on labor markets focuses on possible microfoundations of unemployment and can readily be augmented to pose microfoundations for low-paid, involuntary part-time work. For example, Jeremy Bulow and Lawrence Summers's (1986) "efficiency wage" model could be applied to a dual labor market of full-time and part-time workers. In such a model, firms would pay full-time workers an "efficiency wage" above their marginal product. Such a higher wage is efficient for the company because it makes firing costly to these workers, since if they are fired they cannot count on getting a new full-time job at the above-market wage and may instead have to settle for a part-time job at the lower market wage. Thus, the efficiency wage discourages full-time workers from shirking, rendering them more productive. Part-time workers, who face no threat of lower wages after firing, will be less productive. The workers in part-time jobs are not *inherently* less productive than full-timers; indeed, they may be identical in every respect except that they face a different set of incentives. In this situation, we find involuntary part-time employment: part-timers who would prefer a full-time job. Economists James Rebitzer and Lowell Taylor (1991) have developed such a model.

Similarly, insider-outsider models (Lindbeck and Snower 1985) could be altered to cast full-timers as insiders and part-timers as out-siders. In this model insider full-timers are highly trained, while outsider part-timers are not. Then full-timers extract higher pay by threatening to quit, which would require firms to undertake the costly training of new full-timers. Again, part-timers covet the full-time jobs.

If instead we simply take unemployment to be a fact of life, in the spirit of much Keynesian macroeconomics, then underemployment in the form of involuntary part-time employment is a natural corollary. For many workers, part-time work is preferable to unemployment, even if it pays a lower wage than full-time work. Part-time labor may also be preferable to employers, either because it allows them to retain trained workers during downturns or because it is available at lower wages than full-time labor.

Each of these extensions could also be amended to explain the si-multaneous existence of involuntary part-time and involuntary full-time work. This could be achieved most credibly by assuming that involuntary part-time and full-time work involve two distinct, noncompeting groups in the labor market.

The Institutionalist Theory of the Labor Market and Hours of Work

It is time to switch glasses, but for institutionalist optometrists the pre-scription is not as straightforward as for neoclassical ones. No estab-lished institutionalist theory specifies the determination of hours of work as the standard neoclassical model does. However, the institutionalist no-tion of segmented labor markets offers helpful concepts for thinking about part-time employment. Why do different types of labor markets exist? In the institutionalist view, *firms create the labor markets,* although not in circumstances of their own choosing.

Paul Osterman (1988) of the Massachusetts Institute of Technology presents a very useful discussion of this process of labor market creation, posing it in terms of firm pursuit of objectives subject to constraints. He starts by describing three objectives of firms, based on his interviews with managers: cost minimization, flexibility, and predictability. Cost mini-mization—the most neoclassical of the three in spirit—includes the cost not only of wages, but also of errors, of worker shirking, and so on. Flex-ibility refers to flexibility in both staffing levels and deployment of labor. For companies, predictability in the labor market means the ability to plan on the availability of a labor force with a known set of skills at a known cost.

Unlike the neoclassical framework, which assumes that firms want to maximize profits alone, this approach poses that they in fact have three objectives. How do companies balance them? The main factor structuring their relative importance is the nature of the market for a firm's product. Firms that face stiff price competition will place special emphasis on cost minimization. Firms with large variations in demand or in the mix of products demanded will make flexibility a top priority. Firms experiencing steady growth in demand will stress predictability. Of course, the state of the product market is not strictly exogenous, since firms also make their own choices about their product mix.

It may be argued that in fact all of these goals are subordinated to the goal of maximizing profits. But this claim oversimplifies the firms' decision-making process in five ways. First, it suggests that decision-makers work with a model, implicit or explicit, that tells them the "production function" that converts each combination of cost, flexibility, and predictability into some level of profits. Instead, according to Osterman, managers actually see these three goals themselves as the goals to be monitored. Second, the claim implies that there is unanimity within a firm's management on the single objective of profit maximization, or at least that firms that lack such unanimity will suffer in the market. But in fact, there is often disagreement among managers, as industrial relations scholars Thomas Kochan, Harry Katz, and Robert McKersie (1986) have observed. Personnel managers may stress predictability, while those managing operations may emphasize flexibility and those managing finances may care most about cost minimization. Third, given the uncertainty that firms face, they may "satisfice" rather than maximize, aiming at particular minimum targets rather than attempting to wring every cent of advantage from the available circumstances (March and Simon 1993). Fourth, nonrational factors such as traditions or beliefs about the right way to do business contribute to the decision-making process. Finally, although this account has treated these three objectives as if they were general, in fact they should be seen as specific to particular periods and particular sectors, unlike the timeless profit motive posited by neoclassical economics.

In fact, there may not exist in any meaningful way a single "best" solution *ex ante* to the firm's choice of labor markets. Firms are in effect solving an optimization problem in many variables, over time, under considerable uncertainty, with viable solutions constrained to discrete choices along certain dimensions. In this context it may be essentially impossible to distinguish between the expected profits of one labor market choice and another, and the choice must be made on other bases.

After posing the three objectives, Osterman goes on to suggest three constraints: (1) physical technology (skill, extent of knowledge about production processes, and so on); (2) social technology (the set of relations and beliefs in an organization that establish what is legitimate, acceptable, or customary); and (3) the nature of the available labor force. Susan Christopherson (1988) of Cornell University adds a fourth: state policy (minimum wage, overtime laws, and so on).

These are not constraints in the usual neoclassical sense, because they are—at least in the long run—largely endogenous. One firm can affect all of the first three, and firms collectively can affect the fourth. For example, the firm has a choice over a range of physical technologies. There is often sufficient uncertainty that no one technology can be identified as the least-cost approach. Instead, technological choices are tied to other strategic choices, including labor market choices. As another example, the firm can transform the available labor force by relocating or by inducing migration.

To attain the three objectives subject to the four constraints, the firm fashions a particular labor market structure or set of structures. Senior institutionalist labor economists Peter Doeringer and Michael Piore (1971), among others, emphasized the differences between the labor markets of different firms, particularly between primary labor market firms, which offer steady jobs with promotion ladders, and secondary labor market firms, which offer high-turnover jobs with no prospect for advancement. Osterman (1982) points out, however, that in fact many firms combine a number of labor markets; a firm's markets for managers, clerical workers, skilled and unskilled production workers may be quite distinct.

The same considerations that motivate different firms to create particular labor market structures for their respective workforces can motivate one firm to create several labor market structures for different fractions of its own workforce. The relative importance of cost, flexibility, and predictability for one section of the workforce stems from the role of that section's tasks in production as well as the nature of demand for the product. For example, the standard employment model for large-manufacturing firms stressed predictability among production workers and flexibility among managers; currently, however, many such firms are investigating models that put more emphasis on flexibility and/or cost minimization among production workers.

Classifying the Labor Markets
This account has referred repeatedly to labor market "segments" or "structures." And indeed, in the institutionalist view, labor markets come in types marked by clusters of characteristics. "It is not possible, as it were, to pick a rule from each category and establish a stable set of employment relationships," says Osterman (1985, 58) about rules governing the five categories of job definition, deployment, security, wage rules,

and worker participation in decisions. "Rather, only certain configurations of rules fit together."

From what repertoire of labor markets do firms have to choose? Osterman (1988) offers a typology of industrial, salaried, craft, and secondary labor markets. The industrial labor market, which was the standard model for manufacturing production workers until a few years ago, is defined by long tenure, job ladders, on-the-job skill acquisition, narrow job definitions, little decision-making power, and job security tempered by layoffs. The salaried labor market, on the other hand, corresponds to that of managers or company-based professional/technical workers such as actuaries, and again features long tenure, job ladders, and on-the-job training, but also has broad and flexible job definitions, substantial decision-making power and discretion, and an implicit lifetime employment guarantee. The craft labor market characterizes the situation of workers like the skilled carpenter or computer programmer: short tenure, loyalty to craft rather than to a particular firm, advancement by shifting from one firm to another or by accumulating skill rather than by climbing a ladder in a particular firm, and skills acquired off the job (through apprenticeship or education). Borrowing a term from Doeringer and Piore (1971), the industrial, salaried, and craft labor markets may be called primary labor markets. Finally, the secondary labor market marks a typing pool or custodial staff: short tenure, no job ladder, little skill, and low pay. At a first approximation, the distinction between good and bad jobs is the distinction between primary and secondary labor markets.

Each of the labor markets meets some of the labor market goals of the firm while falling short on others:

- Industrial: High predictability, high flexibility in employment levels but low flexibility in task deployment, high costs
- Salaried: High predictability, low flexibility in employment levels but high flexibility in deployment, high costs
- Craft: Low predictability, high flexibility in both employment levels and deployment, high costs
- Secondary: Low predictability, high flexibility in both employment levels and deployment, low wage costs but may have high costs due to errors or shirking

An employer would be expected to move from one labor market structure to another when either the objectives shift (due to a change in the market) or one or more of the constraints shift. Since firms must choose among a set of discrete clusters of characteristics, thus limiting the possibilities for fine tuning, they are expected to adjust discontinuously in response to large shifts in the environment.

What Do Workers Do?

So far, labor supply—otherwise known as workers—has remained curiously absent from this account. Also, the account has focused on firms and the employment relationship with little attention to connecting these institutions with other societal institutions. But there is more to say about these issues.

Workers are not simply pegs of various shapes that firms match with their holes. Workers appear in labor markets as subjects as well as objects. The institutionalist view holds that because firms are generally more powerful than workers, workers appear as subjects primarily when they act collectively. On a national level, movements like the CIO, the civil rights movement, and the women's movement have transformed labor markets. Certainly the industrial and craft labor market models as we know them have largely resulted from compromises struck between employers and labor movements. On a plant level, unions and other organizations can constrain and push firms in various ways. Even when there is no formal organization, workers in a given plant or community have a set of norms and expectations for worker and manager behavior. Successful attempts to stop plant closings have succeeded not because an entire community was in the same union, but because the community shared certain values about the company's implied commitment.

Workers are far from a monolithic group. They are divided by numerous privileges and conflicts of interest. For example, feminist analysts Michele Barrett and Mary McIntosh (1980) and Ruth Milkman (1980) offer two accounts of how organized male workers have conceived of class interest in a way that subordinated or excluded women in nineteenth century Britain and the nineteenth- and twentieth-century United States, respectively.

The interactions between firms and workers that make up labor markets are tied to a myriad of other social institutions. Perhaps the most obvious connection is with the educational system. For instance, sociologist Thierry Noyelle (1987a), who has studied internal labor market changes for decades, points out that as higher education has grown, it has taken on many of the training functions that were formerly provided by internal labor markets. The requirements of the educational system also create a labor supply of youths looking for part-time jobs.

A Final Comparison of the Two Theoretical Frameworks

The different implications of neoclassical and institutionalist views can be summarized in four areas: the firm's tradeoffs between part-time and full-time employment; employer-initiated change in the rate of part-time employment; the nature of the key economic actors; and the role of history.

Neoclassical theory holds that firms maximize profits and thus seek to minimize production costs. Hence, employers will create part-time jobs if and only if they are less costly (or more productive) than full-time jobs. If workers are unable to find full-time (or part-time) jobs, it must be because it is more costly for firms to employ them as full-timers (or part-timers). Institutionalists do not necessarily question this logic, but emphasize that a labor market feature such as part-time employment comes bundled with job characteristics other than hours. Thus, creating or eliminating part-time jobs generally involves other changes in the jobs that must be considered in the employer's decision about hours.

In a neoclassical view, firms will change their rate of part-time employment when some exogenous parameter in the cost minimization problem shifts; such as workers' desire for time off, the production technology, or the time pattern of consumer demand. The change can be conceptualized as a shift in a supply or demand curve—a movement from one equilibrium to another in the same space. But in institutionalist theory, a change in a firm's environment, rather than invariably leading to adjustment in the same space, can sometimes lead the firm to jump discontinuously from one "bundle" to another.

Neoclassical economics usually assumes that although there may be pockets of buyer or seller market power in the labor market, the market can basically described as a collection of many individuals (firms and workers), each with little market power, pursuing their own self-interests. The institutionalist view of actors in the markets departs from the neoclassical view in four ways. First, collective actors (such as unions and groups of employers) are important. Second, apparently unified entities such as the firm or the household are actually riven by internal conflicts that have an important impact on their actions. Third, power relations that go well beyond the supply-and-demand struggle between individual buyer and seller shape employment practices. And finally, whereas neoclassical actors are rational, institutionalist theory emphasizes that tradition—and the ensemble of supporting institutions outside the firm—shape what firms and workers view as possible options. Thus, the range of possibilities is socially constructed rather than naturally given.

Furthermore, unlike the essentially ahistorical neoclassical model, in an institutionalist model history matters: what has come before in the labor market affects what happens next. For example, past struggles affect the present strength of economic actors. And once an employer has chosen a particular bundle of job characteristics, it may take a large shock to induce them to reconsider.

Each of these four distinctions surfaces in the book, demonstrating that it does matter which glasses you are wearing. The importance of the bundling of job characteristics figures throughout, particularly in the analyses of the two major types of part-time employment (Chapters 4 and 5) and of interindustry differences in the rate of part-time employment (Chapter 6). Economic behavior based on collectivity, struggle within economic units, power relations, and beliefs plays an important role in how firms decide on the level of part-time employment (Chapter 6) and why they change that level (Chapter 7). History—the trace of past decisions, agreements, and confrontations—also figures prominently in these two decision-making processes.

But enough of previews. Now that we have had the chance to try on various pairs of theoretical glasses, it is time to swing open the corporate door and peer inside.

Good and Bad Part-Time Jobs

4

■ LET'S START WITH A SIMPLE QUESTION: DO PART-TIME employees tend to be in high-skill or low-skill jobs? Two managers respond:

> It [a part-time job] would have to be a routine job that we can break up. . . . We don't want people at higher grades to be part-time [because] for these higher grades, there's quite a bit of training. [personnel director at an insurance company]

> You're going to find our more-skilled, higher level people in this [part-time status]. Our senior analysts and above as opposed to just the programmer who's just producing code where the skill level is just technical. [data processing manager at an insurance company]

Thus one manager sees part-time workers filling only low-skill jobs, whereas the other sees such workers in only high-skilled jobs.

Consider another simple question: what are the advantages and disadvantages of hiring a part-time worker? Once more, two managers have divergent answers:

> The pluses of hiring part-time people are the [low] rate of pay that you're able to pay them, the increased [schedule] flexibility that it will allow you, particularly if you have a varying business, varying volume. . . . And also the benefits that are available to a full-time person are not available to a part-timer. . . . [The minuses are] the abilities, experience, and work level that they achieve—their loyalty to the position and the company. . . . I'm talking about absenteeism, I'm talking about tardiness, shrinkage [theft], attitude. . . . [And] the part-time ratio . . . turn[s] over much faster than the full-time ratio. [supermarket manager]

> You probably will not find more committed employees than your part-time population. . . . Part-time people will tell you they work much harder than full-time people. . . . They want to hold on to their position. They want to do it all. They're driven. . . . [But] lack of availability is an issue. You're not as available. It slows things down. It's hard to schedule meetings. . . . [Part-time employment is] also expensive in terms of benefits. [insurance company employee services director]

Again, in one case part-time employment offers employers scheduling flexibility and lower wage and benefit costs but at the price of low productivity and high turnover. In the other case, part-time employment affords exceptionally high productivity but at the cost of decreased scheduling flexibility and increased benefit costs!

What's going on here? The answer is that there are two distinct types of part-time employment in the industries under study. The first manager in each case is talking about *secondary* part-time jobs. Secondary part-time workers have low skills and compensation compared to their full-time counterparts, and are immersed in a secondary labor market with little prospect of advancement. Employers use secondary part-time employment to attract workers, such as housewives and students, who will accept minimal compensation. Secondary part-time jobs are "bad" part-time jobs.

But the second manager answering each question is describing a completely different type of part-time employment: *retention* part-time jobs. Retention part-time workers have skill and compensation levels comparable to or above those of full-timers. Their part-time schedules are special arrangements negotiated to retain or attract valued employees, typically women with young children. Retention part-time jobs are "good" part-time jobs.

Managers are in some cases quite conscious of the distinction between the two forms of part-time employment. Commented a manager of pensions systems at an insurance company:

> In this particular environment that I am in, not everybody would shine as a part-time individual nor would you want them as a part-time individual. It takes a certain mentality, a certain intellect, a certain perspective on life and what you're trying to accomplish and knowledge as to what it is that this person offers you that you can't find anywhere else. Contrast [a part-timer at my company to] the part-time employee at McDonald's. [When McDonald's hires somebody part-time,] it's not because there's all those things I mentioned, it's just because they can't get anybody to work there anyway and the only way they can get them is by offering high [*sic*] salary, flexible hours. It's to attract anybody as opposed to mine which is to attract specific, talented individuals. So there's a contrast in need that causes this willingness to have part-timers.

Most literature on part-time employment has not recognized such differences within the part-time pool. But from time to time, researchers have provided fascinating glimpses of diversity. For instance, Stanley Nollen, Brenda Broz Eddy, and Virginia Hider Martin (1978) explored the manager's view of permanent part-time work in a detailed study that included several surveys and open-ended interviews of principals in firms that used such employment as well as those that did not. They reported that although half the companies they surveyed gave part-time workers no health insurance at all, one-third offered them the full, non-prorated benefit; in effect they were offering more health benefits per hour to part-timers than to full-timers. Even more interesting, although 36 percent of the unit managers and 35 percent of the personnel officers surveyed by Nollen and colleagues described part-time workers as having higher turnover rates than full-timers, another 21 percent of the unit managers and 35 percent of the personnel officers reported that part-timers had lower turnover rates. The survey yielded similar split opinions on the relative productivity of part-time and full-time workers. Nollen, Eddy, and Martin strenuously contended that part-time workers are unfairly maligned, but I suspect that their sample—primarily manufacturing and insurance firms—overrepresented retention part-time workers, leading to somewhat misleading results.

The qualitative literature also refers to nontraditional part-time jobs. For example, in her study of MBAs from MIT's Sloan School of Management, industrial relations scholar Phyllis Wallace (1989) noted that part-time working mothers "have usually been able to negotiate a part-time consulting relationship with their employers" (p. 100).

In contrast to most economists discussing part-time work, Hilda Kahne (1985) did identify two categories of part-time employment: "old concept" and "new concept." According to Kahne, employers viewed the new concept part-time workers as permanent workers with career potential, rather than as temporary or intermittent workers. The new concept part-time job also generally provides fringe benefits, unlike old concept part-time jobs. My secondary/retention split holds much in common with the old concept/new concept distinction.

This chapter describes some of the many dimensions along which secondary and retention part-time jobs differ. It begins with scrutiny of the bundles of job characteristics that make up each of the two types of part-time employment. I argue that these characteristics bundle because the two types are associated with different internal labor markets—a secondary labor market on the one hand, and salaried or other primary labor markets on the other hand. I also examine the distinct institutions outside of work that support each form of part-time employment. The following chapter explores added implications of the secondary/retention distinction, including the rather different advantages and disadvantages that each holds for employers.

The Characteristics of Secondary and Retention Part-Time Jobs

Four sets of key characteristics distinguish secondary from retention part-time employment: skill, training, and responsibility, pay and benefits, turnover, and promotion ladders. This section examines each of the characteristics in turn. In many cases, before presenting the results of my research, I discuss what others have reported about the average characteristics of part-time jobs.

Skill, Training, and Responsibility

Previous research says relatively little about the skill involved in part-time jobs, but my interviews yielded quite a bit of information. Secondary part-time jobs involve low levels of skill, training, and responsibility. In retail stores, full-timers tend to cover the more skilled and responsible tasks, while part-time workers handle low-skill tasks. For example, most supermarkets use only full-time workers in meat-cutting jobs—which are skilled positions—although they employ part-time servers and wrappers in the meat department. On the other hand, a manager at the chain I call SuperValu stated that front-end employees—cashiers and baggers, both relatively unskilled positions—represent the bulk of the part-time workforce. Data from a union-conducted 1987 survey of a Pittsburgh supermarket chain confirm this contrast: only 54 percent of union workers in the meat and deli departments were part-time, compared to 84 percent of union employees in the rest of the store.

Even within low-level job categories like stock clerk in a supermarket or sales clerk in a convenience or department store, management assigns different tasks to part-timers and full-timers. Managers are more likely to give full-time employees responsibilities such as ordering, receiving goods, taking inventory, or doing paperwork. Part-time workers typically just stock the display cases or ring the register. A SuperValu store manager reported: "[The full-timers] come in the morning and get things set up, do the prep. The part-time employees then just maintain it for the rest of the day. It's different to set up and do ordering than to just dump more fruit out there." The distinction between part-time and full-time tasks may be formal or informal. In one convenience store chain,

> They [full-timers] might even do some paper work, some smaller duty that the manager would delegate to a full-time clerk . . . . It's not in their job description, it's just something they're assigned, or they can do it,

and they want to do it. But really, as far as the job description, no, there's no difference between a full-time or a part-time.

Similarly, in a fast-food company, full-timers do meal prep and recovery (cleanup)—a somewhat more varied and complex set of tasks—while part-timers come in during peak mealtimes to cook and serve.

For in-store jobs, use of part-timers appears to be negatively correlated with job training time. Table 4.1 shows reported training times from EZ Mart and SuperValu. While there is some variation around these examples—supermarket cashier training ranges from one day to two weeks among the retailers surveyed—the rank order is found consistently.

In retail office clerical jobs, much the same pattern applies. The personnel director of a convenience store chain explained that his company uses mostly full-time people in office jobs because "our philosophy is: if you want somebody you can ask more of, you have to be in position where you can do more for them."

In insurance, secondary part-timers are found in unskilled service jobs (cafeteria, building service) and in lower-skill clerical jobs with more discrete, less integrative tasks. Part-time clerical jobs were described as being jobs that were "not crucial", jobs found in "your production departments," jobs in which "somebody can put down their work and somebody else can pick it up," "a routine job that we can break up", and

TABLE 4.1
Training Periods and Part-Time or Full-Time Status by Job at EZ Mart and SuperValu

Job	Training period	Part- or Full-Time
EZ MART		
Sales clerk*	24 hours	Mostly part-time
Assistant manager	3 months	Only full-time
Manager	6 months	Only full-time
SUPERVALU		
Cashier	24 hours	Mostly part-time
Part-time grocery clerk	30 hours	Only part-time
Full-time grocery clerk	62–72 hours	Only full-time
Baker	6 weeks	Only full-time

*Combines cashier and clerk functions.
Source: Interviews by author.

"usually just one job, duty—a repeated task," especially "when there are certain times of day that need service". Typical part-time clerical jobs include data entry, filing, mail sorting, direct mail stuffing, and typing in a typing pool.

There is an inverse correlation between training time and the use of part-time employment in claims processing at the health insurer I call Healthco. For example, the main data entry job, which entails two or three days of formal training and takes two to four weeks to master, is staffed completely with part-timers. However, the company uses exclusively full-time workers in claims coding, which takes six to eight months to learn fully. A Healthco manager commented, "Part-timers are in jobs that require a shorter length of training and normally have a faster learning curve."

But all of this is only half the story. The other half is retention part-time jobs, concentrated in technical and professional occupations with high levels of skill, training, and responsibility. For example, the manager of an insurance company's pension systems area said the following about his part-time employees:

> The fact that they're part-timers . . . really serves two purposes. One, they're still raising their children. . . . But the most important thing is that they have a wealth of knowledge and are very critical resources in the area [for whom it] is very difficult to find replacements. [I]t takes three to five years [for a new person] to develop to the level of expertise where they could contribute very heavily to the pension world.

He emphasized that he will grant a part-time job only to "someone who is critical to my goals."

The same reasoning applies to certain retail jobs, although they are a small minority of retail's part-time jobs. The personnel director of a supermarket chain noted: "In the systems area, we have tried to customize the job to fit the job-seeker. It's a very tight labor market. . . . A lot of computer people like to work part-time."

One insurance company's personnel director provided a neat summary of the twofold character of part-time jobs:

> Training costs are . . . minimal for support jobs—routine jobs—collating, printing, shipping, typing. That's one reason we don't want people at higher grades to be part-time. For these higher grades, there's quite a bit of training: there's a mix of classroom, formal, and on-the-job training. So usually if someone is part-time in these grades it's formerly full-time, already trained employees—people who requested part-time hours.

In certain jobs, there is almost no part-time employment of either kind. Managers almost never work part-time, and the few informants who had used part-time managers (on a retention basis) felt that the experiment had been unsuccessful. Part-time insurance agents are also rare.

Pay and Benefits

Unlike skill levels, part-timers' pay and benefits have been quite thoroughly examined by economists. On average, part-time workers earn less on an hourly basis and receive fewer benefits than full-timers. Part-timers in 1993 had a median hourly wage of $5.55, only 62 percent of the full-time median of $7.43—a wage differential of 38 percent. The differential was wider for men than for women (48 percent and 28 percent, respectively).[1] In some cases, companies have paid part-time workers much lower hourly wages than full-timers performing the identical job. For example, the now-defunct People Express and Presidential Airlines paid part-time reservation workers half the hourly wage of full-timers (Nine to Five 1986).

Part-time workers disproportionately crowd the very bottom of the wage distribution. Among part-time workers, 28 percent earned the minimum wage or less in 1984, compared to 5 percent of full-time workers. Part-timers comprise 65 percent of all people working at or below the minimum wage (Mellor and Haugen 1986).

The discrepancy in weekly wages is, of course, much greater. In 1993, part-timers earned $135 a week at the median, against full-timers' $463. Many part-time workers also work only part of the year. While 60 percent of all persons who worked in 1978 worked year-round, only 40 percent of part-timers did so, and a full 31 percent worked less than half the year (Terry 1981).

How much of the full-time/part-time hourly wage differential is due to part-time status itself rather than other characteristics of part-time workers or jobs? Economist John Owen (1978, 1979) found that after controlling for sex, race, education, and experience, a 29 percent full-time/part-time wage differential remained. However, he estimated that as much as 19 of the 29 percentage points resulted from the concentration of part-timers in low-paid industries and occupations. Steuernagel and Hilber (1984) found that segregation of part-timers by industry and occupation explains about one-third of the raw wage differential.

Cornell economist Ronald Ehrenberg and his colleagues (1988) looked at wages separately for 46 industry subsamples, controlling for education, work experience, cost of living, and other variables in addition to part-time status. They discovered negative part-time differentials in all but 4 industries. The employment-weighted average of the part-time penalty across all 46 industries was 13 percent.

But Northwestern University economist Rebecca Blank (1986, 1990) threatened to upset the apple cart by suggesting that part-time employment may have a *positive* wage payoff for women. She started by looking at part-time status as just one of a large number of characteristics that can affect a worker's wage, and found that part-time women workers earn about 21 percent less and part-time men workers about 30 percent less than comparable full-timers. But such simple estimates will suffer from error if characteristics that affect a person's wage also affect the probability that that person will end up in part-time work. So in addition, Blank carefully modeled a three-step process of what determines whether somebody works, whether a worker ends up in full-time or part-time work, and what the wage will be once the worker has been selected into part-time or full-time work. Once this process is taken into account, men still suffer a part-time wage penalty of 18 percent, Blank found. But women working as voluntary part-timers actually receive higher wages (by about 17 percent) than if they worked the same job full-time; women working part-time involuntarily still take a wage hit, however.

How can this apparent positive part-time premium for women be reconciled with the negative effects found in simpler estimates? As Blank pointed out, the premium implies that once the person and the job have been selected, the wage will be higher if the person works part-time rather than full-time. The selection process itself (combining employer and worker choices), then, preferentially selects less productive women or less productive jobs into part-time work, accounting for the overall wage penalty, but once it has been established that a job or person is likely to end up in part-time work, that person or job will garner higher pay if hours are part-time.

An example may illustrate. Suppose a woman has child-care problems that cause her to miss work regularly, especially during nonschool hours. Because of this, she works less productively in either part-time *or* full-time jobs, and receives lower pay as a result. However, she most likely will select part-time work. Since we cannot observe child-care problems in standard data sets like the one Blank used, an economist who saw this woman in a part-time job but ignored the selection process would conclude that she earns less because she works part-time. But in fact, she earns less because child-care needs interfere with her productivity. She will be more productive, and therefore likely to receive more pay per hour, in a part-time job than in a full-time job in which the child-care problems would be even more severe.

But the interview results described above suggest other possibilities that explain the full-time/part-time differential as well. For example, consider a grocery store with part-time and full-time stock clerks. As in many of the retailers discussed above, managers more often assign higher value tasks to full-timers rather than part-timers, so full-timers receive a higher hourly rate. Part-timers' activities, such as restocking fruits and vegetables, are needed on a peak-time basis. Again, the difference between the two jobs cannot be detected in standard data, since they both fall in the same occupational category. But the reduced pay and part-time status of the lower level clerk *both* result from the lower value tasks involved; the part-time schedule does not cause the lower pay. Indeed, if the store manager turned these tasks into a full-time job instead, productivity and pay would be even lower, because the employee would do so little between peak times. This hypothesis—that it is the kind of job rather than the part-time hours that leads to lower pay—conforms with Owen's and Steuernagel and Hilber's findings that occupation and industry account for a large part of the part-time/full-time wage gap. And my interview data confirm that in many cases part-time and full-time jobs, even if they have the same title, *are* quite different.

As a third instance, consider women professionals in a large insurance company—the kind of women who landed retention part-time jobs in the businesses I interviewed. In deciding how to assign promotions or added responsibilities, department managers implicitly assess the likelihood that a given woman will have children and want to take time off to care for them, and therefore will be less productive as a professional. They accordingly shunt some women to the "(likely) mommy track" and others to the "fast track." Assuming the department heads are decent prognosticators, women on the mommy track will more often request reduction to part-time hours. But managers will grant retention part-time status to only the best and most valuable producers in that track. The result: retention part-time women earn *less* than the average woman professional at the company, because they have been selected into the mommy track. But within the mommy track, they earn *more* than women working full-time, because the full-timers include those women not productive enough to win a part-time arrangement. Adding credence to this scenario, Blank found a particularly large, positive payoff to part-time women workers in professional and managerial positions.

One might conclude from Blank's reading of the data that lower wages for part-timers are fair because these workers are less productive. But caution is advised. The two patterns she discusses—lower productivity workers and lower productivity jobs—may interact in a vicious circle. For instance, when employers perceive workers as lacking in experience or responsibility, they will place them in part-time jobs where less experience or responsibility is needed. But part-time jobs also provide less experience and teach less responsibility, leaving the already disadvantaged workers farther behind. Furthermore, employers may sort workers between high- and low-productivity jobs in some discriminatory fashion. Finally, Blank's analysis assumes that pay follows productivity. If in fact part-time workers are actually as productive as full-timers but employers devalue the kind of person they are (say, a woman with children) or the kind of work they do, the results will still look like Blank's.

In any case, this entire discussion overlooks a very important part of the compensation picture: fringe benefits. Part-timers receive fewer fringe benefits than full-timers. Researchers have relied on the U.S. Census Bureau's Current Population Survey for an overview of health and pension benefits. In 1987, only 18 percent of part-timers received health insurance as a benefit, compared to 72 percent of full-timers—a 54-point gap (Piacentini and Cerino 1990). While some receive health coverage through their spouses, the Employee Benefits Research Institute estimated that 48 percent of part-timers (versus 27 percent of their full-time counterparts) have no employer-provided health coverage. A full 21 percent of part-time workers (versus 16 percent of full-timers) lack health coverage from any source, including the government (Employee Benefits Research Institute 1994). As for involuntary part-time workers, Sar Levitan and Elizabeth Conway (1988) of the Washington-based Center for Social Policy Studies found that a considerably higher proportion—almost one-third of those who spent at least one week a year working part-time involuntarily—had no health insurance at all. Similarly, only 11 percent of part-timers have employer-supplied pension coverage, whereas 48 percent of full-timers enjoy such coverage (calculated from Employee Benefits Research Institute 1994, Table 26; also see Rebitzer 1987, Blank 1990).

Using two other data sets—the 1977 Quality of Employment Survey and the 1979 Survey of Job Characteristics—Ichniowski and Preston (1985) confirmed part-timers' benefits shortfall. They reported that the probabilities of having sick leave, paid vacation, pension, and health insurance are significantly decreased for part-timers. Depending on the specific benefit and data source, part-timers are from 11 percent to 33 percent less likely to obtain these benefits.

The benefit gap looms even larger in small businesses, where more than half of the part-time workforce toils (Employee Benefits Research Institute 1994). A special U.S. Bureau of Labor Statistics (1991) survey of small establishments (those with fewer than 100 employees) found 69 percent of full-time workers and only 6 percent of part-timers receiving health coverage. But large firms are not immune. A 1985 survey of 484 medium-to-large employers by Hewitt Associates, a Chicago consulting firm (Worsnop 1987), indicated that benefit coverage drops off sharply with hours worked. For example, 99 percent of these employers offer health insurance to full-timers, and a substantial 73 percent offer this benefit to part-timers working 30 hours or more, but only 13 percent provide such coverage for people working less than 20 hours a week. This general pattern is echoed for dental, life, accidental death and dismemberment, and long-term disability insurance, paid sick leave, paid holidays, and paid vacation.

Research indicates that otherwise identical workers and jobs receive fewer fringes when they are part-time. Ehrenberg and his colleagues (1986) estimated pension and health insurance differentials, controlling for worker characteristics and other variables, and found that part-timers are less likely to receive these benefits in every one of 46 industries. And on this point Blank (1990) agrees, reporting that even after controlling for the selection process, part-time women and men workers are substantially less likely to be included in health and pension plans.

Not all part-timers get less. Eleven percent of the companies quizzed by Hermine Zagat Levine (1987) pay full benefits to part-timers. And in a 1977 survey of mostly large companies, Nollen, Eddy, and Martin (1978) discovered that although half give part-timers no health insurance at all, one-third offer them the full, non-prorated benefit. In effect, the latter companies pay out more for health benefits on a per hour basis for part-timers than for full-timers.

My retail and insurance industry interviews recast these compensation patterns in terms of the distinction between secondary and retention part-time workers. Secondary part-time workers receive reduced fringe benefits and in some cases lower hourly pay than full-timers. Differentials in fringe benefits are widespread, particularly in retail trade with its large mass of secondary part-timers. As a fast-food company's personnel director observed, "traditionally American business doesn't provide fringe benefits to part-time workers." Every retail company surveyed pays lower fringes to part-timers. Retailers commonly exclude part-time employees from one or more of the insurance benefits (health, life, disability). The SuperValu supermarket chain estimates that it spends 20 percent of base pay for benefits for part-timers, compared to 36–41 percent for full-timers. Given that there is also a difference in hourly wages (see below), this means that part-time benefit costs are roughly one-quarter of the full-time costs on a per-hour basis—and total part-time hourly compensation is about 43 percent of that of full-timers. In Pittsburgh area supermarkets, the lowest rung of part-timers, customer service clerks—better known as baggers—receive no benefits at all.

The majority of the insurance companies also reduce benefits for part-timers. For example, two offer part-timers only prorated vacation and holidays (versus sick pay and health, life, and accident insurance for full-timers in one case). The insurance companies offering reduced benefits to part-timers include those where secondary part-time employment is most common, particularly the three health insurers, which are the only insurance companies to adopt deliberate strategies of expanding part-time employment.

Lower hourly wages for part-timers are standard at supermarkets. SuperValu's personnel director estimates that the company pays part-timers, on average, half the hourly wage of full-timers. Nationwide, supermarket chains surveyed by the magazine *Progressive Grocer* (1993) reported an hourly starting wage of $4.93 for a part-time clerk in 1992, roughly three-quarters of the $6.37 starting wage for a full-time clerk.

Other types of retail establishments, however, tend to pay full-time and part-time workers identical hourly wages. A reduced hourly rate for part-timers is also rare among insurers, although one company provides its part-time employees with longevity raises only every two years instead of once a year.

One-third of the surveyed retail companies reported that they even have employees working a full 40 hours who are considered part-timers and thus receive lower fringe benefits. One of them explained:

> I do have people working forty hours a week in baggers' jobs. But they are not considered full-time people. . . . The difference is the rate of pay that they're able to get. And also the benefits that are available to a full-time person are not available to a part-timer. It's really just a job title more so than the work performed.

But once more, there is another side to the issue. Five of the 12 insurance companies provide full benefits to all employees working above some cutoff in the range of 18 to 24 hours a week, which ends up covering the bulk of part-timers. "Full benefits" in these cases means full insurance benefits and prorated other benefits. In all of these companies, retention part-time employment is the main form of part-time employment.

In contrast with the retailers who have "part-timers" working 40 hours, at least one insurance company had a "full-timer" working 20 hours:

> MANAGER: When Carol ——— was ill, did she work part-time for a while?
> EXECUTIVE SECRETARY: The one that had the heart condition? Yes. She worked half-days but she was still considered a full-time—
> MANAGER: She was a full-time, regular employee.

This contrast accords well with Blank's notion that it is the person and the job, not the part-time hours, that make the difference in terms of pay.

Setting benefit levels for part-time workers can pose certain problems for employers, for it is not practicable to offer full benefits to some part-time workers (the retention part-timers) and partial benefits to other part-timers (the secondary ones). Thus, it is not surprising to find generous fringe benefit provisions for part-timers at the companies that use the most retention part-time employment, and reduced fringe benefits at those where secondary part-time employment is most common.

Turnover

On the average, part-time workers stay at jobs for much shorter periods than full-timers. Employers of secondary part-timers are aware of and indeed obsessed with this fact. Those who manage retention part-timers, on the other hand, use part-time employment precisely to reduce turnover.

The average job tenure of part-timers is 3.4 years, well below the average of 5.7 years for full-time women workers and 8.1 years for full-time men workers (Rebitzer 1987). Furthermore, more than 1 in 4 part-time workers surveyed in a given month has left the labor force altogether 12 months later, compared with only 1 in 19 full-time women workers and one in 34 full-time men workers! Nollen and his colleagues (1978) asked both individual unit managers and chief personnel specialists to compare the turnover of part-time and full-time employees. Unit managers, who are more sour on part-time turnover, generally responded that it was worse (36 percent) or no different (44 percent) than full-time turnover. Personnel specialists, on the other hand, were almost evenly divided in ranking part-timers' turnover as "worse," "better," and "no different" than that of full-timers.

High turnover is the bane of managers employing secondary part-timers. Retailers universally report higher turnover among part-timers than among full-timers. At the SuperValu grocery chain part-time turnover, at 116 percent annually, exceeds full-time turnover (11.5 percent) by a factor of ten! EZ Mart, the Boston-area convenience store chain, experiences 312 percent part-time turnover annually, dwarfing the 134 percent among full-timers. Part-time turnover is overwhelmingly composed of quitting in most settings—"easily" 90 percent or more, according to a SuperValu manager.

The high turnover of retail part-timers stands in striking contrast to full-timers in retail, who are remarkably stable, especially where a union contract improves wages and working conditions:

> They *marry* those jobs. [union official]

> The turnover rate with the full-timers is very, very slim, almost nil. You know, we're talking a full-timer leaving probably only because of retirement, and some chance of them finding a higher-paid job. [supermarket store manager]

Specifically, one independent supermarket and one department store reported *zero* turnover among full-timers in the previous year (part-time rates were 200 percent and 78 percent, respectively). While turnover rates of 200 or 300 percent are exceptionally high, the full-time/part-time disparity holds up in national data. Grocery chains queried by *Progressive Grocer* in 1990 reported that they had hired 45 percent of their part-timers and only 9 percent of their full-timers during the preceding year.

Insurers also commented on higher turnover among some part-timers. Managers at two health insurers employing large bodies of secondary part-timers were particularly emphatic:

> Part-time[rs] have a much higher rate of turnover.
> My guess . . . based on my experience is I'd run a 15 to 20 percent turnover rate in the full-timers annually, and I'd run closer to a 40 to 50 percent turnover on part-timers.

But among retention part-timers, part-time employment is an *alternative* to turnover:

> INTERVIEWER: What's your sense of what would happen if you said to these women, "No, you can't have part-time hours"?
> MANAGER: I think in every case they would terminate their employment. And that . . . comes from the fact that their skills are very marketable. . . . I suppose the tradeoff that's mentally taking place by me and by other managers when these situations are coming up is that . . . here are my choices: [if I say yes, you may work part-time,] I get less work for the same position; if I say no, how am I going to replace the skill set?

In many cases, retention part-timers eventually move back to full-time hours, sometimes as a result of company pressure:

> We don't like people to stay on part-time forever. . . . Some departments will tolerate part-time employees for 6 to 12 months. Then they'll look at them again after a year. The vast majority of employees who go part-time return to full-time after a year.

Promotion Ladders

Part-timers face special barriers to promotion. The unit managers and personnel specialists surveyed by Nollen et al. tended to consider part-timers "less promotable" than full-time workers. According to Nine to Five (1986), company policies block the promotion of part-timers in many cases. For example, Control Data Corporation, the University of Cincinnati, Los Angeles Community College, and Cigna Corporation treat applications for full-time jobs from part-timers within their organizations no differently than applications from outsiders. "Peak-time" work in banks (part-time work matched to busy banking hours) has been designed to exclude advancement. Says Stuart Martin, the originator of peak-time work, "Peak-time is not meant to provide job security rights or career mobility. The point is to get workers who want to remain in part-time jobs" (quoted in ibid., 30).

This profile fits secondary part-time jobs, which tend to be both entry level and dead-end. Retention part-time jobs, however, are generally located part of the way up a promotion path. In both cases, promotion beyond a certain limited span means moving to a full-time job.

In all kinds of retail establishments, for example, secondary part-time jobs form the bottom of a ladder that extends upward to full-time jobs and thence into management. Many food retailers have a formal requirement that full-timers be hired exclusively from their part-time ranks, not from outside the company, and still others apply this policy de facto. But although most full-timers in retail food were once part-time workers, few part-timers become full-timers. The explanation for this paradox is that there are very few full-time jobs—less than 20 percent of the jobs in the store, in quite a few cases—and that full-timers turn over slowly. Most people leave part-time retail jobs the same way they came in: through the door.

At insurance companies, secondary part-time jobs are often cut off from the rest of the workforce by nonstandard shifts or geographically remote locations (a feature at Boston-area health insurer Healthco). One of Healthco's suburban part-time facilities, with 280 employees, is 93 percent part-time—more segregated than any of the supermarkets surveyed. Thus, moving to full-time from a secondary part-time job may involve a change in shift and/or job location. Some companies also have additional rules designed to minimize such mobility. For example, a Pittsburgh insurer requires part-timers to stay at least a year before moving to a full-time job.

Retention part-time workers, on the other hand, perch in the middle of job ladders. Retention part-time arrangements are usually worked out for employees with substantial company-specific training, such as underwriters, or workers with very marketable skills, such as systems analysts.

However, working a part-time schedule at this level generally means forgoing further promotion—at least until the worker returns to full-time hours. Eternal Life's employee services director noted succinctly, "We don't hire part-time people and run them up these ladders as part-timers." Part-timers are also generally barred from management positions at the top of the job ladder. In the words of Eternal Life's data processing manager, part-time schedules are only tolerated among "individual contributors," not "team leaders."

Summarizing the Differences

These differences between secondary and retention part-time employment are not just isolated examples but rather reflect widespread patterns, at least within my sample of 29 retail and insurance companies. To document this, I classified informants' comments on skill, compensation, and so on according to whether they referred to secondary or retention part-time workforces. The key characteristic used to distinguish between the retention and secondary groups is the stated reason for employing part-time workers. If managers stated the major reason was to retain or attract people with valued skill or experience, the jobs were classified as retention part-time. If the main reason cited was lower costs or schedule flexibility, the jobs were classified as secondary.

At 22 of the 29 firms, respondents reported on only one of the two types of part-time employment. At the other 7 companies, interviewees commented on both types, and the statements had to be sorted according to which portion of the part-time workforce they were referring.[2]

The data on all 29 companies confirm the generalizations made above about job demands, compensation, and turnover. Secondary part-time workers almost invariably have jobs involving less skill, responsibility, and training than their full-time co-workers. Retention part-timers tend to have greater skill and training than their co-workers but less responsibility, reflecting the fact that they are barred from manager or "team leader" roles. Secondary part-time workers have lower fringe benefits than full-timers and in some cases lower hourly wages as well; retention part-timers tend to have the same fringes and wage rates. Turnover is elevated for secondary part-timers, depressed for retention part-timers.

Tabulating the relationship between part-time jobs and job ladders is a trickier matter, but once more the data support the claims made above. Secondary part-time workers usually were originally hired on a part-time basis, whereas retention part-timers most often started on a full-time basis and were granted an hours reduction later. For secondary part-time workers, a move to a full-time job would represent a promotion, whereas for retention part-timers it is simply a change in hours.

The Link Between Part-Time Employment and Internal Labor Markets

A picture of secondary and retention part-time employment is emerging. The former is marked by minimal skill, training, and responsibility; low benefits and/or hourly wages; high turnover; and little connection to promotion ladders. The latter exhibits an opposite set of characteristics.

But this is precisely the distinction between secondary and primary labor markets. Secondary and retention part-time jobs are the way they are because they occur in particular internal labor markets—a secondary labor market in the case of retail clerks and insurance claim coders, a salaried labor market in the case of technical and professional workers, a craft labor market in the case of computer programmers.

In other words, part-time jobs are good or bad for the same reasons that full-time jobs are. There is nothing inherent to part-time jobs that dictates that they must have low productivity and compensation. Even in a retail food store, where the boundary between high- and low-compensation jobs in the stores is the line between full-time and part-time, it is the secondary labor market embodied in the part-time jobs—not their shortened hours—that brands them as inferior. A part-time systems analyst working for the same retail food company has a productive, high-paid job.

The Link Between Part-Time Employment and Supporting Institutions

In addition to various internal labor markets within the workplace, secondary and retention part-time employment are supported by certain institutions outside the workplace. Secondary part-time work builds on the distinction between breadwinners and secondary earners as well as the institutions that strengthen that distinction. Retention part-time work depends on the erosion of the distinction.

The tipoff to identifying these supporting institutions comes from a look at who works the part-time jobs. Secondary part-time jobs are mainly filled by housewives, students, and a smaller number of moonlighters. These are workers supplementing income from other sources, whose main life activity lies outside this job. Their limited employment aspirations and their limited attachment to any job form a match with the minimal rewards of a secondary part-time job. The prevalence of these groups in the secondary part-time population, in turn, legitimizes different treatment for full-timers and part-timers. As one supermarket manager put it: "A full-time employee is usually [a man] that has a family, or is planning a family, or planning to get married. The part-time employee is a kid looking for a car payment."

Some retailers even screen for supplementary earners when they hire for part-time jobs, as the personnel director of a Boston-area convenience store chain reported: "[Our company] require[s] that part-time employees have another source of income—they [have] to be either full-time students, a spouse, [or] living at home with their parents—because we [know it is] unreasonable to think that they would live on this income alone."

The distinction between breadwinners and secondary earners may seem like a natural one, but in fact, the factors that reinforce this distinction are man-made. Students become secondary workers because the U.S. educational system generally requires full-time study, rather than using apprenticeship or cooperative education models to integrate paid work with classroom learning. Housewives become secondary earners because child care is not widely available, and because of the social norm that individual women bear the primary responsibility for housework and child-rearing.

A turning point in the separation of primary and secondary earner roles was the struggle for the family wage that began in the early nineteenth century in the United States (Buhle 1981, 8; Milkman 1980, 108–10). Under the banner of the family wage, male trade unionists fought for a wage sufficient for a single male breadwinner to support his family. As a corollary, they fought to exclude married women and children from the workforce—or at least from the skilled trades over which they had some control. To the extent that this movement was successful, it defended the standard of living of the working class family, but also represented the adoption of the ideology that "a woman's (or child's) place is in the home" by the most organized and influential sectors of the working class. The ongoing distinction between breadwinner and secondary earner is a sequel to this contention championed some 150 years ago.

If further evidence of the unnaturalness of the breadwinner/secondary earner distinction is needed, retention part-time employment provides it. Retention part-timers in the companies sampled are mainly women with young children. Because these women are skilled and provide an essential part of their family's income, they are unwilling to give up their jobs to care for their children. Because the companies value their skills highly, they are unwilling to give them up for the sake of maintaining a full-time workforce.

For the retention arrangements to work, the employees need various supports outside of work, such as husbands who assist with child-rearing and day-care facilities that allow them to return to work full-time once the children reach a certain age. There also has to be a shift in attitudes. A union official who has represented insurance workers and other clericals reflected: "Parenting as a reason for part-time work has become more acceptable. Before, they [management] would say, you're crazy, or too bad you're doing that, or you can't stay." Thus, retention part-time workers are neither breadwinners nor supplementary earners. And they are lucky enough to obtain a work arrangement that recognizes their position.

Frequencies of Secondary and Retention Part-Time Employment

Although employers do not count their secondary and retention part-time employees separately, it is fairly clear that in both retail and insurance the secondary labor markets harbor more part-time workers than do the primary labor markets. In retail, secondary part-timers work in the stores in clerk and cashier jobs, whereas retention part-timers mainly work in professional and technical jobs in the back office. Among the retail firms surveyed, the rate of part-time employment is uniformly much higher in the stores (an average of 72 percent, after weighting by firm employment size) than in the offices (12 percent, on average). The contrast would probably be still greater if professional and technical workers were considered separately from office clericals.

In insurance, secondary part-timers are clerical and service workers, and retention part-timers once more inhabit the professional and technical occupations. The distribution of part-time jobs by occupation ranges from the situation at Eternal Life, where the majority of part-time workers are at the technical level or above, to that at Healthco, where hundreds of low-skilled claims processors make up the vast bulk of the part-time workforce. A distribution between these two extremes is probably typical: many part-time clericals, especially in the lowest employment grades, and a scattering of part-time technical, professional, and service workers. Certainly informants at every insurance company surveyed agreed that part-timers at the professional or technical level are rare indeed.

It is not surprising, on the face of it, that part-time jobs are more common in secondary labor markets than in primary labor markets. Retention part-time employment is by its nature exceptional, extended to one employee at a time on a negotiated basis. Secondary part-time employment, on the other hand, is applied to whole job categories. The reasons for this are explored further in Chapter 6.

Generalizing to the Retail and Insurance Industries

Quite a few patterns in part-time employment have emerged from the interview data presented in this chapter. How representative are the sampled companies of their industries?

As a first cut at this question, consider the informants' answers. Retailers generally reported that their companies discussed labor issues regularly with other retail companies in addition to staying in touch through the trade literature. Retail informants tended to view their experience as typical of the industry—and in some cases of the entire economy:

> SUPERMARKET MANAGER: Everyone's probably pretty much in the same boat we are, with pretty much full-time meat departments, and then maybe just a few full-timers sprinkled throughout the store. Part-time is basically where it's at, right now.

CONVENIENCE STORE PERSONNEL OFFICER: I think you'll find the same trends in all convenience stores.

FAST-FOOD CHAIN PERSONNEL DIRECTOR: The volume of use of part-time is pretty much identical in food service.

UNION OFFICIAL: The country has more or less basically gone part-time. No matter where you look, if you look at the banks, they're part-time. Even if you look at the wholesale industry, they've become part-time. I think the country, with the man and wife working now, is basically a part-time work force.

Insurance companies, like retailers, communicate with other insurers and large clerical employers about labor-related policies. But part-time labor is not as central a concern in insurance as it is in retail, and most insurance managers were not particularly conscious of how other companies used part-time employment. Managers from some companies at the extremes were aware that their firms' practices were exceptional. For example, a high-ranking Healthco manager remarked that relatively few companies have followed Healthco's suit by rapidly expanding part-time employment: "Other companies have pursued it, but not as aggressively and not as widespread as I would have expected." On the whole, insurance informants agreed that "insurance companies tend to be middle of the road. . . . Insurance companies will usually try things that other companies have tried."

The Nationwide Data

Moving beyond these opinions, the generality of this chapter's findings on part-time employment within the retail and insurance industries is testable with larger, more representative data sets. The central claim of this chapter is that there exist two categories of part-time jobs, secondary and retention, with distinct characteristics, that are linked to secondary and primary labor markets, respectively. A strong test of this hypothesis would depend on a multidimensional measure of the characteristics of part-time employment and a measure of the type of internal labor market, neither of which is readily available. But an alternative, indirect measure can be used to tap Current Population Survey data.

To arrive at an indirect gauge of the type of part-time employment, note that in secondary part-time employment, the part-time characteristic is usually inherent to jobs, not people. But in retention part-time employment, part-time people are accommodated in jobs that are ordinarily full-time. In both of the industries studied, there is evidence that secondary part-time jobs outnumber retention part-time jobs. Therefore, a high rate of part-time employment can be used as a marker of secondary part-time work, and occupation can be used as a marker for primary and secondary labor markets. Thus, a weaker test of the hypothesis is to examine whether the connection between occupation and the rate of part-time employment is the same in a representative sample as in the interview sample.

Several specific predictions can be made based on the interview results:

1. *The highest concentration of part-time employment should be found in low-skill occupations.* In retail, high rates of part-time employment are expected in the broad occupational categories of sales, service, and operative/laborer jobs. Somewhat lower rates are expected in clerical jobs. In insurance, high rates of part-time employment should be found in clerical and service jobs. The part-time employment rate in professional and technical jobs in both industries is also expected to be above the rate in managerial jobs, reflecting the retention category.

In both retail trade and insurance, the ranking of occupations by rate of part-time employment is as predicted. In retail, sales, service, and operative/laborer jobs indeed have the highest rates of part-time employment (Table 4.2). Clerical jobs have a lower rate, and technical and professional jobs lower still. Part-time employment is lowest in managerial jobs, as expected. The same patterns prevail in the grocery subsector.

In insurance, service and clerical operative employees have a high incidence of part-time employment, as expected (Table 4.3). Managers,

TABLE 4.2

Percent of Part-Time Employment by Occupation in the Retail and Grocery Industries, March 1992*

	Retail			Grocery		
Occupation	Involuntary Part-Time	Voluntary Part-Time	All Part-Time	Involuntary Part-Time	Voluntary Part-Time	All Part-Time
Managerial	2.0	5.4	7.4	0	6.8	6.8
Professional	6.9	17.2	24.1	20.4	0	20.4
Technical	2.9	20.3	23.2	0	26.0	26.0
Sales	8.5	28.6	37.1	9.2	30.8	40.1
Administrative/ clerical	8.5	23.4	32.0	10.7	27.1	37.9
Service	14.8	39.3	54.0	14.0	36.5	50.6
Craft	4.0	9.3	13.3	5.7	16.0	21.7
Operative/laborer	11.3	31.8	43.2	12.6	46.1	58.7
All occupations	9.4	27.7	37.1	10.1	32.6	42.7

*Grocery is a subset of retail. Retail sample = 11,447 observations; grocery sample = 1,738 observations.
Source: Data from Current Population Survey tapes.

TABLE 4.3

*Percent of Part-Time Employment by Occupation in the Insurance Industry, March 1992**

Occupation	Involuntary Part-Time	Voluntary Part-Time	All Part-Time
Managerial	0.8	2.6	3.4
Professional	0.6	3.5	4.1
Technical	1.1	2.5	3.6
Sales	1.2	5.1	6.3
Administrative/clerical	2.8	9.2	12.1
Service	0	11.1	11.1
Craft	0	0	0
Operative/laborer	0	10.8	10.8
All occupations	1.8	6.5	8.3

*Sample size = 1,365 observations.
Source: Current Population Survey tapes.

professionals, and technical workers are unlikely to work part-time. The estimated part-time employment rates in professional and technical categories slightly exceed the managerial part-time rate, although the differences among these three turn out not to be statistically significant[3] given the small sample sizes.

2. *A person's job should help to determine his or her probability of part-time employment even after controlling for observed personal characteristics.* In other words, the probability of working part-time is at least in part attached to jobs rather than people. There are three reasons to expect this outcome. First, workers will be sorted by unobserved personal characteristics (such as their desire for part-time work or high propensity to quit) to jobs where the work hours that fit with these characteristics are accommodated most profitably. (Secondary labor markets are particularly hospitable to part-time work, for reasons that are explored further in Chapter 6.) Second, in primary labor markets, some workers with a preference for part-time work will be in full-time jobs; that is, workers who otherwise have certain characteristics of part-timers will hold full-time jobs because of their occupation. Third, in secondary labor markets, some workers who otherwise have certain characteristics of full-timers will involuntarily hold part-time jobs because of their occupation. The second reason applies only to voluntary part-time employment, the third only to involuntary employment, and the first to both. Thus, the expected job effects should show up in both voluntary *and* involuntary part-time employment.

I estimated linear probability regression models for the probability of involuntary and voluntary part-time employment among currently employed workers in the retail and insurance industries.[4] These models estimate the amount that various personal or job characteristics contribute to a person's probability of working part-time: for example, how much more—or less—likely is part-time work among managers?

Many, although not all, of the occupational variables are indeed significant determinants of the probability of part-time employment, with effects in the expected directions. In the retail industry, workers in sales, service, and operative/laborer jobs are all significantly more likely to be employed part-time both voluntarily and involuntarily. Managers have less probability—by a statistically significant margin—of holding either type of part-time employment. Clerical workers fall in between these two extremes.

In insurance, most jobs have the expected effects. Managers, professional/technical workers, and sales workers (agents) all have a lower probability of working part-time voluntarily than clerical workers. Service workers' likelihood of part-time employment unexpectedly falls below that of clerical workers after controlling for factors other than the job, although the difference is not statistically significant.

3. *The probability of part-time employment is expected to be determined differently in retail than in insurance.* For example, employment in sales occupations is expected to have different implications in the two industries. We would expect retail sales workers (cashiers) to have a high rate of part-time employment, but insurance sales workers (agents) to have a low rate.

Statistical tests reveal that overall, the probability of both voluntary and involuntary part-time employment *is* determined differently in the two industries.[5] Specifically, while the effects of being in managerial, service, and operative/laborer occupations are strikingly similar between the retail and insurance samples, the effect of being in a sales job differs clearly between the two industries. As expected, retail sales clerks are more likely than the base group of clericals to work part-time; insurance agents are less likely.

Thus, this set of tests generally supports the hypothesized relationships between part-time employment and particular job groups in these two industries. Nationwide, part-time work in the retail and insurance industries seems to reflect the bifurcation into secondary and retention part-time employment that emerges from the interviews.

Implications of the Distinction Between Good and Bad Part-Time Jobs

5

■ TYPOLOGIES SUCH AS THE DISTINCTION BETWEEN SEC-
ondary and retention, or "bad" and "good," part-time jobs classify the
world, sorting messy events into neat boxes. A new typology generally
offers a fresh look at something we had previously thought we had
known. But that classification scheme's value is greater if it not only describes but also explains. The secondary/retention dichotomy can indeed
help to explain a number of the systematic features of part-time employment.

This chapter addresses two such features. When managers speak of
the advantages and disadvantages of part-time work, they sometimes appear to contradict each other flatly, citing utterly opposite advantages.
The dichotomy between secondary and retention part-time work demonstrates that there in fact is no contradiction—just two utterly different
types of part-time jobs. Another puzzle is the coexistence of involuntary
part-time *and* involuntary full-time work. But by taking into account the
difference between bad and good part-time jobs, we can not only explain
this coexistence but also predict with some success where each of the two
involuntary groups will cluster in the economy.

Finally, although extrapolating beyond the range of one's data is always risky, it seems important to consider the usefulness of the secondary
and retention categories outside the retail and insurance industries. The
chapter ends with a brief discussion of the possibilities of generalizing this
typology to other industries and extending it to accommodate other
forms of part-time employment.

"Hiding the Dog," and Other Advantages and Disadvantages of Part-Time Workers

"It's easier to hide a dog that's a part-timer than a full-timer," a Pittsburgh supermarket manager told me when asked about the advantages of hiring a part-time worker. Management representatives suggested a wide, wide range of pluses and minuses to hiring part-timers. The responses ranged from commonsensical to seemingly irrational, from cynical to idealistic, from bureaucratic to creative.

But running through most of the responses like a backbone—only occasionally visible but constantly shaping the contours and tensions of the part-time/full-time tradeoff—was the secondary/retention distinction. Employers reap markedly different benefits and costs from retention and secondary part-time work because they bundle very different job characteristics with part-time hours.

Previous Research on the Pros and Cons of Part-Time Workers

Some of the researchers who have tackled this question of advantages and disadvantages of part-time workers have simply compiled lists. For example, Hermine Zagat Levine (1987) surveyed 73 employers who used permanent part-timers and found that the advantages they most often cited were, in declining order, better coverage of the workplace, reduced labor costs, reduced benefit costs, reduced overtime costs, and better work schedules. The disadvantage most often cited was higher turnover.

Managers told Stanley Nollen, Brenda Eddy, and Virginia Martin (1978) that part-time employment often yields greater productivity and requires lower compensation but entails more difficult supervision. However, in their sample these considerations were not decisive in explaining where part-time employment is used. Nor did Nollen and his colleagues find organizational climate a primary determinant of part-time use. Instead, they concluded that technology and the pattern of demand and output over time are important in determining where part-time workers are used.

Susan Christopherson (1988), reviewing a corpus of case study literature, placed the Nollen et al. findings in a historical and sectoral context. She noted that up to the 1960s part-time work was limited to certain "backward" sectors of the economy (agriculture, household service, retail trade, and so on) or to "back-up" rolls for full-time labor, filling in the spaces that full-time workers could not. However, firms in a variety of other industries then began to allot part-time employment a central, integral place in their labor force. Christopherson argued that part-time workers are part of a growing periphery of labor that absorbs demand fluctuations.

In summary, earlier studies have pointed to two main motivations for using part-time employment: solving scheduling issues involving coverage and fluctuating demand, and reducing labor costs.

Evidence from the Retail and Insurance Interviews

Manager responses in my interviews repeat these earlier key findings, but go beyond mere replication to offer a much richer picture of the costs and benefits of hiring part-time workers in two particular industries. The frequency with which managers cited each advantage and disadvantage of part-time employment is tabulated in Table 5.1. Although idiosyncratic responses abound, the main pattern is clear and simple. Secondary part-time employment brings schedule flexibility and low compensation, but at the expense of high turnover and low productivity. Retention part-time employment, quite to the contrary, yields lower turnover and higher productivity, but decreased scheduling convenience and in many cases higher compensation. In Osterman's (1988) terms (see Chapter 3), managers use secondary part-time employment to meet the goals of cost minimization and flexibility of both employment levels and deployment, even though they must sacrifice some predictability. Managers use retention part-time employment to make the opposite tradeoff.

Consider the advantages and disadvantages of part-time workers in each of four categories: scheduling, compensation, turnover, and productivity.

Scheduling

Scheduling flexibility was cited as an advantage of part-time employment by managers from almost every retail and insurance company surveyed—25 out of 29. Such flexibility has several dimensions: the ability to increase employee hours without paying overtime or decrease hours without violating a commitment; the ability to cover peak hours; the ability to cover odd shifts such as evenings, nights, and weekends; and access to a pool of workers who can be used to fill in gaps or be moved from one time to another.

These advantages apply to secondary part-time employees, who work more or less at the pleasure of the employer—"more or less" because in fact even secondary workers can have bargaining power, as an EZ Mart convenience store manager in a student area of Boston explained:

INTERVIEWER: [It sounds like] it's not so much that you're asking them to fit into your schedule but you're fitting around their schedule.

MANAGER: And . . . that can metamorphosize itself into, yeah, they're fitting into my schedule. It depends on what the help situation is like. Towards the end of the summer I couldn't hire somebody if I tried. . . . However, once the first week of October came around, all of a sudden I had all these people who wanted to work. . . . Once I had a whole bunch of people who wanted to do all kinds of hours; all of a sudden I said, "Look, you're going to fit into my schedule and you're going to do it my way. . . ." That is a definite struggle. The balance between the two. Come Christmas time I'm going to be back in the same boat, because there's going to be nobody around.

Unlike secondary part-time jobs, retention part-time jobs are characterized by employer *in*convenience in scheduling. Managers at nine insurance companies listed the scheduling drawbacks of allowing a worker to reduce her or his hours: the loss of week-long availability of the employee, difficulty in coordination with other employees, and discontinuity in work flow. A typical comment was: "Sometimes . . . a part-time worker is in a job where he or she should really be making a trip to such-and-such a place, and she's not available to go. There's not as much flexibility for the employer."

Compensation
Secondary part-time employment comes with a special low price tag. Managers at every retail company surveyed, and most of the insurance companies, spend less on benefits and/or wages for part-timers than for full-timers. One store manager explained that he employs all part-timers except for management positions because "in a store like this you can't afford . . . to pay much more than a minimum wage."

Why are employers able to offer secondary part-timers reduced compensation? The personnel director of a convenience store chain offered an answer: "[Convenience stores have always] concentrated on part-time employees because they expected less in wages. They needed less because this was usually a second job for them."

There are two points here. First, creating part-time jobs gives companies access to a labor supply of people who are blocked from obtaining other jobs and people who are seeking secondary income. But in addition, staffing secondary jobs as part-time jobs also limits the expectations of the persons taking these jobs, since "traditionally American business doesn't provide fringe benefits to part-time workers," in the words of another retail manager. All of the workers—both part-time and full-time—interviewed in this study felt that the full-time/part-time benefit differential at their company was fair. In fact, a union representative

TABLE 5.1

Advantages and Disadvantages of Part-Time Employment for the Employer

Advantage	Number of Companies Responding*		Disadvantage	Number of Companies Responding*	
	Retail	Insurance		Retail	Insurance
SCHEDULING	16	9	SCHEDULING	4	9
Can increase or decrease hours	7	—	Lack of availability, coordination, continuity	2	9
Can cover peak hours or partial jobs	8	9	Inflexibility in scheduling, need to work around employee schedule	3	3
Can fill in without overtime or work variable hours	9	1			
Other	2	—			
COMPENSATION	17	7	COMPENSATION	—	7
Fewer benefits provided or used	17	7	Higher cost of benefits per hour	—	4
Lower hourly wage	5	1	Prefer not to have employee who is not covered by benefits	—	3
LABOR SUPPLY	5	9	LABOR SUPPLY	5	4
Tap into different pools of workers	5	9	Harder to find part-timers (or anybody) so each person's hours must be maximized	2	3
Not using part-timers but would if it were a way to get a valued person	—	2	Harder to find part-timers in specific jobs or areas	3	1
TENURE AND TRAINING	1	9	TENURE AND TRAINING	15	6
Higher retention	1	9	Higher turnover	15	4
Means of regaining former employees	—	2	Longer training (or more people to train), not as many work hours as payoff to training investment	2	3
PRODUCTIVITY	1	7	PRODUCTIVITY	13	7
More job commitment	—	3	Less job commitment	11	6
Exert more effort on job	—	4	Exert less effort on job	9	1
More freshness toward job	1	2	Less freshness toward job	1	—
Efficient utilization of capital	—	2	Inefficient utilization of capital	—	2

TABLE 5.1 Continued

Advantage	Number of Companies Responding*		Disadvantage	Number of Companies Responding*	
	Retail	Insurance		Retail	Insurance
More productive due to selection effect or coverage of peak hours	1	1	Less productive due to selection effect or less experience	9	—
RELATIONSHIP TO JOB LADDERS	3	3	RELATIONSHIP TO JOB LADDERS	3	2
Helps recruit full-timers	—	3	People take part-time jobs to gain access to full-time jobs	1	1
Helps screen full-timers	3	—			
Must promote by seniority, so people are kept part-time to avoid promoting unwanted workers	2	—	Need full-timers as a pool for promotions	2	1
ADMINISTRATIVE ISSUES	—	2	ADMINISTRATIVE ISSUES	3	6
Easy way to get budgeted for full-timers is to create part-timers and expand	—	2	More people, harder to manage	3	5
			Budget mandates fixed number of people regardless of hours worked	—	2
Other	—	1			
EFFECTS ON OTHER WORKERS	—	1	EFFECTS ON OTHER WORKERS	—	1
Morale boost	—	1	Resentment	—	1

*Number of insurance and retail companies where a respondent cited each advantage or disadvantage. Numbers next to category headings (Scheduling, Compensation, etc.) indicate the number of respondents who cited any of the reasons within a given category.
Total number of retail companies = 17; total number of insurance companies = 12.
Source: Interviews by author.

who attempted to organize part-time workers at the Healthco insurance company complained that

> the company has inculcated in [the workers'] brains . . . [that] you don't deserve any more than you're getting because you're only part-time. And they try to get these folks to compare themselves with 20-hour-a-week waitresses or high school kids working in Burger King for 20 hours a week.

But lower compensation is not an advantage of part-time employment for all employers. In insurance companies where full benefits are offered above a certain hours cutoff (the same companies where retention part-time jobs are most common), managers commented that part-timers are often *more* expensive to employ.

Turnover
Secondary part-time workers have elevated turnover rates, whereas retention part-timers have decreased turnover rates. Employee turnover has several kinds of costs. In addition to the direct costs of recruiting, hiring, and training, there are the indirect costs of present and future sales lost due to understaffing or employee inexperience. Managers worry about these indirect, or "soft," costs. Lamented the personnel director of a department store whose chain had aggressively shifted toward hiring more part-time workers:

> We're losing credibility as a company. We never would get customer complaints that . . . employees didn't know their merchandise. Now we get them all the time. . . . I hear over and over again: "I used to like to come to [this company] because the sales clerks knew what they're talking about, but these days they don't know anything."

A "SuperValu" grocery store manager added: "If you're down a cashier and a customer has to wait in line too long, they may never come back. That's $150 times 52 weeks a year. It's an intangible cost, but I think it's bigger than the direct costs."

Overall, turnover is probably the major disadvantage of secondary part-time employment, as the personnel officer of a supermarket chain declared: "The biggest drawback of the part-time workforce is greater vulnerability to turnover, and knowing that a replacement supply is not available [because of the labor shortage]. It's not the work ethic, it's not productivity." But some turnover is functional for the employers. According to a Boston union official: "A supermarket prefers a mix of people—some at 6 months, some at 12 months, some at 18 months—so they can pay a mix of rates. They don't want all their people at the top of the scale. They bank on turnover."

Personnel officers from a supermarket chain and a health insurer, respectively, both employing large numbers of secondary part-timers, agreed:

> Some turnover is healthy, because as people stay, they progress in rates. And we want to have a certain portion at the starting wage.

> We're experiencing a high turnover among part-time, which is a plus in terms of dollars and cents, because you don't really want them to get those higher benefits [that accumulate over time].

On the other hand, the advantages of the decreased turnover of retention part-timers are substantial. Because these part-timers tend to be skilled, the cost of losing them in terms of training new workers, disruption, and lost sales would be much greater than the cost of losing secondary part-time workers.

Productivity

Most managers employing secondary part-time workers agreed that such part-timers are less productive than full-time workers. Although none of the companies had directly studied the relative productivity of full- versus part-time employees, most of the informants—particularly store managers—had strong negative opinions about part-timers' productivity. The reason most commonly given was that part-time employees are lacking in what is labeled "commitment" in Table 5.1. This somewhat nebulous concept encompasses a variety of terms supplied by managers: commitment, reliability, responsibility, loyalty, pride, dependability, attitude. While the concept often includes other categories such as effort and experience, it in fact seems to be broader than any of these categories.

At many of the companies, informants stated that part-timers are also less productive because they exert less effort on behalf of the employer. Again, "effort" is defined as a broad category including all of the ways in which employees give less by choice, such as shirking, carelessness, absenteeism, tardiness, theft, and failure to put in "extra" effort.

Finally, at the majority of the retail companies, managers noted that at least part of the productivity difference between part-time and full-time employees was due to the higher turnover of part-timers and to the fact that many of the best part-time employees are promoted to full-time jobs. Several informants argued that in fact these reasons account for all or most of the productivity difference. A SuperValu manager expressed the following opinions:

> INTERVIEWER: Do you find a difference in productivity or effort between part-timers and full-timers?
> MANAGER: Effort, no; productivity, definitely. . . . In my produce department, one good full-timer can do as much work as any three part-timers.
> INTERVIEWER: Per hour?
> MANAGER: Per hour. They just can crank it out. And they know what's important to the customers. And they bring out the important things, where the part-timer will fiddle around with something that is not important. Because they are not as experienced. . . .
> INTERVIEWER: So it's basically a question of experience. If you had a part-timer that had actually been there that length of time, would they probably be equally good?

MANAGER: They would be equally good. Yes. It's just that you don't get the part-timers that are willing to stay on with you for that period of time. Not in this location. There are a number of stores that had part-timers working for 15, 20 years or longer. And equally productive or better than a full-time person. But they're few and far between.

Implicit in this viewpoint is the fact that although formal training times are short for secondary part-time jobs, useful learning continues well beyond the actual training period: "To be a clerk and be a good clerk might take several months. . . . If your job is to stock shelves, we've got eight or ten thousand items out there, and it's just a matter of knowing where they are."

In contrast with the negative evaluation of the productivity of secondary part-timers, managers reported increased commitment and effort from retention part-timers. A personnel officer from the Eternal Life insurance company, herself a former retention part-timer, explained:

> This is my personal bias: part-time people will tell you they work much harder than full-time people. There's a tendency to try to keep up, try to prove your worth. . . . Professional part-time people are generally very committed people. They want to hold on to [their] position. They want to do it all. They're driven. It's interesting to think that part-time people may actually be *more* committed.

One insurance company's personnel director even commented on both productivity effects:

> There's certainly a lot to be said for the good will [of] . . . being able to help people [who need part-time hours] and accommodate them, and maybe for that reason, some people are very grateful, and therefore are clearly very dependable. . . . The downsides are those that are less dependable. . . . [For example,] the younger people coming in that don't have the same type of values, and therefore don't necessarily show up.

Against Their Wills: Involuntary Part-Time and Full-Time Workers

One of the key problems associated with part-time employment is bad matches—involuntary part-time and involuntary full-time employment. What is the relationship between the secondary/retention dichotomy and the voluntary/involuntary distinction? And what do the interview data tell us about the reasons that involuntary part-time and full-time employment persists?

Where the constrained workers are

Pools of secondary part-time workers generally include some fraction of involuntary part-timers. At every company surveyed, involuntary part-time employment took the form of workers who were unable to obtain full-time jobs—*never* former full-time workers whose hours had been re-duced against their will, either temporarily or permanently.[1] Although full-time workers sometimes move to a part-time schedule at these com-panies, that move is invariably a voluntary one.

In high-unemployment Pittsburgh, most retail companies reported that half or more of their part-time employees would prefer to be full-timers. One incredulous Pittsburgh store manager commented: "Some people here have three jobs. I have CPAs, electrical engineers working for me. They haven't been able to find jobs." And a Pittsburgh insurer that had just introduced part-time jobs was having a hard time shaking its im-age as a full-time employer and attracting applicants who actually wanted part-time work:

> We have noticed that the part-time people do want to go full-time— even though they swear up and down that they don't—"No, no, I just want part-time!" They can only go full-time after a year. But I would anticipate that a lot of people, because there is a shortage of jobs in Pitts-burgh, [are] going to say they want part-time, but stay there a year and then they want to move to full-time.

In Boston, with its tighter labor market at the time of the interviews, rates of involuntary part-time employment were considerably lower. In-dividual SuperValu store managers estimated that from 5 to 17 percent of their part-timers would prefer full-time work. SuperValu's company-wide list of "exceptional" part-timers queuing for full-time jobs num-bered 217—about 2.5 percent of its total part-time population. Boston union officials stated that an average of 7.5 to 10 percent of the part-timers at the supermarkets they represent were involuntary. The manager of a Boston-area Healthco insurance part-time facility employing 260 part-timers noted that only about 20 of its part-time employees had changed to full-time—a move that also required relocating to another fa-cility—in the last several years.

Unlike secondary part-time employment, retention part-time em-ployment is by definition voluntary. However, not everybody who wants a retention part-time arrangement gets one, so the labor markets hosting retention part-time employment also tend to have a slice of involuntary full-timers queuing for part-time jobs. For example, the personnel direc-tor at Eternal Life stated, "It's easier to go from part-time to full-time than it is the other way around." The personnel director of another in-surance company agreed:

> INTERVIEWER: Do you know of any . . . situations where part-timers are working part-time, but would really prefer to be full-time . . . ?
> PERSONNEL DIRECTOR: No. You know, it's interesting, because what we find is, we're generally able to accommodate those folks in a fairly quick period of time. . . .

INTERVIEWER: Do you think the opposite is common? Having a full-time employee who would rather be part-time?
PERSONNEL DIRECTOR: Yes. I do.

Involuntary Part-Time and Full-Time
Work Nationwide
Economywide statistics confirm that secondary labor markets harbor involuntary part-time employment, whereas primary labor markets host involuntary full-time employment.[2] This analysis employs the May 1985 Current Population Survey, which provides a rare opportunity to measure involuntary full-time employment (Shank 1986). The survey asked respondents, "If you had a choice, would you prefer to work the same number of hours and earn the same money, fewer hours at the same rate of pay and earn less money, or more hours at the same rate of pay and earn more money?" For the purposes of this analysis, full-time workers who opted for "fewer hours, less money" were classified as involuntary full-timers. Economywide patterns of part-time employment for men and women diverge markedly, so I looked at men and women separately.

In operationalizing the concept of involuntariness using these data, two problems were anticipated—one with involuntary part-time work, one with involuntary full-time work. First, the secondary/retention model is based on evidence from service industries where the main reason for involuntary part-time work is the inability to find a full-time job, but the sample will also include manufacturing and construction workers with temporarily reduced hours, who fall outside this model. To deal with this, I limited my attention to the involuntary part-time employment of those who reported they "could only find part-time work," as opposed to those whose work week was temporarily shortened. As a shorthand, I refer to these individuals as "could-only-find" part-time workers.

A second problem is that the operationalization of involuntary full-time status simply depends on whether full-time workers express a preference for fewer hours, but there is no way of determining whether they would like to reduce their hours all the way to a part-time schedule. "The category of "involuntary full-timers" thus could include people who are working mandatory overtime but seek a reduction to regular full-time hours. To minimize this possibility, analysis of involuntary full-time status was limited to persons working 45 hours or less.

Before examining the results by occupation, it is necessary to assign major occupations to either primary or secondary labor market status. There is no one-to-one correspondence between occupation and labor market segment, but we could roughly classify managerial, professional/technical, clerical, craft, and operative occupations as part of primary labor markets. Service occupations (particularly domestic service) and laborers are part of secondary markets. Transportation and materials moving are ambiguous. Sales is a special case: for men, who predominate in upper level positions, sales jobs are chiefly primary labor market jobs; for women, who are concentrated in lower level cashier jobs, sales generally represents a secondary labor market location.

Tabulations of the proportions of involuntary part-time and full-time workers by occupation generally confirm the expected variation of involuntariness by labor market segment.[3] Among part-time men and women workers alike, private household workers are most likely to work part-time involuntarily due to the inability to find full-time jobs; managers are least likely to do so. Other service workers, transport workers, and laborers also have above average probabilities of "could-only-find" part-time status among both genders, whereas more skilled or white-collar jobs fall far below the average. Even sales exhibits the expected pattern: the proportion of part-time sales workers who could only find part-time jobs stands below the overall rate among men, but above the overall rate among women.

The reverse pattern shows up among full-time workers, also as expected. Involuntary full-time employment is far more common for women than for men, which is consistent with the interview finding that retention part-time jobs are primarily held by women. And among full-time women, the occupational pattern is clear: white-collar women (managerial, professional/technical, and clerical workers) are most likely to want part-time hours, and service workers are least likely to want them. For full-time men, almost none of the interoccupational differences are statistically significant. However, the estimated proportions provide some confirmation for the influence of labor market segmentation: white-collar men and operatives (as well as, unexpectedly, service workers) have above average probabilities of working full-time involuntarily; laborers have a probability far below the average of doing so.

Finally, for both men and women, occupations with above average odds of "could-only-find" part-time status generally have below average probabilities of involuntary full-time status.

Occupation is not a completely satisfactory indicator of the primary/secondary labor market distinction. An alternative analytical strategy starts from the notion that primary labor market workers enjoy some sort of wage premium, perhaps because they have a greater payoff to education and experience than secondary labor market workers, as argued by Paul Osterman (1975) and Russell Rumberger and Martin Carnoy (1980). I computed a wage premium variable, which shows the amount a given person's hourly wage falls above or below the wage that is predicted based on his or her education and experience.[4]

If the story I've spun about secondary and retention part-time work is correct, then people enjoying a higher wage premium should have a lower probability of involuntary part-time employment and a higher probability of involuntary full-time employment. This is precisely what happens among both men and women. The associations are strong and highly statistically significant, except for the small group of involuntary full-time men (among whom the expected effect is found but is not statistically significant).[5] This offers very striking evidence for the generalizability of the secondary/retention distinction in part-time employment.

In short, the findings from both occupational and wage premium analysis uphold the secondary/retention model's prediction that labor market status should have opposite effects on the probabilities of involuntary full-time and involuntary part-time work. The finding that involuntary part-time employment is associated with secondary labor markets while involuntary full-time employment occurs in the primary labor markets that generate retention part-time jobs also clarifies why the involuntary part-timers and involuntary full-timers cannot simply "trade places": they are essentially noncompeting groups, in totally different kinds of jobs. The professional and technical workers longing for part-time hours would not accept a part-time sales clerk job. And the managers of these professionals would not hire frustrated sales clerks in their places.

But why does involuntary part-time and full-time employment exist in the first place? To answer this question, it is necessary to take a closer look at firms' decision-making about part-time employment.

Why Involuntary Part-Time and Full-Time Work Exists

The reasons for involuntary part-time employment in secondary labor markets and involuntary full-time employment in salaried labor markets are essentially symmetrical. Here a fairly detailed discussion of the former is followed by a more schematic presentation of the latter.

Involuntary part-time employment in the secondary workforce exists for several microeconomic, firm-level reasons.[6] First, temporary mismatches placing persons desiring full-time jobs into part-time positions may be a by-product of rational hiring and job search processes. Second, given the differences in compensation and marginal productivity between part-time and full-time employees, increasing the number of full-timers would drive up unit labor costs. Third, firms are reluctant to alter the difference in compensation between part-time and full-time employees, because it plays an important incentive role in their internal labor markets. Let's explore each of these three factors.

Some involuntary part-time employment in the form of mismatches is to be expected, given the nature of secondary part-time employment. From the employer's standpoint, the costs of such mismatches are minimal. The major advantages of secondary part-time employment for the employer—schedule flexibility and low compensation—do not depend on hiring people who *wish* to be part-time. Involuntary part-timers may tend to leave more quickly than others, but the expectation of high turnover is already built into the situation, and employers can retain outstanding involuntary part-timers by offering them the promise of promotions at a later date.

On the other hand, it would cost the employer to avoid such mismatches by either granting full-time jobs to all applicants who want them, thus running the risk of investing training time and higher compensation on someone who may be unsuitable, or conducting costly screening to determine a prospective employee's trainability and likelihood of staying. As a result, employers of secondary part-timers simply tend to define a job and hire whomever shows up, rather than creating a part-time or full-time job depending on the wishes of the applicant. Employees are then screened for promotion based on their ability to perform in the part-time job. A number of managers commented on this. This is what the Pittsburgh supermarket manager meant by saying, "It's easier to hide a dog that's a part-timer." As a convenience store chain personnel director said, "Management . . . want[s] to hire someone on part-time, and check them out, before hiring them full-time."

Indeed, part-time jobs serve as the port of entry for most retail job ladders. According to a SuperValu store manager: "Quite a few of the full-time people come from the part-time ranks. Probably 80 percent of them, in the chain as a whole."

From the employee's standpoint as well, temporarily taking a part-time job on the way to a full-time job may be the preferred option. The case is clearest when changes in a part-timer's life leads the person to prefer full-time hours; this occurs, for example, when a student graduates. In such a situation, the worker is more likely to retain the part-time job while searching for full-time employment than to quit immediately. In fact, if the worker is in retail and chooses to remain in retail, where part-time jobs serve as a port of entry, it often makes sense to wait for a full-time job with the current employer, since moving to another retailer would simply involve taking another part-time job—with less seniority. Similarly, a jobless person searching for a full-time job may find it advantageous to take a part-time job while continuing to look.

In short, there are reasons for both employers and employees to engage in frictional, or search-based, involuntary part-time employment that simply results from delays in matching people with full-time jobs. Is this likely to explain much of the observed involuntary part-time employment? Probably not. Involuntary part-time employment is frequently protracted. According to Current Population Survey (CPS) data, 71 per-

cent of involuntary part-time workers experienced such employment for
5 or more weeks during 1985, and 38 percent experienced it for 15 weeks
or more. Data from the Survey of Income and Program Participation
paint an even gloomier picture, indicating that during 4-month periods
in 1985, involuntary part-time employment lasted 5 or more weeks for
74 percent of those experiencing it; it lasted the full 4 months for 45 percent (U.S. Bureau of Labor Statistics 1987).

The share of the total number of weeks spent in involuntary part-
time employment is even more slanted toward long-term involuntariness.
Let's arbitrarily designate one- to four-week spells of involuntary part-
time employment as "frictional." Based on the more conservative CPS
data, although 29 percent of part-time workers had short, frictional
spells, only 5 percent of all the weeks spent in involuntary part-time work
was accounted for by such spells—and 49 percent was accounted for by
persons involuntarily employed part-time for 27 weeks or more![7]

In addition, company informants referred to very long waits for full-
time jobs *within* companies. For example, a personnel director and store
manager at SuperValu respectively described the situation as follows:

> Up to about four years ago [when the current labor shortage began,]
> . . . it was not uncommon to wait one to two years to get a full-time po-
> sition.

> You could have somebody who's on the part-time list [waiting for a full-
> time job] for six years. There was a girl in [a certain store] who was on
> the list for nine years—waiting for the new store to open up.

Such long waits must be accounted for by nonfrictional forces.

A second reason for involuntary part-time employment is that, given
the relative cost and productivity of full-time and part-time workers in
certain functions, businesses can minimize expenses by employing a small
number of full-timers and a large number of part-timers. Most retail informants agreed that some core of well-trained, responsible full-time employees is necessary to run a retail business smoothly:

> Without some of the full-time employees that I have in this store, the
> store would just not operate the way it does, because of their long-term
> experience, their willingness to accept some additional responsibilities,
> and more or less to manage some subdepartments.

But when asked why the company didn't hire more full-time workers,
managers responded that the cost in higher wages, benefits, and lost
schedule flexibility would be too high:

> CONVENIENCE STORE CHAIN PERSONNEL DIRECTOR I: We're adding a
> few more full-time positions in order to stabilize the workforce. But we
> can't go entirely with full-time.
> INTERVIEWER: Why not?

> PERSONNEL DIRECTOR I: Because of the cost of benefits. Also, full-time employees need more per hour in wages.

> INTERVIEWER: What would be the disadvantage of having a store completely staffed with full-timers?
> CONVENIENCE STORE CHAIN PERSONNEL DIRECTOR II: I think most of it is flexibility on the schedule.

The implication is that the marginal product of the first few full-timers is high, but that it drops rapidly with added full-timers.

To explain involuntary part-time employment in secondary part-time jobs, however, it is not sufficient to state that given compensation and productivity differences, the cost-minimizing mix of part-time and full-time employment implies that some people preferring full-time jobs will be stuck in part-time positions. The question, then, is why not narrow the difference in compensation between part-time and full-time jobs? In particular, why don't firms take advantage of the excess supply of full-time labor by decreasing the compensation of full-timers and hiring more involuntary part-time workers into full-time positions?

In response to these questions, incentive arguments surface. Full-time and part-time wages are not simply designed to fill the two groups of jobs in a spot market for labor. Instead, the full-time/part-time differential serves other purposes as well. One of its functions is to induce full-timers to take more responsibility, exert more effort, and stay on at a job:

> CONVENIENCE STORE CHAIN PERSONNEL DIRECTOR: Among the office employees, 90 percent are full-time . . . [because] our philosophy is: if you want somebody you can ask more of, you have to be in position where you can do more for them.

> INTERVIEWER: Are there any jobs . . . that are not appropriate for a part-timer to take on?
> FULL-TIME CONVENIENCE STORE WORKER: Yeah, I think so, because they don't get paid to do any of the paperwork. . . . If they're taking on all that responsibility, they don't get paid the salary for the responsibility. . . . If they're going to do the same work as me, then they should get paid [the same].

> INTERVIEWER: If you could hire people full-time but at the minimum wage [which is the wage for part-timers in the store], would you do it?
> GROCERY STORE MANAGER: Yes, I would do it. But, when you hire a person at minimum wage for full-time, you really put a lot of responsibility, you entrust [sic] them too much. . . . At that kind of wage, you're just not going to find . . . that good a person. . . . You can't put that much trust, 40 hours of trust, into one person at that kind of wage. . . . And if they're that good that you'd want them for full-time, they're not going to be around that long. They'll find something better.

The differential also helps to elicit effort from part-timers by fostering the aspiration of upward mobility:

[Hiring people part-time] acts as an incentive. Somebody who wasn't hired full-time would have a reason to try a little harder. [supermarket manager]

We give full-time to those people that have worked for it. So it's kind of like a reward system. [convenience store chain personnel director]

In fact, retailers seeking to reduce labor costs have cut part-time wages and benefits, through two-tier arrangements that set lower compensation for new part-time workers, rather than reducing full-time wages.

The reasons for involuntary full-time employment in salaried labor markets are largely analogous to those for involuntary part-time employment in secondary labor markets. Full-timers who start to prefer part-time work may linger in their full-time jobs while searching for or attempting to create part-time opportunities. Unit labor costs for a given employee tend to be higher on a part-time basis, since per hour compensation is often higher, while per hour productivity may be lower due to the loss of week-long availability and other scheduling limitations. Thus, companies extend retention part-time jobs only to people whose productivity exceeds that of a possible full-time replacement.

Then why don't these companies decrease the wages and/or benefits for part-timers? Once more, incentive considerations are one key. Several insurance managers argued that decreasing benefits to part-timers is counterproductive. "You really can't cut out people who need those benefits," one personnel director said. Getting managers to explain why high benefits for part-timers served the company's interests proved difficult, but the answer in at least one case boiled down to a need to retain the employees:

PERSONNEL DIRECTOR: I would much rather provide full-time employment, for full fringe benefits.
INTERVIEWER: Well, let me play devil's advocate. What would happen if you didn't?
PERSONNEL DIRECTOR: If they're working less than 20 hours a week, they're not eligible for our earned vacation and holidays, etc, which I think is a detriment. We have a very nice fringe benefit package . . . .
INTERVIEWER: It's clear to me that being ineligible for the benefits package is a detriment to the employee. In what ways is it a detriment to the company?
PERSONNEL DIRECTOR: I don't like to see anyone employed by [this company] who is not getting the full benefits. I think our benefits are such that we retain employees. Retention is a significant factor.

This, of course, is precisely the concern that motivates the creation of retention part-time jobs in the first place.

In some salaried labor markets—in particular, in some of the insurance companies sampled—another reason for involuntary full-time employment emerges. In these companies, the resistance to the creation of part-time jobs seems to be based more on tradition and prejudice than on any assessment of the economic costs and benefits of part-time employment. As one insurance manager noted:

> I think you have a tendency to look at a part-timer and think of the negatives, and say, Jesus, I've only got him four hours, . . . there's a lot more people to deal with, . . . do I really want to get into those headaches? And I think that might cause some reluctance on the part of line managers. Until they get exposed to it, and learn how to manage those headaches.

This observation echoes the finding of Nollen and his colleagues that nonusers of part-time workers imagined numerous disadvantages that users rarely reported. However, such ill-informed beliefs about the differences between part-time and full-time workers are unlikely to explain much involuntary *part-time* employment, since retail firms and the like generally employ large numbers of full-timers as well as part-timers. The role of traditions and beliefs is examined more closely in the next chapter.

In summary, although involuntary part-time and full-time employment is in part frictional in nature, it also results from rigid compensation differentials between part-time and full-time jobs. These differentials, designed to structure employee incentives, are a feature of primary labor markets: in one case (retail), a primary labor market limited to full-time jobs; in the other case (insurance), a primary labor market encompassing both part-time and full-time jobs. In the case of involuntary full-time employment, another source of labor market rigidity may be strongly held beliefs about the superiority of full-time labor.

These microeconomic reasons for involuntary part-time and full-time employment sit in a macroeconomic context. Thus, as the labor market improves for workers and they face more job alternatives, the rate of involuntary part-time employment in secondary labor markets and of involuntary full-time employment in salaried labor markets would be expected to fall. A simple model for this process is developed in Chapter 7.

Is That All There Is? Generalizing to the Rest of the Economy

So far this chapter has revealed relatively little about the use of part-time employment beyond the confines of the retail and insurance industries. A small set of interviews of informants outside retail and insurance sheds some light on this issue. The set includes data from manufacturing (specifically, a newspaper), transportation, wholesale trade, noninsurance financial services, education (a university), health care, building service, and local government. In addition, I studied in more detail one large employer: the U.S. Postal Service (Tilly 1991b). Much less information was accumulated from these interviews than from the retail and insurance interviews, but two tentative conclusions are possible:

1. *The categories of retention and secondary part-time employment are durable, proving useful in other industries as well as retail and insurance.* Examples of secondary part-time jobs are the more widespread. Health-care providers employing part-timers trade off peak-time coverage against increased turnover and reduced experience. A wholesaler who uses "casual," on-call part-timers trades off lower compensation, peak-time deployment, and the ability to screen people for full-time jobs against higher turnover and availability problems.

The U.S. Postal Service displays some of the same tradeoffs. Part-time workers turn over four times as frequently as full-timers among letter carriers and nearly twice as frequently among clerks. Part-time Postal Service employees also lag behind full-timers in their amount of education, although by only a fraction of a year. Nonetheless, the Postal Service has pushed—against strenuous union opposition—to expand part-time employment (as well as "casual" and "transitional" workforces), primarily to increase schedule flexibility as the level of automation escalates.

But retention part-time employment also appears occasionally in other industries. A university department hires a researcher or faculty member part-time to gain access to the specialized talents of someone who has another career, but in so doing forgoes the person's ongoing interaction with other employees. And while the Postal Service's large "part-time flexible" category manifests high turnover and low productivity, a smaller corps of "part-time permanents"—chiefly people for whom this is a long-term second job—is quite stable and productive.

2. *The categories of secondary and retention part-time employment do not exhaust the types of part-time work. Certain patterns of part-time employment in other industries have no parallel in retail or insurance.* For example, in a university, student employees are simultaneously consumers and workers. University departments may use part-time employment as a way of attracting students qua consumers. In the U.S. Postal Service, "part-time flexibles" are essentially waiting for full-time employment under nearly full-time conditions. They receive the same benefits as full-timers, in many cases work 40 hours a week (although the hours are not guaranteed), and rest secure in the knowledge that full-time jobs are *only* available to those in the part-time pool, primarily on the basis of seniority.

Still other forms of part-time employment did not appear in this limited set of interviews. For instance, in some blue-collar occupations (particularly the building trades), part-time work results primarily from temporary hours reductions during slack times as an alternative to layoffs.

TABLE 5.2
Industry Composition of Part-Time and Total Workforce, 1993*

Industry	Percent of Part-time Workforce	Percentage of Total Workforce
Mining	0.1	0.6
Construction	3.5	5.3
Durable manufacturing	2.3	10.4
Nondurable manufacturing	3.4	7.6
Transportation, public utilities	3.6	7.5
Wholesale and retail trade	36.0	21.5
Finance, insurance, real estate	4.1	6.9
Service industries	45.2	34.8
Public administration	1.8	5.4
Total	100.0	100.0

*Includes only nonagricultural wage and salary workers at work.
Source: Data from U.S. Bureau of Labor Statistics, *Employment and Earnings*, January 1994.

After all is said and done, are secondary part-timers the most common group of part-timers economywide? The data summarizing average wages, benefits, job tenure, and so on certainly fit the profile of secondary part-time work. And to the extent that we can match broad industries and occupations with primary and secondary labor markets, this results confirm the sprawl of secondary part-time employment. The great majority of part-time jobs—over four out of five—reside in the trade and service industries, which are also home to extensive secondary labor markets (Table 5.2). Part-time employment is greatly overrepresented in these industries and underrepresented in every other major industry. A slim majority of part-time jobs are located in sales, service, and laborer occupations, also secondary labor market sites, and another large group sit in clerical jobs, where there are substantial numbers of secondary part-timers (Table 5.3). Again, part-timers are found disproportionately often in these four occupational groups and disproportionately seldom in every other major occupation.

Finally, part-time workers crowd in small businesses, where secondary labor markets predominate. A 54 percent majority of part-timers work in firms with fewer than 100 employees, compared to 41 percent of full-timers (see Table 5.4). Put another way, the proportion of the workforce with part-time hours falls from one-third in firms of less than 10 employees, to just over one-sixth in firms boasting 100 or more workers. All signs indicate that secondary part-time employment *does* account for the lion's share of the part-time workforce.

TABLE 5.3
Occupational Composition of Part-Time and Total Workforce, 1993*

Occupation	Percent of Part-Time Workforce	Percent of Total Workforce
Executive, administrative, managerial	4.9	13.4
Professional specialty	12.2	14.2
Technicians and related support	2.6	3.5
Sales occupations	17.1	12.4
Administrative support, including clerical	16.8	16.1
Service occupations	28.6	14.2
Precision production, craft, repair	5.7	11.5
Machine operators, assemblers, inspectors	3.2	6.4
Transportation, material moving	3.1	4.3
Handlers, equipment cleaners, helpers, laborers	5.9	4.0
Total	100.0	100.0

*Includes only nonfarm workers at work.
Source: Data from U.S. Bureau of Labor Statistics, *Employment and Earnings,* January 1994.

TABLE 5.4
Firm Size Composition of Part-Time and Total Workforce, March 1993

Number of Employees	Percent of Part-Time Workforce	Percent of Total Workforce
Fewer than 10	31.6	21.0
10–24	10.6	9.1
25–99	12.2	13.5
100–499	10.8	14.3
500–999	4.6	5.6
1,000 or more	30.2	36.4
Total	100.0	100.0

Source: From Employee Benefits Research Institute, *Characteristics of the Part-Time Workforce,* Special Report and Issue Brief, No. 149 (May 1994), Table 8; reprinted with permission.

■ In Chapter 6 we shall use the concepts of secondary and retention part-time employment to explain the divergent levels of part-time employment in retail and insurance, and to examine in more detail how managers decide on the mix of part-time and full-time workers that is appropriate to each environment.

How Businesses Set the Level
of Part-Time Employment

6

■ PART-TIME EMPLOYMENT SPREADS QUITE UNEVENLY across industries and occupations. By major industry, the rate of part-time employment ranged from a negligible 4 percent in mining and durable manufacturing to a hefty 30 percent in trade in 1993 (Table 6.1). Major occupational groups vary even more dramatically—from 7 percent of managers to an overwhelming 61 percent of private household employees (Table 6.2). Surveys of firms indicate that the variance within industries is also large (Nollen and Martin 1978).

Clearly, this variation reflects differences in how managers perceive the advantages and disadvantages of part-time employment across industries, occupations, and companies, as discussed in Chapter 5. Other researchers have conducted statistical searches for the factors that explain the highs and lows of part-time employment. The retail and insurance case studies done for this book shed additional light on the subject. In particular, they illuminate how different actors within (and outside) the firm interact to set the level of part-time employment.

Previous Studies on the Amount
of Part-Time Employment

Statistical studies have identified two determinants of employer demand for part-time workers: compensation differentials and quasi-fixed costs of labor. Quasi-fixed costs are those that are incurred per worker rather than per hour worked, hiring and training costs being chief examples. Quasi-fixed costs are higher per hour of part-time labor than per hour of full-time labor.

TABLE 6.1
Percent of Part-Time Employment by Major Industry, 1993*

Industry	Part-Time Involuntary	Part-time Voluntary	Total Part-Time
Construction	7.6	4.4	11.9
Durable manufacturing	1.8	2.2	4.1
Nondurable manufacturing	3.9	4.2	8.1
Transport, communications, utilities	3.2	5.4	8.6
Wholesale and retail trade	8.4	21.9	30.3
Finance, insurance, real estate	2.3	8.7	11.0
Service	5.9	17.6	23.6
Public administration	1.3	4.6	5.9
Mining	1.5	2.0	3.5
All industries	5.2	12.9	18.1

*Wage and salary workers in nonagricultural industries only.
Source: Data from U.S. Bureau of Labor Statistics, *Employment and Earnings*, January 1994.

TABLE 6.2
Percent of Part-Time Employment by Major Occupation, 1993*

Occupation	Part-Time Involuntary	Part-time Voluntary	Total Part-Time
Managers	1.7	5.3	6.9
Professional	3.1	13.0	16.1
Technical	2.5	11.3	13.8
Sales	6.3	19.5	25.8
Clerical/administrative support	3.8	15.9	19.7
Private household service	19.7	41.7	61.4
Service, except private household	11.0	25.3	36.4
Craft, precision production, repair	6.0	3.2	19.2
Machine operators	5.4	3.9	9.3
Transport, materials moving	5.7	7.7	13.5
Laborers	10.9	16.7	27.7
All occupations	5.5	13.3	18.8

*Nonagricultural occupations only.
Source: Data from U.S. Bureau of Labor Statistics, *Employment and Earnings*, January 1994.

John Owen (1979) and Ronald Ehrenberg and his co-researchers (1988) found that employers hire more part-timers in settings where wage and fringe benefit differentials are greater. Owen also observed that the demand for part-timers goes down as the absolute wage level in a sector (after controlling for worker characteristics) increases. He speculates that high pay is linked to training, promotion, and complex organizational structures—many of the traits of primary labor markets. These features could be antithetical to the use of part-timers, since part-timers offer less payoff to training (because they both tend to stay at jobs for shorter periods and use their training for fewer hours per week) and are seen by managers as less promotable. However, James Rebitzer (1987) suggests a contrary interpretation: higher levels of part-time employment may undermine the wages of full-timers.

Economist Mark Montgomery (1988), using a unique survey of over five thousand private employers, reported that lower quasi-fixed costs of employment (based on reported time spent recruiting and training employees), smaller firm size, and a larger wage gap between part-time and full-time workers tend to lead to a higher use of part-time workers. Montgomery hypothesized that because per-worker supervision costs rise with firm size, size is a stand-in for this quasi-fixed cost; the variable could also be an indicator of secondary labor markets, which are most common in smaller businesses. His results also indicated that service industries tend to have more part-timers, after controlling for a variety of other firm characteristics.

Part-Time Employment in Retail
Versus Insurance

The rates of part-time employment in retail and insurance diverge sharply, making this pair of industries good candidates for exploring the causes of interindustry differences. As of March 1992, 37 percent of retail employees and only 8 percent of insurance employees worked part-time, straddling the economywide average of 21 percent.[1] The gap between retail and insurance is even wider among the companies sampled for this book. The weighted average rate of part-time employment is 60 percent for the retail units, 5 percent for the insurance units. Even the insurance company with the highest rate of part-time employment, 24 percent, falls far below the retail company with the lowest rate, 43 percent (Figure 6.1). Why?

Although many of the considerations raised by previous researchers resurface in the retail/insurance distinction, the various influences on part-time employment—such as compensation differentials, training levels, and scheduling issues—connect in a deeper institutional structure.

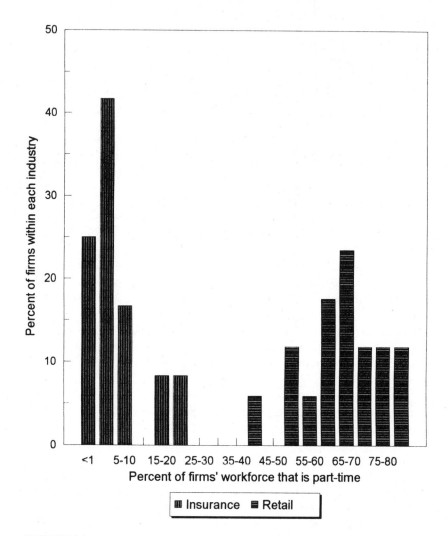

FIGURE 6.1
Distribution of Surveyed Retail and Insurance Firms by Rate of Part-Time Employment

Note: This chart shows, with each of the two industries, the percentage of surveyed firms that fall in each range of part-time employment, from less than 1 percent part-time to more than 80 percent part-time. *Source:* Interviews by author.

The distinction between secondary and retention part-time employment is central to explaining interindustry differences in the rate of part-time employment. I make the argument in four steps below. First, I consider the possibility that the different utilization of part-time work can be completely explained by different time-dependent patterns of demand in the two industries, so that the secondary/retention distinction need not enter the explanation at all. However, considerable evidence weighs against this possibility. Second, I compare the internal labor markets of the two industries. Both combine salaried and secondary labor markets, but in retail the secondary labor market is much larger than its salaried market, whereas in insurance the salaried labor market is dominant. Thus part-time employment is chiefly secondary in retail and mainly retention in insurance. But secondary and retention part-time jobs are not equally compatible with their respective labor markets. The third step is then to identify three reasons why part-time employment is particularly compatible with a secondary labor market, and thus why secondary part-time jobs tend to be more numerous than retention ones. Fourth, I examine a number of firms that represent exceptions to this pattern to demonstrate that there is an element of choice in the process and that the firms' decisions are not absolutely predetermined. After this discussion, I turn to the question of *who* determines the rate of part-time employment in different settings.

Beyond the Time Pattern of Demand

One obvious reason that retail uses part-time workers more heavily than insurance lies in the difference in the time pattern of demand in the two industries. A closer look indicates that this difference is important, but not sufficient to explain the gap between retail and insurance in the utilization of part-time employment.

Retail trade has a distinctive time pattern of demand for several reasons. People prefer to shop at certain peak times of the day and week. Extended hours are used as one basis of competition among stores. There are also predictable fluctuations in demand over the month (for example, because of the timing of food stamp distribution) and year (for example, because of holidays). Insurance has a few similar workload patterns (for example, quarterly billings, a surge of claims before the end of the year, competition via 24-hour claims phone lines), but to a much lesser extent than retail.

However, retail respondents reported that their use of part-time employment has gone well beyond the level necessary to meet peak-time needs. In addition to covering peak times, part-timers can be used to fill gaps in staffing, but part-timers also create such gaps, since quite a few managers report that they have higher absenteeism. Furthermore, a substantial proportion of part-time employees in retail work hours that are fairly fixed or that change according to the employee's needs. In addition, schedule concerns fail to explain why more part-time employment is not used in insurance, since a nine-to-five workday in itself does not preclude the use of part-timers.

If the scheduling issue does not fully explain the different levels of part-time employment in the two industries, what other forces are at work? To answer this question, it is necessary to look at their internal labor markets. Both retail and insurance combine salaried and secondary labor markets, but in very different proportions.

Internal Labor Markets in Retail and Insurance

The typical retail firm has a small core of salaried employees surrounded by a large periphery of secondary employees. The salaried core includes full-time clerks, managers, and much of the office staff. Within this core, retailers promote from within, because, according to a SuperValu store manager, "that way you have a person who is about 100 percent trained. And it shows [employees] that the company has growth from within."

The secondary periphery in retail companies comprises the mass of unskilled workers in the stores, who happen to be part-timers. One measure of the unimportance of training in this secondary labor market is the low cost of an employee turnover. For example, a convenience store chain cited in a study by the National Association of Convenience Stores (1986) estimated the total direct and indirect costs of a clerk's turnover at $334, compared to $7,898 for a manager.

Retailers seek to have as much of the workforce as possible in the periphery, but there are practical limits:

> We can't turn all the jobs into part-time jobs. Department managers must . . . be full-time. The body of the store—the clerks—can be part-time. But we like to have at least one full-time, mature, committed person in each department, to keep things running smoothly. [grocery chain vice president]

> [Before the labor shortage compelled us to create more full-time jobs,] we would only keep a limited number of full-time people. Number one, to maintain stability; number two, to provide a pool for promotion into management; and number three, to augment [managers]. [fast food chain personnel director]

The expansive use of a secondary labor market has its costs in higher turnover and lower productivity, but most retailers accept this as a fact of life. An independent store manager philosophized: "Everybody knows it's a high turnover [business]. . . . The less skill, the less money, the higher turnover. That's just the way it is."

Insurance companies, on the other hand, usually have a large complex of salaried internal labor markets, taking in higher level clerical workers, technical and professional workers, and managers. These salaried labor markets involve many small steps, with additional training and responsibility at each step. A typical labor market structure is to have two promotion pyramids, one for clerical workers and another, atop the first, for professional workers:

> We hire at the entry level—office support people and professional people—and then promote from within. . . . Typically, [our company's] culture was[2] that we hired at the entry level, and moved people up at a steady rate—not extremely rapid. . . . For example, if you come in with a BA, you start out a grade seven or eight and work your way up. When a BA reaches [a higher] level, they're very loyal, and very aware of our corporate culture. It takes longer each step up—it's a pyramid structure.

Insurance companies, particularly the more traditional ones, tend to see themselves as lifetime employers:

> We do not look for people that might last just a year. We hope they'll retire with us.

> The people that we have here do not turn over. . . . We have 650 or 700 people with over 20 years of experience, out of 6,000. . . . It's a very secure, stable company. It's almost like a parent.

> Most of the employees here have never worked anywhere else.

The emphasis on internal training, promotion, and retention in insurance has its basis in the importance of detailed, firm-specific knowledge for many jobs:

> We do fill [jobs] from within. We're typically trying to bring people up, particularly in the line departments. . . . [We do this because] the work can be extremely technical—no, not technical so much as complicated. For example, say you're thinking about a policy change. Change a policy, and it sets off waves—ripples in all directions, things you wouldn't even think it would affect.

One indication of the importance of specific training is the size of the costs of a turnover. One insurance personnel director reported, "Our latest scenario is that we clock for every employee that terminates, we have lost something like . . . 3.4 times their annual salary to replace them as a fully efficient, quality person." Applied to this company's minimum entry-level salaries for technical employees (based on the 1987 Pittsburgh salary scale), this ratio yields an estimated turnover cost of $60,520 for the lowest-paid technical employee. Quite a contrast to the $334 cost of a convenience store clerk's turnover!

The stable, paternalistic, salaried labor market does not apply to all insurance employees. Service jobs and some low-level clerical jobs are organized in secondary labor markets. One indicator of this is higher turnover rates: "Companywide, our turnover rate right now is about 21 percent. And in grades one through six, it's 43 percent" [Eternal Life vice president]. But in insurance the salaried core is typically much larger, and the secondary periphery typically much smaller, than in retail.

Implications of Internal Labor Markets for Part-Time Employment

Once we know that most retail employees reside in secondary labor markets and most insurance employees in salaried labor markets, it follows that there is likely to be more part-time employment in retail than in insurance, for secondary labor markets favor the creation of part-time jobs far more than do salaried markets. In other words, secondary part-time employment thrives in a way that retention part-time employment does not. The use of secondary part-time employment is strategic, whereas the use of retention part-time employment is opportunistic. The type of internal labor market affects the frequency of part-time employment through three channels: the degree of continuity of tasks, the importance of career ladders, and the target workforce.

Continuity of Tasks

In a salaried labor market, jobs involve considerable discretion, responsibility, and specialized knowledge. People in these jobs are most productive when they are continuously available throughout the business week to deal with situations as they come up. Secondary labor market jobs, on the other hand, entail discrete tasks requiring little specialized knowledge. The loss of continuity that results from creating part-time jobs is not much of a loss in a secondary labor market. At the Eternal Life insurance company, the personnel director elaborated on this point:

> It's different in retail. That's a transaction-oriented business, as opposed to a service-oriented business like ours. . . . I think in, let's say, a retail business, where you clunk somebody down at Jordan Marsh [a Boston-area department store chain] who can sell a sweater to somebody and go home and it doesn't matter; the next person can come on the cash register, it really doesn't matter. But here, for the most part, the kinds of jobs that we have, there is some continuity in terms of the servicing we're providing to clients and the training; overall, people's effectiveness increases with training and experience, and there's a lot of com-

munication, departmental and interdepartmental communications, and those opportunities are lost—they're not lost, but they're thwarted—when you have people, well she's gone home or he's gone home, or he won't be in till three o'clock, and things get lost and they fall between the cracks.

Of course, some tasks in retail, such as ordering merchandise, *are* service oriented. These are precisely the jobs that are organized in a salaried labor market and staffed with full-timers.

Career Ladders
Salaried labor markets are characterized by career ladders built around firm-specific training. Part-time employment does not mix well with such career ladders for two reasons. First, using part-timers drives up training costs per hour worked. A manager at the Healthco health insurance company pointed out, "One obvious minus [of part-time employment] is that you have to invest more in training, 'cause you're training . . . two people to do the same work." Second, part-time workers are most often people with major commitments outside of work, and they may be less committed to a career than full-timers, as Eternal Life's personnel director stressed:

> When you're doing something on a full-time basis, you're more immersed in it. It occupies you more fully; you think about it more, you're just into it more. And that part-time work, it's a piece of somebody's life but there are lots of other pieces. . . . The emotional involvement . . . on a part-time basis just may not be there to the degree that a full-time worker's involvement is there.

Or as another insurance company's personnel director put it:

> We have never been a part-time employer in any big way. We're a career company. . . . It's better for an employee to become full-time. You're eligible for promotions, eligible for benefits. So if you're a career employee, you'll generally want to get a full-time job.

Of course, the same considerations lead insurance companies—reluctantly—to create retention part-time jobs for their career employees.

In secondary labor markets, these concerns are peripheral. Contrast the insurance informants' emphasis on careers with the attitude a store manager at the SuperValu grocery chain displayed toward a retail job: "It's a good first job. Almost everyone that starts out working, starts out working in a supermarket."

The two labor markets stand even farther apart when it comes to involuntary part-time employment. In a salaried labor market, the employer nurtures the employee's long-term commitment with an implicit employment guarantee; compelling a prospective or current employee to accept part-time hours would be antithetical to this process. In a secondary labor market, however, involuntary part-time employment becomes just another unpleasant necessity.

The Target Workforce

Secondary labor markets run on low-cost labor. As noted in Chapter 5, creating part-time jobs helps employers to obtain low-cost labor, both because it gives them access to potential workers with fewer job options and because part-time jobs are generally recognized to merit lower compensation. Part-time jobs can be used to target low-cost labor.

Indeed, when evaluating the advantages of part-time employment, retail informants rated low compensation equal in importance to scheduling flexibility. Two SuperValu store managers expressed this consensus:

> Both are essential. Both are equally important.

> They are of equal importance, but I really don't think I could say one was more important to me than the other.

Although employers would certainly like to lower their costs in salaried labor markets as well, they have a different target labor force for these jobs: workers who are likely to end up as long-term, committed employees. Tapping the labor supply of supplementary earners that part-time employment opens up does not help to meet this need.

An Eternal Life manager who has managed at both the insurance company and a department store highlighted the difference in worker expectation in the two industries:

> A lot of times when people are looking for a job in an insurance company, it's more like a career path. Whereas a lot of people working part-time in retail are just working for the time being, or they're in school, or whatever. They don't look for benefits so much.

The Element of Choice

So far, the story runs as follows: most retail employees are in secondary labor markets, and most insurance employees are in salaried labor markets. Part-time employment is more compatible with secondary labor markets, and therefore the rate of part-time employment is higher in retail. If each employer's choice of labor markets were dictated by technology and the tastes of actual and potential workers, this would be the complete story.

But to enliven the situation, there is the element of choice: employers actively choose their labor markets. This is not to say, for example, that insurers could staff skilled professional jobs using a secondary labor market, or that retailers could guarantee promotions and lifetime employment while remaining competitive. Such changes would require major shifts in the product markets for retail and insurance. What the element of choice does mean is that even without changes in the product market, the boundary between the salaried and secondary labor market is somewhat elastic; given the thousands of tasks necessary to running a business, employers have some choice about which tasks to bundle into jobs in a secondary labor market and which to bundle into jobs in a salaried labor market. They actuate this choice by altering the constraints of physical technology, social technology, and labor supply discussed in Chapter 3.

In the retail and insurance industries, such choices often directly affect the use of part-time employment. Looking at the following companies in each industry that are exceptional in their use of part-time employment tells us something about where different employers have drawn the boundary between salaried and secondary labor markets.

Altering the Physical Technology Constraint

The importance of having workers continuously available flows from physical technology: certain jobs can only be done well if someone keeps track of all the details. Similarly, when the technology is such that some tasks can only be performed by people with extensive, firm-specific training, career ladders are a logical response. But firms can and do change the technology that underlies the tasks.

Consider, for example, a health insurer that we shall call Wellcorp. Wellcorp adopted a new computerized system for paying claims, which was in place by 1982. In the process, they broke down the benefit approver's job:

> Prior to 1982, every benefit approver had a telephone on [his or her] desk. They were answering phones and processing claims. . . . We took the telephones off the desk. We made them dedicated to paying claims. We set a telephone center up, so that all people calling up for information or about a claim talk to the telephone center. . . . We found we could divide up the benefit approver's job. . . . Approvers have a nine-month training period. They have to learn coverage, and so on. Data entry is just keying in. . . . So we tiered the work. . . . There's a prescrub [triage] of claims. The easy claims go to data entry. Benefit approvers get the more complex claims.

Before-and-after comments by two Wellcorp workers illuminate this change:

I had to do all the figuring, making sure all the math was correct, the wording was correct, and everything was in its proper place before the claim was typed up.

All you have to do . . . is put a claim in front of you, punch some numbers, take another claim, and punch some numbers.

In creating de-skilled data entry and telephone service jobs, Wellcorp moved tasks from a salaried labor market to a secondary labor market. At the same time, they found that they could staff data entry and telephone service jobs with part-time workers, with significant savings in labor costs. The result: according to the human resource director, the company's rate of part-time employment rocketed from "probably less than 1 percent" before the change to 16 percent in 1987.

Altering the Social Technology Constraint

The career orientation of an insurance company's workforce is anchored in the traditions and implicit agreements that can be considered part of the company's social technology. But insurance companies are not the only places where a strong career orientation is the norm. Some convenience store chains also expect their employees to treat their jobs as careers! The personnel director of one convenience store chain commented on this:

PERSONNEL DIRECTOR: Some convenience store chains offer all full-time jobs. They pay a higher wage, higher benefits. They build up a very high commitment among their employees.
INTERVIEWER: Are their costs higher?
PERSONNEL DIRECTOR: I think their costs are similar—maybe they're higher. Their turnover is lower, that's for sure. They pay a person $6.10, $6.20, $6.50 [a high wage at that time].

One such chain is EZ Mart. EZ Mart's personnel director, upon being told of the preceding quote, remarked, "He's talking about us." She continued;

[Managers'] expectation of who should work in stores is very blue collar, very smokestack. This is the culture. It's very unsympathetic to any life interruptions in schedule. . . . The culture is that you work hard, sustain exceptionally long hours. [Managers are] often divorced men. Men whose wife would stay home and take care of the kids.

In short, managers try to run the stores based on a primary labor market. In this context, part-time employment is not very welcome, as the EZ Mart personnel director explained:

They resist [part-time employment], because they see CSRs [customer service representatives, i.e., sales clerks] as people who should follow *their* path, and work long hours. For example, [a certain] store had 15 people—that was a big joke [with other managers]. Managers would say, "He can't manage well," because he had so many people.

Indeed, EZ Mart had the lowest rate of part-time employment of all the retail companies surveyed—43 percent in mid-1987. In contrast, the other Boston convenience store chain surveyed had a rate of 59 percent, and two Pittsburgh-area chains had rates as high as 68 percent.

Altering the Labor Supply Constraint

Finding a new source of workers can dramatically widen an employer's options in terms of internal labor markets. For decades, the health insurer Healthco had the internal labor market structure of a traditional insurance company. That structure still persists in Healthco's downtown offices:

> They promote from within the department or the company. . . . If you're good, you'll move along.

In the late 1970s, Healthco computerized its claims processing system, just as Wellcorp would do a few years later. Unlike Wellcorp, however, they initially tried to use the same workforce: "What happened was we had mostly long-term people, claims examiners that we tried to teach how to use a keyboard. And I think our first year we had a 150 percent turnover."

Given the tedious nature of work on the automated system, these workers exercised their option to "move along" by moving to other jobs. So Healthco looked for new help:

> Then we found we were having great difficulty just getting any labor at all in the city of Boston that was qualified. And out of 72 positions in exam entry [claims processing]—I remember this distinctly—we had 16 open [jobs] at one point and we put in big ads in the *Sunday Globe,* something like quarter-page ads . . . [on] two or three consecutive Sundays. We had two applicants. No hires. I remember one of the applicants—I had to help him fill out the application because he couldn't read.

The solution? Healthco began relocating its claims processing facilities to the suburbs. When the company surveyed potential workers there, they found a population of housewives and students who wanted part-time work, and were willing to accept reduced benefits:

> [It's] easier to find part-timers. . . . You hit a different labor force. . . . When we went to [a suburban location where Healthco opened a part-time facility], we hit what [a colleague] referred to as a latent labor force. Didn't show anywhere on the statistics, because they were moth-

ers who had been out of work for 10 or 12 years, bringing up their families. And they were hiding down there in their bedroom communities, until all of a sudden, here came an opportunity for them to earn some money. [Healthco department manager]

Many of the women that are at their locations feel that having [Healthco] come in and open up a "factory" is kind of a bonus, that if [Healthco] hadn't come in and opened up their operation there wouldn't be any jobs at all. And these women wouldn't be working at all, or if they were working they'd . . . have a seasonal job as waitresses, or cranberry people, whatever. [Union organizer who attempted to organize Healthco workers]

Healthco's first suburban facility opened in 1979. Although no earlier figures are available, its rate of part-time employment rose from 7 percent in 1983 to 24 percent in 1987.

From Why to Who

So far, this chapter has made a particular argument about why the retail industry has more part-time workers than does the insurance industry. Differing time patterns of demand explain only part of the interindustry difference. Employers in the two industries have also chosen different internal labor market structures—predominantly secondary and salaried, respectively. While each market implies a different type of part-time employment, secondary part-time employment makes a better "fit" with a secondary labor market than does retention part-time employment with a salaried labor market. Thus, secondary part-time jobs are the center of an employment strategy in retail, whereas retention part-time employment remains an exception in insurance.

This argument has been framed as if firms first chose their internal labor market structure and then accordingly decided whether to use part-time employment, subject to scheduling needs. In fact, however, as the examples of Wellcorp, EZ Mart, and Healthco illustrate, the decisions tend to be more simultaneous. The possibility of using part-time employment affects the decision about whether to organize particular tasks in a secondary labor market, as well as vice versa. Arguably the choice of internal labor markets is the more fundamental decision. In any case, whatever the multiple directions of causation, there is a robust correlation between a secondary labor market and part-time employment.

This chapter has also taken a conceptual shortcut by talking about how "firms" make decisions about part-time employment. Firms are made up of many people with some degree of de jure or de facto decision-making power, who are influenced by a variety of forces. Now I shall go on to decompose the decision-making process by looking at the key actors who affect where and how much part-time employment will be used.

Part-Time or Full-Time: Who Decides?

Who decides what jobs will be part-time? According to Stanley Nollen, Brenda Eddy, and Virginia Martin (1978), the decision not to use part-time employment is generally made by default, whereas the decision to use part-time employment usually originates—and ends—with the unit or departmental manager as a case-by-case problem-solving response. But can this be true in an industry like retail trade? After all, as a supermarket manager pointed out, "Part-time employment is not only necessary, it's an absolute must in this business, in order to maintain the bottom-line profitability." The answer is that Nollen et al.'s model is a special case. When part-time employment is not a strategic issue for the company, unit managers *do* hold the decision-making reins, as the model suggests. But when part-time employment is a critical strategic issue, as it is indeed in retail trade, top management gets directly involved in decisions about which and how many jobs will be part-time. This does not eliminate the role of unit managers, because they still play a central part in implementing—or failing to implement—top management's policies.

It is useful to think of the unit manager—store manager in retail, department or branch manager in insurance—as the center of a web of sometimes conflicting influences with respect to part-time employment (Figure 6.2). This chapter discusses the goals and instruments of each major actor in the web, first for the case where part-time work is a strategic issue, then for the case where it is not. One potentially powerful force that does *not* appear as a major actor is the state, and a final section of the chapter looks at the very limited influence of public policy on employer decisions about part-time work.

The Strategic Case

In the sample of employers surveyed, part-time employment is a strategic issue not only in the retail companies but also among the three health insurers, all of whom decided to convert a significant proportion of their operations to secondary part-time jobs. Within these companies, high-level management lays down a policy on part-time employment and attempts to induce unit managers to follow it. Unit managers retain some decision-making power, which they sometimes use to pursue interests that are at odds with the company's policy. In some cases unions influence the policy on part-time work either as collective bargaining agents or as potential organizing threats.

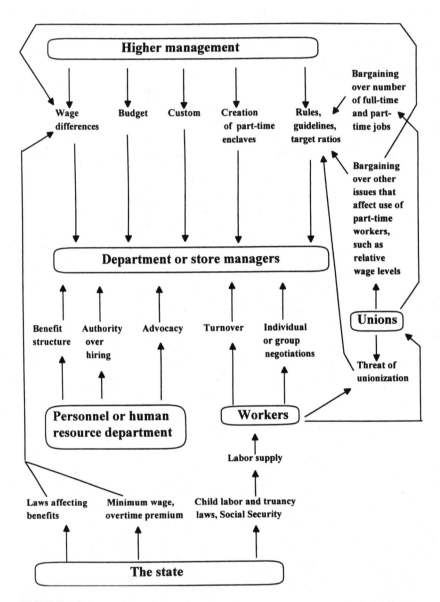

FIGURE 6.2
Influences on the Department-Level Manager in Determining the Mix of Part-Time and Full-Time Jobs

Top Management in the Strategic Case

In the companies where part-time employment is a strategic issue, high-level managers—typically executive or operations officers—worry about the rate of part-time employment as one of the major determinants of labor costs. In terms of Paul Osterman's (1988) troika of objectives—cost minimization, predictability, and flexibility—they are particularly concerned about cost minimization.

The part-time staffing issue comes up somewhat differently in retail and insurance. In retail, each store employs a mix of part-timers and full-timers, and management tends to think in terms of maintaining a particular ratio between the two groups. In insurance, companies staff some functions with full-timers, but designate other job functions as either exclusively or preferentially part-time. Thus, insurance management thinks about which functions to move into the part-time realm. At health insurer Wellcorp, for example, a simple governing principle has been adopted:

> INTERVIEWER: Are there company guidelines on when to use part-time employment?
>
> DIRECTOR OF HUMAN RESOURCES: Pretty much if you can do it with a part-time person, do it.

Once top managers have set their goals for part-time employment, they use a variety of methods to encourage or enforce their implementation. In the insurance companies, management's main instrument is fiat: simply mandating that particular areas of the company shift to part-time employment. Of course, a decision from the top by itself may or may not be sufficient to change managers' practices. At Healthco, a high-ranking manager noted that many managers had misgivings about the move to part-time employment, but that "they didn't really have a choice. It was a top-down decision." At another health insurer, on the other hand, a personnel assistant admitted that the new CEO's part-time initiative had not really caught on yet:

> INTERVIEWER: How do you find that managers are reacting to the idea of part-time in the clerical functions?
>
> PERSONNEL ASSISTANT: I think they like it. . . . But not a lot has been done yet on that, as far as actually taking action to use it.
>
> INTERVIEWER: Can you generalize at all about which divisions have been most anxious to try it?
>
> PERSONNEL ASSISTANT: Let me think, okay, the customer service [division] really is the one. . . . And also, health-related services. . . .
>
> INTERVIEWER: So, the other senior vice presidents [division heads] are mulling it over, but have not said, okay.
>
> PERSONNEL ASSISTANT: Right. . . . Sometimes it just takes a while for things to get going, as far as new ideas, accepting new ideas.

At the retail companies, given their longer experience with part-time employment and their explicit numerical goals, top managers use more fine-grained methods of control, such as rules about the use of part-time employment, budgetary parameters, target ratios, and limits on store managers' hiring authority. First, operations executives promulgate rules and guidelines to shape the way that part-time employment is used. For example, several chains have or had a rule that full-time jobs are to be given only to workers showing an interest and potential for moving into management. Of course, rules are subject to interpretation, as the personnel director of a convenience store chain related:

> Management wanted to hire more part-time in the stores for a very good business reason: because they wanted to hire someone on part-time and check them out before hiring them full-time. But the stores [i.e., store managers] interpreted it even more strongly. It's like playing telephone when you're a kid. When you go down a couple of levels, the message gets changed. Plus [district] supervisors give it their own twist. Top management says hire part-time when possible; the supervisor goes and says hire a part-time person. We ended up with maybe too many part-time people.

In fact, even at a department store chain that had adopted a flat policy of *no* new full-time hiring below the management level, a store-level personnel director told of subverting the directive as the labor shortage tightened: "The region oversees any decision we make—if we want to hire somebody full-time, we're supposed to ask them. Now we hire full-time first and then tell them. . . . We're doing our own thing for our needs."

Rather than relying on rules alone, top management in retail generally also provides managers with a set of budgetary parameters that indirectly influence the use of part-time employment. An EZ Mart convenience store manager explained the system at that company as he saw it:

> If you're doing x-amount of sales you need x-amount of people. . . . What I get handed is a budget as far as man-hours. I have a pay scale that I'm supposed to use and I do use. . . . For every week of the fiscal year I'm supposed to run a certain amount of man-hours. I am budgeted like this week, for instance, 520 man-hours. Out of those 520 man-hours I'm budgeted 16 hours of overtime. . . . That 520 . . . is also based on a projection, a sales projection.

To meet budgeted person-hours, wage rates, and overtime quotas, a store manager is compelled to use some part-time labor. The personnel director of another convenience store chain described the process:

> PERSONNEL DIRECTOR: [The staffing formula is] not etched in stone. It gets done by . . . [district] supervisors. They have a budget they've got

to follow. There's a certain percentage [of sales] they strive for in labor [costs].

INTERVIEWER: Does the company just tell the manager the total number of hours, or do you give them some guidance on the mix of part-time and full-time?

PERSONNEL DIRECTOR: Definitely give them guidance. . . .

INTERVIEWER: But it's ultimately up to the manager?

PERSONNEL DIRECTOR: It's up to the manager. If you have all full-time people working for you, it cuts back on the people you have. If one full-time person is out sick, you have to find someone to cover, and that gets into overtime. Each store has its own budget. . . .

INTERVIEWER: Do you run into a problem with managers wanting to hire more full-time than they really should?

PERSONNEL DIRECTOR: *I* don't run into a problem. *They* find themselves running into a problem. Again, if somebody calls in sick, then they have to cover and use overtime [and risk running over their budget].

In supermarkets, where hourly wage rates for part-timers and full-timers are quite different, the payroll budget itself provides more direct incentives for using part-time employment. A store manager at the SuperValu grocery chain remarked: "We're assigned a certain number of hours, sales per hour, and payroll per each department [in the store]. Controlling the average hourly rate—that's how you control payroll. And part-time gets a lower hourly rate."

But like the rules, the budget does not guarantee that unit managers will make precisely the decisions about part-time employment that higher managers might prefer. One reason is that the budgets typically link hours with wage rates, but not with fringe benefit costs. A Healthco department head pointed out the resulting incentive problem:

INTERVIEWER: Now one thing you didn't mention [in summarizing the advantages of part-time employment] is differences in compensation between part-time and full-time. Is that not as significant a consideration [as schedule flexibility and access to different workforces]?

DEPARTMENT MANAGER: It certainly is from an overall management viewpoint. But you sometimes don't necessarily think about that when you're out fighting with the next guy just trying to get a body in the door. Obviously the benefits are less for part-time. And overall, they're cheaper, but just from a benefit standpoint. Because we pay them identical to full-time on an hour-by-hour basis. So my direct budget doesn't show any difference.

Also, like rules, budgets are made to be broken, as a convenience store manager illustrated:

It's hard to set up a budget for everything. . . . When they set up the budget, they're only going to budget for one full-timer as in vacation pay and sick pay and stuff like that, whereas right now I have four people. So it's four people on vacation pay, so I might go over the budget that way, but . . . that's life. I just hope they don't hear me say that [laughs].

In most of the grocery and department stores in the sample, operations management explicitly directs store managers to target a particular rate of part-time employment, in addition to giving them person-hour and payroll budget targets. For example, SuperValu's central management proposes an optimum part-time rate for each grocery store. And SuperValu's store managers listen:

> INTERVIEWER: Do you feel like you get a message from higher up in terms of what you should be doing with part-time and full-time?
> STORE MANAGER: Oh, without a doubt. They want to decrease the full-time ratio and increase the part-time ratio. . . . We would want at least a three-to-one ratio, three part-time people to one full-time.

In some supermarket chains, store managers are only empowered to hire part-timers, with full-time hiring to be carried out by representatives of personnel or operations. This further limits a manager's freedom to change the part-time ratio.

Finally, top management also exerts some control over the rate of part-time employment via the channels of custom and culture. In a fast-food company, for example, the personnel director insisted: "There's no pressure on the stores [i.e., store managers] to hire part-time versus full-time. It's just been a habit in this industry." The cultural link is often a close one, since operations officials have typically risen from unit manager positions.

Unit Managers in the Strategic Case
The description of all the methods used by top managers to control unit managers' use of part-time employment suggests that the top managers see unit managers as unruly subordinates fighting a guerrilla war against part-time jobs. While this picture is overdrawn, it is somewhat accurate. Unit managers themselves expressed their main concern to be keeping the store or office staffed with dependable people. Whether they lean toward part-time or full-time people depends in large part on which half of this formula—staffing or dependability—is seen as more of a problem.

If the critical issue is finding the bodies to cover the schedule, then managers are likely to favor part-time employment: "Managers would rather have more part-time. More part-time means more [schedule] flexibility." On the other hand, if dependability is the main problem, managers tend to lean toward full-time employment. Quite a few store managers expressed a wish to employ more full-timers because they are perceived as being more committed:

> Having more . . . full-timers does have major advantages. It's their ca-
> reer. They are more responsible and they do more work. I know it's not
> the ideal situation as far as the company is concerned, because I'm also
> paying them four and five dollars more an hour than the other person,
> but they do a better job. . . . If I had my way, if it was my business, I'd
> like to have a lot of full-time people working for me, because I think
> they do a great job.

The personnel director of a convenience store chain elaborated:

> INTERVIEWER: Is there a reaction among managers to converting to or
> using part-time employment?
> PERSONNEL DIRECTOR: There's always a resistance to keeping people
> part-time. If things are allowed to go naturally, you get to know a per-
> son, you develop confidence in a person, so if that person wants more
> hours, you try to satisfy them and make them full-time. That happens.
> Once [i.e., one extra full-time person], it's not too bad. Twice, and if
> somebody leaves, it's a crisis [because so many hours are suddenly left
> unstaffed]. . . . If full-time workers [i.e., managers and assistant man-
> agers] had their way, they would prefer to have more full-time people.
> The number one thing that keeps them on the job is interaction with a
> peer group at work. They feel like they want to relate to other people
> who are up to their neck in it, who can really sink their teeth into it.
> They see a stigma that part-time people are not as involved, not as com-
> mitted, that they're not there to stay.

In fact, one manager of a supermarket with a workforce that was over 80
percent part-time stated that he would prefer a workforce that was 80
percent full-time. When asked why their companies could not increase
the full-time ratio, he and other managers gave a variety of reasons: the
need to control costs, in some cases the unavailability of full-time workers at their company's wage level, in other cases union rules of promotion by seniority that bar a manager from granting full-time jobs on the
basis of merit.

The evidence suggests that in at least some cases, the store managers
who favor more part-time employment may have a more accurate sense
of how to minimize production costs than the top management. Recall
the SuperValu store manager who reported that full-time produce clerks
are three times as productive as part-timers. The ratio of hourly compensation between part-time and full-time employees at SuperValu is 2.3
to 1, according to the company's personnel director. Although other costs
enter into the cost minimization problem,[3] this store manager concluded
that replacing part-timers with full-timers would cut costs overall. Higher
management, to the contrary, "want[s] to decrease the full-time ratio and
increase the part-time ratio" in the store. Here it appears that rigid company guidelines, based on the overall cost advantage of part-time over

full-time jobs, prevent the minimization of costs in a specific situation. In general, it may be easier for higher level operations managers to see savings in payroll than losses in sales resulting from a lower quality workforce, whereas unit managers tend to be acutely aware of the workforce quality issue.

At insurance companies like Healthco, secondary part-time employment clashes with the dominant culture that has grown up around a salaried labor market. At these companies, unit managers are, if anything, even more resistant to the use of part-timers than are the retail store managers. Commented a Healthco department manager:

> You could classify me with a handful of other managers that have had . . . experience [with the suburban part-time facilities], and their preference is to go more part-time. Then you've got the other majority of line managers who have not had that exposure, would probably still have a tendency to [go] full-time, but are learning about the benefits of part-time, and are slowly making a transition.

Healthco's personnel director seconded this analysis:

> Businesses are very slow to change. They'll change one piece, and they'll say about something else, "We've always done things this way; we can't change this." Some areas have part-time quality control [workers], others have full-time quality control [workers]. The difference is that some managers are slower to change than others.

Unions in the Strategic Case
Unions are common only in the supermarket and department store sections of retail trade, and are a rarity throughout the insurance industry. However, all three of the health insurers surveyed were targets of union organizing drives. The retail and insurance unions have somewhat different agendas on part-time employment. The retail unions interviewed have three stated objectives: (1) expand full-time employment; (2) increase guaranteed hours of part-timers; and (3) equalize the benefits of full-time and part-time employees. The insurance unions emphasize equal benefits far more than the other two issues.

How successful have the unions been at achieving these goals? As far as expansion of full-time employment, as a representative of a Boston retail local put it, "The tide has been running the other way." Even so, the unions have not given up the battle. In the words of a Pittsburgh union official: "We're always out fighting [for] full-time jobs. . . . When we go in to bargain, we always try to bargain [for] full-time jobs." Pittsburgh retail union officials believe that without the union's intervention, the store owners would "push it to the limit," converting almost all jobs to part-time. Typical contract language mandates the one-for-one replacement of full-time people that leave, either as a general rule or at least as long as business conditions remain the same.

Some retail unions have resisted the introduction of part-time jobs more successfully than others. According to several informants from supermarket chains, the low rate of part-time employment in supermarket warehouse, trucking, and meat-cutting jobs is largely due to the efforts of the Teamsters and the former meat-cutters' union (now merged with retail clerks into the United Food and Commercial Workers).

Retail unions have obtained contractual hours guarantees for part-time employees, although the guarantees are limited to 16 or 17 hours at the companies sampled. The unions' goal of equalizing benefits, however, suffered a major setback in the concessionary multitier contracts that swept the retail industry (and other industries) beginning in 1980. These contracts, which establish a lower level of pay and benefits for new hires, have widened the gap between newly hired part-timers and more senior full-timers.

Even at the insurance companies, where no union is recognized, the mere threat of union organizing has affected the use of part-time employment. At Healthco, where a union drive was in process at the time of the interviews, the personnel director suggested that the union threat was one of the factors deterring the company from moving toward converting even more of their operations to part-time:

> If we keep converting to part-time, labor would say, "Hey, wait a minute—you're creating slave labor without any benefits." We don't want to face the labor people and say we're converting entirely to a part-time workforce, all 6,500 people.

Furthermore, as union pressure mounted, Healthco narrowed the benefits gap between part-time and full-time workers.

In some cases, unions have negotiated changes that have had unplanned consequences for part-time employment. For example, two Pittsburgh union officials talked about the creation of the "customer service clerk"—a bagger job without fringe benefits:

> UNION OFFICIAL I: When they established a customer service clerk, things were good, and that was just to give the kids some spending money, and pay for [your] gas and buy yourself a car, that's what that job was made for.
> UNION OFFICIAL II: That was the intent of it. But it didn't work out that way.
> UNION OFFICIAL I: No, that classification is in deep problems.
> UNION OFFICIAL II: It's embedded. Very hard to get out of contracts. . . . Believe it or not, we've had steel workers go and apply for a customer service clerk's job, because their unemployment ran out. And those rates of pay were like $3.50 an hour.

Less obvious examples of unintended results are the repercussions of union rules mandating that promotions take place by seniority. While some managers expressed agreement with this principle, others cited it as a major impediment to creating full-time jobs:

> If I create a full-time job for a person . . . eventually he is going to leave. . . . Now when he leaves, I have to fill that position with the next most senior person in the store. He might be my worst employee. Now he's in a full-time position. And that's basically what we can't afford to do. . . . We're shackled with those types of rules.

The Nonstrategic Case

Part-time employment is not a strategic issue at most of the insurance companies surveyed, where the attitude of top management toward part-time employment ranges from indifference to reflexive hostility. In this policy vacuum, unit managers exercise considerable discretion, which some have used to create retention part-time jobs. Other actors such as personnel officers and even individual workers also wield some influence over the use of part-time employment.

Top Management in the Nonstrategic Case

At the companies where part-time employment is not a strategic issue, the most common attitude of top management toward part-time work is indifference. A human resource professional at the Eternal Life insurance company stated:

> I think [a controller is] not going to have much to say about part-time employment. Theoretically they could tell you benefits cost more [for part-time employees], because the premia [paid by part-timers] are less. But when [part-time employees] go to visits, they go to the dentist just as often. . . . But really, most operations people don't even think about part-time. There are so few [part-time employees] in the company, it's just not something they think about—because they don't have to.

Behind this indifference is an assumption that, with a few minor exceptions, the labor needs of the company can best be met with full-time employment:

> INTERVIEWER: Does the company have opinions or a policy about part-time work?
> PERSONNEL DIRECTOR I: We don't have a policy, but we have an opinion. It's that all positions are full-time positions unless we choose as the company that they will be part-time.
>
> PERSONNEL DIRECTOR II: The company has discouraged the use of part-time workers, because we feel like the work product is better with full-time workers.

This latent hostility toward part-time employment only becomes overt when top managers see the use of part-timers having seriously adverse effects on costs. For example, the personnel director at a property and casualty company that was forced to downsize and become "lean and mean" due to a financial squeeze described the following situation:

PERSONNEL DIRECTOR: What we said to [managers] was, "If you think you can fill a head-count with this 20-hour person, go ahead." Then it's up to them, and a lot of times they decide they can't get the work done that way. . . . Since we can't guarantee the staffing [for job-sharing positions], it's the manager's problem, and a lot of them will just decide to use a full-time person.

INTERVIEWER: So Personnel has reined in managers compared to past practices?

PERSONNEL DIRECTOR: Absolutely. We had to. Because of the company's problems, there wasn't any opportunity for any give. Say there was one person available for 20 hours, and one available for 20 to 25 hours—we didn't say, "Well, [the sum of the two is] close enough [to 40 hours]." We couldn't.

But despite its prevailing indifference, high-level management does affect the use of part-time employment through several channels. First, in some companies top management must approve the creation of part-time jobs: "A department head will ask for permission to have part-time [workers]. It's up to our executive department [in company headquarters] to decide if they want to get into part-time. Generally we prefer to avoid it." Such direct control is only used in a small number of companies.

A second form of top-level influence is the department budget. The budget usually specifies either the number of full-time equivalents (FTEs) or a head-count in addition to a total dollar limit. Various aspects of the budgeting process affect the desirability of employing part-timers. The budget may include partial positions, which can only be filled with part-time employees. If, as at Eternal Life, the head-count is fixed, regardless of the hours per head, department managers must decide if they can get the work done with part-timers.

The treatment of fringe benefits in the budget might be expected to influence the use of part-time employment, but in fact it does not seem to have much of an impact. Eternal Life charges each department the same rate for overhead for every position, whether it be part-time or full-time, as the company's personnel director spelled out:

All of our departments are charged, through their budgets, for benefits costs and the per-employee overhead costs, things like the cafeteria and security, . . . are factored in and charged to departments on a head-count basis, so it turns out to be more expensive for them [when they cover a job with part-timers] because they're charged for two people instead of one."

But, she added, "That's not a big deal," and other Eternal Life managers confirmed her assessment. The remarks of one department manager were typical:

> DEPARTMENT MANAGER: In a sense [the greater per-hour cost of fringe benefits for part-time employees is] a hidden cost with regard to a departmental budget. . . .
> INTERVIEWER: The message I'm getting is that's not a very important consideration, compared to other things that you're thinking about.
> DEPARTMENT MANAGER: In this environment it's not. To say it's not an important consideration in the whole spectrum is crazy, because costs are a number one issue [since] we're trying to leverage costs down, but in leveraging costs down you have to be able to deliver the service. . . . In this particular environment, those costs are not deemed as extensive with regard to what we get in the way of results.

The final way in which top management affects department managers' decisions about part-time employment is—as in retail—via the corporate culture. A statement from management such as, "We really don't want to encourage part-time work—this is a full-time career company," presumably reflects a consensus that probably has more effect on the utilization of part-time employment than most of the budgetary levers.

Unit Managers in the Nonstrategic Case

Given the limited intervention by higher management in decisions about part-time employment, most decision-making power rests with department or branch managers. At Eternal Life, the personnel director reported: "We haven't changed policies on recruitment of part-timers in a long time. We let management drive that process. If management is interested in part-time workers, we recruit part-time workers; if they're not, we don't."

And insurance line managers, on the whole, are *not* very interested in part-time workers. They tend to feel that part-timers are second-rate employees, both because they are not available all week long and because they are less committed to the job (see Table 5.1). One personnel director summarized managers' attitude toward employing part-timers in professional and managerial jobs in words that could apply to the use of part-timers in most insurance jobs: "If they have a need, they want to fill it with a full-time person. This is a company that likes to feel like the employees that come into this kind of position are theirs. It's a very old-time philosophy." In fact, over and over again in the interviews, managers asked, "If I could get a full-timer, why would I want to get a part-timer?"

The employee services director at Eternal Life bemoaned this managerial reluctance to consider part-time employment:

> EMPLOYEE SERVICES DIRECTOR: The Human Resource [Department's] position is to keep somebody on part-time if you have a valuable employee. But there is resistance in management. . . .
> INTERVIEWER: Is the management resistance due to culture or to the higher costs of employing part-timers?
> EMPLOYEE SERVICES DIRECTOR: It's cultural. Traditionally, people have worked full-time, and it's expected. But it's also easier to manage full-time people. That's an issue of both cost and culture. It's easier for a manager to know someone is here when they need to be here.

She added, in another interview, that the resistance is more passive than active:

> Somebody told me years ago that managers follow the path of least resistance. And as a manager, I know that's true. Unless somebody approaches you and asks you to consider part-time employment or unless you're unable to fill jobs with full-time, you're not going to think about part-time.

Informants at a number of other companies concurred with this general assessment. It also accords with Nollen et al.'s (1978) finding that nonusers of part-time employment tend to anticipate costs and obstacles that users rarely report in practice.

Nonetheless, unit managers do create retention part-time jobs, most often because they are dealing with exceptional situations:

> INTERVIEWER: The [managers] I spoke to [here at Eternal Life] were all positive toward part-time employment, and every one of them said they were atypical.
> EMPLOYEE SERVICES DIRECTOR: They're not as atypical as they think. Everybody likes to think that they're a little more liberal than the rest. Even the ones who don't use part-time workers—they won't admit they're actually negative to part-time work. What they're going to say is that . . . either they haven't been approached, or the opportunity to run a job as part-time isn't there.

When a manager sets up a retention part-time arrangement, it is explicitly an individual deal between manager and employee: "The full-time person who negotiates a part-time arrangement, that just sort of happens. They just do their thing and the managers are happy about it, and sometimes we [Personnel] don't even know about it; they just do it." And employers prefer to keep such agreements individual. A union representative commented: "[The right to return part-time after childbirth is] not contractually guaranteed—employers have really fought that. It's a privilege they give someone."

Other Actors in the Nonstrategic Case

With top management paying little attention to part-time employment, other actors in addition to the unit managers may have significant influence. The initial impetus for retention part-time jobs, of course, comes from the employees involved. At Eternal Life, for example:

> In 1974–75, professional women started . . . coming back from maternity leave and wanted part-time work. These were women out of college, five to ten years into their career. So awareness of the issue developed. They were a very vocal group. . . . They represented an enormous investment [in training] by the company. The company realized if it didn't give them part-time, they were gone. . . . They negotiated with management, and got pretty much what they wanted.

The source of the above statement, Eternal Life's director of employee services, herself a former retention part-timer, emerged as a strong advocate for part-time professionals. Among other things, she redrafted the company's fringe benefit policy to accommodate part-timers better. According to another Eternal Life manager:

> The administratively generous provisions that were added a couple of years ago were done deliberately with the focus on the working woman, and . . . our corporate policy is to be supportive and make every effort to assist women and make their life at work as comfortable as possible and so forth, as part of our equal opportunity effort, and . . . a number of those changes were made with that spirit in mind, [even though] they were administratively more complex and difficult for the company to handle. In my mind, the women won out in that situation.

This woman's degree of personal involvement in the issue of part-time work is unusual, but her sentiments are not. The personnel director of another insurance company said, almost apologetically: "[This company] is sort of insular. Most of the employees have never worked anywhere else—so we tend to get somewhat out of touch with what's going on out there. I'd like to be able to argue with managers for more openness to part-time." And a third company's personnel director added:

> I think [the concept of part-time professionals] is an issue today, and I think it's something that we've got to be conscious of. If you look at the early '70s and you look at EEO [equal economic opportunity], and look at . . . women coming in, . . . a lot of people who have really start[ed] to rise in the corporations and then, all of a sudden decide, forget it, I'm going back to raise my family or whatever. I'm not sure if you would have the same issues if . . . they ha[d] the opportunity to work part-time.

Effects of Public Policy

Absent in the entire discussion of decision-making about part-time work up to this point has been any mention of public policy. And in truth, public policy seems to have little if any direct effect on part-time employment.

Retail managers did note the indirect effects of several laws. The overtime premium creates an incentive to use part-timers when hours are variable. Child labor laws lessen the supply of teen-agers, one of the main groups of part-time workers in retail. At the time of this study, the minimum wage constituted a floor for part-time wages in retail in the Pittsburgh area (and indeed several of the companies started part-timers at minimum wage).

Little was said about other laws. A striking omission was federal laws mandating equal coverage of employees working over a certain number of hours, such as the Employee Retirement Income Security Act (ERISA) and Section 89 of the Tax Reform Act of 1986. ERISA requires—with certain exceptions—that an employer offering pensions to any employees must allow all employees working 1,000 hours a year (20 hours per week) or more to vest. Section 89 would have made health insurance and certain other benefits taxable unless they were extended to all employees working over 17.5 hours per week, effective in 1989. However, Section 89 was rescinded before it took effect (but after these interviews were conducted) due to intense business lobbying. Some insurance managers had an imprecise notion that such equal coverage laws existed:

> Isn't it mandated in Pennsylvania if you do more than 1,000 hours you must pay them the full benefits you're paying other employees? [branch manager]

> I believe there are certain state laws or whatever, I don't know if they're state or federal actually, that indicate if you work over x amount of hours, hours a year, you have to provide benefits. [personnel director]

No retail informant seemed to be aware of Section 89, although retail industry spokespeople led the public criticism of it (Repko and Martingale 1988). It would have been interesting to return to these managers in the midst of the recently swirling health-care debate and find out if they were contemplating the likely effects of the various reform proposals.

In short, it appears that most of public policy's effects on part-time employment are either unintended or unnoticed. In one interesting exception, however, an insurance informant commented that the threat of legislation was one of the forces pushing her company and others to expand the use of retention part-time employment:

> The working parents issue is gaining much more national attention. There is a feeling in companies that if we don't respond, some state or

federal regulations will be imposed. Companies like us don't tend to like to be regulated in this way. We prefer to be proactive. The parental leave act is coming up again—and there's a good chance it will pass. The problem with regulations is that they're generic—they don't necessarily fit our needs.

Can policies with more substantial effects on part-time employment be adopted? Overall, the findings of this chapter do not offer much grounds for optimism. The difference between the strategic case and the nonstrategic case implies that top management is much more involved with the creation of secondary part-time employment than with the creation of retention part-time employment. Employers can be expected to strenuously resist policies placing restrictions on secondary part-time employment, since such restrictions would conflict with their chosen strategies for dealing with labor. Unfortunately, it does not follow that employers would accept with equanimity policies increasing worker access to retention part-time jobs. The testimony of the union representative who said "employers have really fought" the right to return to work part-time after having a baby and the manager who commented that "we prefer to be proactive" in issues such as parental leave policy suggests that companies will jealously guard their management prerogatives.

However, this chapter's findings also indicate that in regard to both secondary and retention part-time employment, the position of "management" is rarely unanimous, even within a company. Thus policy-makers may find unexpected allies—or at least abstentions—on issues of part-time employment.

Policy options will be taken up once more in the concluding chapter. First, though, it is necessary to complete the study of part-time work in the retail and insurance industries by looking once more at the reasons for change, both cyclical and long-term, in the rate of part-time employment in Chapter 7.

Cycles and Trends

7

■ THE RATE OF PART-TIME EMPLOYMENT RIDES A ROLLER coaster: it rises and falls with the unemployment rate, but after each recession over the last quarter-century, it has remained a little higher (Figure 7.1). It is involuntary part-time employment that propels the ups and downs, and recently the upward drift as well. In Chapter 2, we saw the beginning of an explanation for the long-term increase: the growth of industries that use part-time employment heavily and a strategic shift within industries toward wider use of part-time schedules. Later in this chapter, I shall complete this story of the long-term part-time expansion.

But now it's time to turn an inquiring eye on the roller coaster's short-term fluctuations. To deal with the problem of involuntary part-time employment, this relationship between part-time work and the business cycle must be understood. After explaining why the conventional wisdom about this relationship no longer works, I shall draw on the interviews to suggest an alternative theory.

In addition, in the last few years we have witnessed the disturbing spectacle of a roller coaster that refuses to come down again. Despite the economic recovery that officially began in March 1991, involuntary part-time employment continued to rise during 1991 and 1992, and has decreased relatively little since then. So I shall close by speculating about whether the cyclical pattern's nature has changed.

Refuting the Conventional Wisdom

The cyclical pattern of part-time work means that when unemployment rises, involuntary part-time employment does too. Analyses by Bernard Ichniowski and Anne Preston (1985), Rebecca Blank (1990), and myself

121

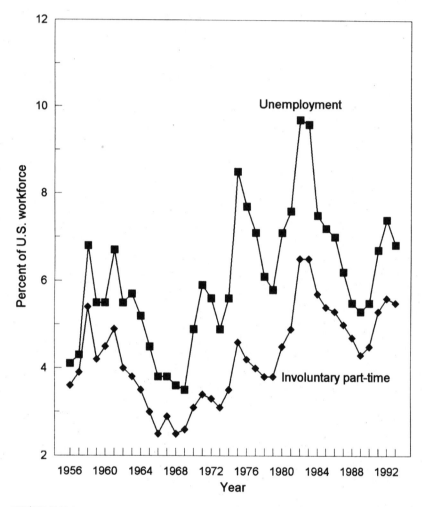

FIGURE 7.1
*Unemployment Rate and Rate of Involuntary Part-Time Employment,
1956–93*

Source: Unemployment rate from U.S. Council of Economic Advisors (1994). Involuntary part-time employment rate from U.S. Bureau of Labor Statistics (1988b), with additional data from the U.S. Bureau of Labor Statistics, based on the Current Population Survey.

(see Tilly 1989, Appendix B; 1991a) all estimate that if the unemployment rate climbs by 1 percentage point, the rate of involuntary part-time employment on average follows with an increase of about 0.5 point.

The cyclical ups and downs of part-time employment have been studied most closely by Bureau of Labor Statistics analyst Robert Bednarzik (1975, 1983), who has suggested that the fluctuations are caused primarily by temporary hours reductions among normally full-time workers. But are they?

The answer is no—or at least not any more. Hours reductions explain only a minority of involuntary part-time employment. Most involuntary part-time workers state that they usually work part-time, and do so because they are unable to find a full-time job. Figure 7.2 shows that such workers have made up the majority of involuntary part-timers since 1971 and that this majority has grown over that time. Ichniowski and Preston (1985) estimated the effects of the unemployment rate on the involuntary part-time employment of those who usually work part-time and those who usually work full-time, and found that changes in the unemployment rate triggered responses of equal size in both groups. Thus, only half of the cyclical fluctuations are due to changes in hours by workers who usually work full-time.

Furthermore, much of the cyclical pattern comes from industries whose output and employment are not cyclical! Look at the roller coaster's swoop over the business cycles of the last 15 years. From a trough in 1979, involuntary part-time employment climbed until 1983, fell to a new low in 1989, and then rose once more to a 1992 peak. Trade, finance, and services accounted for 77 percent of the net rise in involuntary part-time jobs between 1979 and 1983, 72 percent of the 1983–89 drop, and 91 percent of the increase from 1989 to 1992. But trade, finance, and services, unlike manufacturing and construction, are industries whose employment levels are little affected by business cycles. So the major part of the cyclical fluctuations of part-time employment remains unexplained.

Do Changes in the Industry Composition of Employment Offer an Explanation?

One possibile reason for the rise and fall in the rate of part-time employment over the business cycle may simply be an artifact of fluctuations in the industry composition of employment. Since the service industries, which are noncyclical, have the highest rates of part-time employment, the overall rate of part-time employment goes up during recessions, as other industries contract, and goes down during expansions, as other industries rebound. In more stylized terms, in a recession, factories shut

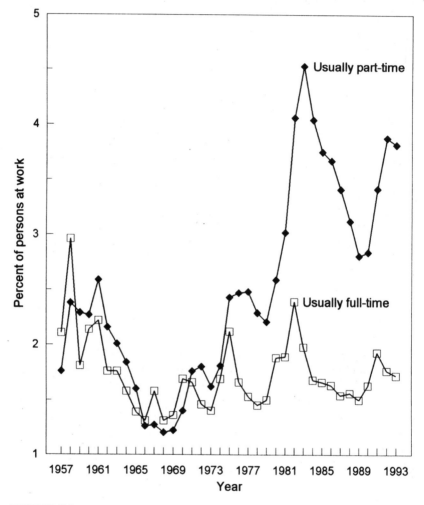

FIGURE 7.2
Components of the Involuntary Part-Time Workforce, 1957–93

Note: All involuntary part-time workers are classified as either usually full-time or usually part-time.
Source: U.S. Bureau of Labor Statistics, *Employment and Earnings,* annual summary issues, various years

down and stores stay open; in an expansion, both factories and stores are open; and stores use more part-timers than factories.

This explanation can be evaluated using a time series regression analysis that compares different points in time to see which factors are most closely associated with changes in the rate of part-time employment. I shall consider three factors: the unemployment rate, the industry mix (the proportion of the workforce in each major industry), and a time trend that simply denotes the passage of time.

I shall test two opposite hypotheses. First, perhaps all unemployment-related movements in part-time employment are due to changes in industry composition, not to unemployment itself. In other words, if part-time work is more common in high-unemployment years, this may simply reflect the fact that on average the industry mix happens to differ in those years. Then once the industry changes are taken into account, the unemployment rate should not offer any added information useful in predicting the rate of part-time employment.

Inversely, perhaps any apparent relationship between the industry mix and the rate of part-time employment is simply an illusion. Maybe what is actually happening is that the business cycle (measured in this simple model by the unemployment rate) affects both the part-time rate and the distribution of employment across industries. In this case, once unemployment is accounted for, the industry mix should no longer exhibit any independent association with the level of part-time employment.

The first hypothesis is dead wrong: with or without the industry mix variables, the rate of part-time employment remains strongly associated with the unemployment rate.[1] Years with high unemployment also have high part-time employment, regardless of what sectors provide the jobs. The data also firmly reject the second hypothesis, indicating that industry composition as well has an independent tie to the rate of part-time work.[2] So both the unemployment rate and industry shares contribute in different ways to determining the rate of part-time employment. Credit for a substantial part of the cyclical pattern goes to the unemployment rate. In other words, much of the cyclical movements in the rate of part-time employment are taking place within industries.

A Hidden Reduction in Compensation

Now we are left with a puzzle. What remains to be explained is the cyclical pattern of part-time employment within noncyclical industries. Since the industries involved are relatively insensitive to the boom and bust of the business cycle, the explanation does not lie in changing demand for the services they produce. Instead, it must involve their reaction to the tightening and loosening of the labor market.

A natural supposition is that when unemployment is high, employers find workers more willing to accept secondary part-time jobs and therefore expand secondary part-time employment. Since these part-time jobs have lower compensation than the full-time jobs they replace, this expansion represents, in effect, a hidden reduction in average compensation—even if the respective compensation rates of full-time and part-time labor remain unchanged. When unemployment rates fall, secondary part-time employment contracts, and there is a hidden increase in compensation.

But exactly how does this hidden wage reduction mechanism work? A closer look at the retail and insurance industries helps to answer this question.

Cyclical Patterns in Retail and Insurance

In the aggregate, retail and insurance manifest totally different cyclical patterns in the rate of part-time employment. In retail, as in the economy as a whole, involuntary part-time employment varies contracyclically, rising, with unemployment, when the economy slumps (Figure 7.3). Retail thus appears to be a good place to look for the expansion and contraction of secondary part-time employment.

In the insurance industry, on the other hand, the rate of involuntary part-time employment shows no discernible cyclical fluctuations. Instead, the rate of voluntary part-time employment varies procyclically, rising when an expanding economy drives down unemployment (Figure 7.4). This suggests that retention part-time employment expands and contracts based on the tightness of the labor market, leading to a contracyclical pattern in involuntary full-time employment. Interview findings support these suppositions for both industries.

Retail Managers on Part-Time Employment and the Business Cycle

The picture that emerges from interviews with retail managers is that retailers do indeed increase secondary part-time employment when unemployment is high and decrease it when unemployment is low. Managers from 5 of the 17 surveyed retail companies stated explicitly that their companies had cut their part-time employment because the labor market had tightened. In all, 11 of the 17 companies reported a decreasing part-time ratio in the recent past as the economy had expanded, 3 reported little or no change, and 3 reported increases. Most reporting a recent decrease in part-time employment added that previously the rate had been

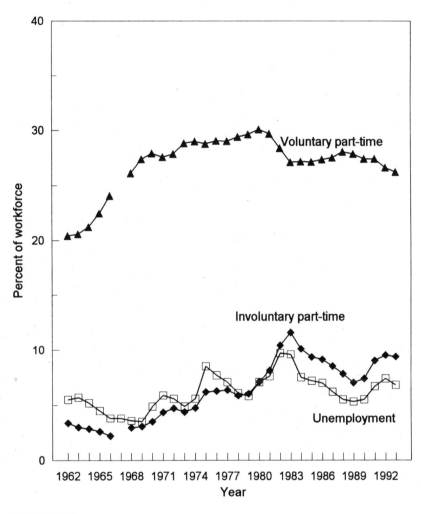

FIGURE 7.3
Rate of Part-Time Employment in Retail and Unemployment Rate, 1962–93

Note: From 1968 on, employment figures include people with a job but temporarily absent from work.
Source: Unemployment rate from U.S. Council of Economic Advisors (1994). Retail data from U.S. Bureau of Labor Statistics, unpublished Current Population Survey data, provided by Thomas Nardone.

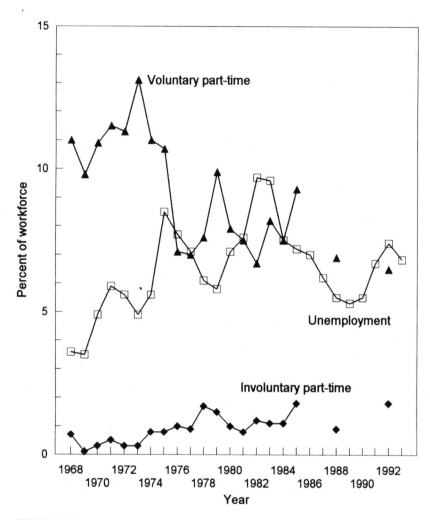

FIGURE 7.4
Rate of Part-Time Employment in Insurance and Unemployment Rate, 1968–92

Note: Insurance data based on the March Current Population Survey only, rather than annual averages. This is one reason for the observed volatility.
Source: Unemployment rate from U.S. Council of Economic Advisors (1994). Insurance data from Current Population Survey computer tapes.

increasing. In fact, during the last recession 4 of these companies had adopted a general policy of hiring just part-timers, only to relax or abandon the policy during the expansion.

The same pattern emerges from comparing retailers in high-unemployment Pittsburgh and low-unemployment Boston in 1987. Within each category—supermarkets and convenience stores—the rate of part-time employment was higher in Pittsburgh. This offers further evidence for the positive effect of unemployment on part-time employment. Furthermore, as noted in Chapter 2, the reported rate of involuntary part-time employment stood much higher among Pittsburgh retailers than among Boston retailers.

The data from the interviews paint a more vivid picture of how retail managers viewed the 1987–88 labor market and how they were reacting to it by adjusting part-time employment. Informants from 13 of the 17 retail companies volunteered staffing as one of their major personnel-related challenges; in 11 cases, it was *the* major challenge. Interviewees described the crisis in dramatic terms:

> [Our biggest challenge is] getting a sufficient number of qualified people. It's a Massachusetts problem. That damned Governor Dukakis and his economic revival is causing the problem. [personnel director, Boston]

> [I]t's very different—it's a much more competitive [labor] market [than it used to be]. . . . If there's a major recession, then this won't be a problem. [personnel director, Boston]

> I've had people just leave, and I don't even know where they are. You know, "Where's Sally?" "Shit, I don't know, she's gone." Sally calls me a week later and says, "Gee, I got tired and I decided I'm going to work for [a nearby restaurant]." [store manager, Pittsburgh]

> Boston, I guess all of New England, has a very tight labor market. Pittsburgh has a much more open labor market. But even that's been changing in the last six to eight months. You used to be able to put an ad in the paper and get 50 people lined up for the job. Now you're lucky if you get 5. Unemployment rates have been falling dramatically. Once you get below 6 percent, it starts becoming a problem. [personnel director, Pittsburgh]

As the last informant indicated—and contrary to the views of some Boston retailers—the labor shortage was not just a Massachusetts problem. Pittsburgh retail managers agreed that the labor market there was tightening, and some classified the state of affairs as a labor shortage, although it was clearly not as acute as in Massachusetts.

Retail companies felt the labor shortage in three areas: attraction, retention, and quality of employees. Weakness in attraction and retention, of course, translates into vacancies. A personnel official from one supermarket chain commented, "We could probably use 800 to 1,000 part-time employees right now."

Informants particularly emphasized the impact of turnover: "It used to be an employer's business. Now it's an employee's business. You keep 'em happy, or they're going to go to work the next place they have lunch." One supermarket chain hired 3.7 times as many people in 1986 as in 1980, for "basically the same employment and staffing level."

Retailers tend to agree that the three problems particularly affect the part-time population. Attracting full-time employees is not difficult when there are part-timers who want full-time jobs:

> Most of the jobs we're trying to fill are part-time right now. When you have a part-time workforce, and full-time positions [open], it seems like the part-time person slides in there automatically, so there is not much problem filling the full-time positions.

Chains can also move full-time employees from store to store, as a SuperValu store manager pointed out:

> MANAGER: The unemployment rate in [a certain] area has been around 2 percent now since the store opened. And it has just not allowed us to increase our part-timers at all.
>
> INTERVIEWER: Why does a low unemployment rate in a tight labor market particularly pinch you on part-timers as opposed to full-timers?
>
> MANAGER: We've been able to promote people from other areas of the company to full-time positions where they had been waiting to get a full-time position in other stores that . . . didn't need the position as a full-timer.

The supermarket industry's press confirmed that the labor shortage had particularly increased the difficulty of finding entry-level part-timers (*Progressive Grocer* 1986; Sansolo, 1987; *Supermarket News* 1985, 1987).

In addition, part-time turnover was much higher than full-time turnover and had risen disproportionately in most cases. Part-time turnover at a representative SuperValu store roughly doubled between 1985 and 1987, whereas full-time turnover increased by only 29 percent. A nationwide survey of supermarket operators by *Progressive Grocer* (1988) revealed that this pattern was widespread: 61 percent of the grocers reported higher part-time employee turnover, and only 20 percent reported increased full-time turnover.

The decreasing quality of workers was also most severe among part-timers:

For part-time, we've had to drop our standards considerably. We used
to be very selective in terms of having a stable job history and what their
current situation was. For example, if someone was a high school student and it's April and he was going to graduate in June, we wouldn't
hire him. . . . Now we don't have as much choice. . . . For full-time, we're
still holding the line on a stable job history, looking for people who will
be with us for a while. [SuperValu personnel director]

In fact, some retail managers described the labor shortage in part as a
mysterious change in people's schedule preferences:

It just doesn't seem like there is an interest in part-time positions any-
more. I don't know what the reason is.

[Five years ago] there were more people in the market to pull from, pick
from. . . . People only want full-time jobs these days.

Retail companies responded to the labor shortage in a number of
ways. They redoubled recruiting efforts. Most also raised wages, but
managers were dubious about this strategy. One reason is that close com-
petitors tend to match wage increases:

One of the problems with the part-time workforce is that everybody
needs them so desperately, that as soon as one makes a change, the rest
follow. If we raised our pay a dollar, [two other supermarket chains]
would follow right on our heels. [supermarket personnel official]

We have meetings with other stores. They all have [the] same pay
scale[s] for retail and clerical. . . . All retail is within 5 to 25 cents of
each other—[lists three other department store chains as examples]. We
come to an agreement. [department store personnel director]

Also, the whole pay scale is pegged to the entry-level wage: "If we move
up [our] entry-level pay, there's pressure on all wages. Right now our
strategy is to hold the entry-level wage fixed and hope that turnover is
not too great" [grocery chain vice president]. The potential expense of
raising wages was large. A SuperValu store manager complained that
even the chain's top rate on entry-level part-time wages—$6.27 an hour,
well above the official entry-level wage of $3.65—was not high enough
to allow him to staff his store adequately.

Thus, retailers pursued an additional strategy of increasing full-time
employment. The personnel director of a fast-food chain eloquently described how the company's hiring policies had changed:

INTERVIEWER: How do you decide how many part-time and full-time
positions to use?
PERSONNEL DIRECTOR: Three years ago, that question would be an-
swered differently than today. We use to be—in all businesses—deter-
miners of our own destiny. We'd hire part-time because they were less

expensive. . . . These days, we'll hire whatever we have to hire or whatever capacity they want to work. Instead of limiting their hours—it used to be that if they asked for more hours, we'd say take it or leave it. Now we will beg them to stay. . . . If there's a person coming in off the street who wants a full-time job, we'll take them. . . . If we had the freedom of choice, we'd take the part-time. [But] we have mitigating circumstances. We're no longer saying are we looking for part-time or full-time. We're just looking for anybody who's willing to take the responsibility to work at [our company].

Other companies—particularly in the Boston area—reported similar changes.

A final note about this cyclical pattern in retail: the evidence from the interviews strongly indicates that retailers reduced part-time employment during the particular economic expansion then in effect. The findings are much more mixed about whether firms had made analogous adjustments at previous cyclical turning points. It is possible either that the cyclical pattern is becoming stronger or that changes in the late 1980s changes represented something more than a cyclical adjustment. These possibilities are discussed later in this chapter.

The Insurance Industry on Part-Time Employment and the Business Cycle

Unlike retail companies, insurers tend to increase retention part-time employment during expansions and decrease it during recessions, although the pattern does not emerge as powerfully in the interviews as retail's cyclical movements. Informants from 5 of the 12 insurance companies listed a tightening labor market as a reason for increasing their rate of part-time employment; one added that as the labor market slackened after the late 1960s, her company had *decreased* its use of part-timers.

A comparison between insurance companies in Boston, New York (recall from Chapter 2 that the Boston sample was supplemented by two insurers based in the New York City area), and Pittsburgh also points to a procyclical pattern of the rate of part-time employment. Sector by insurance sector, Boston- and New York-based companies utilized more part-time employment than their Pittsburgh counterparts.

Insurance informants did not appear to be as overwhelmed by the labor shortage as their retail counterparts. Informants from 7 of the 12 companies—mostly Boston- and New York-based insurers—listed staffing as one of their major personnel-related challenges. Compared to the retailers, their rhetoric was muted, and the managers linked the shortage to the "baby bust" as often as to the economic expansion:

INTERVIEWER: What would you say at this point is the company's biggest challenge in terms of human resources or personnel?

PERSONNEL DIRECTOR: Well, I think it's going to be, you know, as you look over the next five to ten years, it's certainly going to be [the] attraction or retention of good, qualified personnel. . . . And, you know, that has a lot to do with . . . the demographics . . . the whole "baby bust" generation and the fact that there just are going to be fewer people and . . . more companies competing for them.

There were the inevitable stories about employees going to lunch and not returning. For example, a Healthco employee testified: "We've been finding good help is very hard to find, especially recently. . . . [Healthco has] been hiring a lot through a temporary agency, and they just haven't been able to get people that stay. They go to lunch and don't come back." In Pittsburgh, on the other hand, some insurance employers were almost smug about the state of the labor market:

It's our marketplace right now, and it has been for about four or five years. Therefore, our recruiting tends to be less proactive. In the lean years, when you've got a 2 to 5 percent unemployment [rate], you have to go out and actively seek. . . . Now, unfortunately for people seeking employment, we can find MBAs working at McDonald's, which is rather sad.

The labor shortage hits insurance companies in the same ways as it does retailers, causing problems with the attraction, retention, and quality of workers. Comparisons over time or between geographic areas highlight these problems:

In the last three years . . . the full employment that's in Massachusetts is starting to create a problem. So I think our [companywide] turnover . . . hasn't reached any crisis proportion yet or anything like that, but you can start to see the trend. . . . So far my [departmental] turnover isn't any higher, but what we're beginning to see is that going out in the marketplace to find somebody to fill a position in the higher skill levels, we just don't find them. And so there's some inkling that there's going to be some further problems there. [department manager]

I was at a meeting with a group from a lot of different companies in New York. Somebody who was in New York, and is now in Milwaukee, was discussing "the New York worker"—someone who comes in late when they feel like it, takes a one-and-a-half-hour lunch—and this goes for the mailroom clerk as well as the vice president. They stay out sick, and don't even give notice when they leave. . . . In Milwaukee, they have the "Midwest work ethic": they come in on time, they warn the supervisor if they're not feeling well, so [the supervisor] can figure out coverage for a sick day next day. In New York, they can easily find another job. [personnel officer]

Like retailers, insurance companies have intensified recruiting efforts and escalated salaries in order to deal with the labor shortage. Both tactics have their limits, as Eternal Life's personnel director indicated:

> The recruiting process is one that requires multiple activities on a variety of fronts on an almost constant basis. And when you put it all together, you get enough people to keep your head above water, but there aren't any magic answers. . . . [We'll] probably be increasing the salaries, too. Actually, we're already at a point where the secretaries—entry-level secretaries—make as much as entry-level four-year grads. . . . You find really bizarre things like that happening when the labor market gets out of control and crazy.

In a response opposite to that of retail companies, insurance businesses have increased their part-time employment to adapt to the labor shortage. A personnel director painted the picture:

> I suspect you'll find a lot more flexibility here in the greater Boston area because of the state of the labor market. That's true of other companies, and it's also true of us. Our general desire would be to fill full-time positions with full-time people. But if you can't, part-time is better than no time. . . . We're thinking this weekend of advertising for part-time people in programming [data processing]. . . . The desire previously was not to go into part-time employment. Now, we're saying we'll do anything as far as data processing to meet our needs. . . . I'm finding managers are saying, "If you can find somebody good who can work 30 hours, maybe I can live with that, as opposed to having nobody."

Other Boston- and New York-based insurance respondents echoed these views. The same themes and even the same phrases recurred: "It's better to get a 20-hour person than 0 hours if you can't get 40. Before, we could be picky. Now, it's: 'Are you a body? Can you breathe?'"

Among insurers in the Pittsburgh area, managers' sentiment was that they would hire more part-timers *if* confronted by a labor shortage. A manager who currently employs no part-time people declared:

> The only thing I would possibly consider [in terms of part-time workers] . . . [would be] if the workforce became scarce and we wanted some professionals, and let's suppose we had a couple of individuals who would want to work half a day. . . . I would consider it if I needed professionals and I could only get them for a half a day.

Pittsburgh Versus Boston: What Kind of Difference?

I have contrasted Pittsburgh and Boston as respectively high- and low-unemployment areas in 1987. But do their labor markets differ in more profound ways? A closer comparison of Pittsburgh and Boston shows that although the disparity in their unemployment rates generates very different levels of retention and secondary part-time employment in the two cities, it does not lead to qualitative differences in how part-time jobs are used by employers. However, a closer look also reveals other determinants—in addition to the degree of labor market tautness—of the difference in part-time employment between the two cities.

The most striking comparative finding is that despite the big difference in the tightness of the two labor markets, the basic structure of part-time employment in retail and insurance, as outlined in the two preceding chapters, is essentially identical in the two areas. Both cities have secondary and retention part-time jobs. In both cities, retail employment is dominated by a secondary labor market of part-time jobs, whereas insurance employment is primarily a salaried labor market of full-timers peppered with a few retention part-timers. Given these similarities, it seems quite appropriate to suppose that in the two cities similar structural forces set the average levels of part-time employment and that differences in the unemployment rate lead to variation around these averages in a fashion that is analogous in both cities.

Despite the basic similarity, some differences in the structural determinants of part-time employment are apparent in Boston and Pittsburgh. In particular, two differences—other than the difference in unemployment rates—help to explain Pittsburgh's lower rate of voluntary part-time employment. First, Pittsburgh has much lower labor force participation among women than Boston (U.S. Bureau of Labor Statistics 1988a; 1993, Table 23). Pittsburgh families are more likely than those in Boston to have a single, full-time wage-earner. Second, Pittsburgh's insurance companies tend to be much more traditional in their labor policies than Bostonian insurers. Tradition, in this case, includes eschewing retention part-time jobs. Such traditionalism probably affects other industries as well.

Summary of Interview Findings about
Cyclical Changes

In summary, the retail and insurance interviews show two completely different types of behavior. Retail firms increase the rate of secondary part-time employment as unemployment rises and decrease it as unemployment falls, when it becomes more difficult to attract and retain part-time rather than full-time employees. Insurance companies, on the other hand, decrease the rate of retention part-time employment as unemployment climbs and increase it as unemployment drops, when it becomes more difficult to attract and retain full-time employees.

A Formal Model

These findings can be formalized in a mathematical model of the cyclical adjustment in part-time employment in noncyclical industries. Developing the model has two payoffs. First, it demonstrates that under plausible assumptions about how businesses behave, a simulated economy generates many of the same results observed in reality, thus further bolstering the notion that much of the cyclical pattern of part-time work represents hidden changes in compensation. Second, it suggests certain side effects of the hidden compensation changes mechanism. Here the model is simply outlined; a full mathematical description can be found in the Appendix. Any such formal model, of course, must greatly simplify the real-life processes observed through the interviews.

This model supposes the following: (1) as unemployment falls, people who are working a schedule other than the one they prefer become more likely to find a job with their preferred schedule and quit; and (2) since turnover entails costs for firms, the firms adjust their mix of part-time and full-time jobs to try to satisfy more workers. The reverse mechanism operates when unemployment rises. Each mechanism operates within a particular institutional structure, and since retail and insurance have different institutional structures, the outcome of the model is different in the two industries.

Several points about the model are important to note:

- Wages and the full-time/part-time wage differential are fixed in the model.
- Unemployment is taken as given in the model. This is not a macroeconomic model that specifies how unemployment is determined.
- This is a model of *firm* behavior. It takes worker behavior as given, rather than having firms and workers simultaneously make choices.
- All firms are assumed to be identical.
- The model removes much of the institutional detail of the last two chapters, and flattens firms into unitary profit-maximizers rather than collections of agents with conflicting interests.

All of these features can be relaxed, and I consider the consequences of relaxing some of them after presenting the model.

First consider a submodel of the retail labor market, or more generally of a labor market in which secondary part-time employment is the main form of part-time work. For simplicity, assume that the relevant labor market is closed in that workers cannot choose to enter or leave it, but that unemployment varies due to an influx or outflow of workers from the pool of the unemployed, with the size and direction of the flow determined outside this model. Suppose that some people in the labor market want part-time work and that some want full-time work. However, in general firms offer fewer full-time jobs than the workforce desires. Thus, some people work part-time involuntarily. To keep things simple, assume that all workers who *prefer* a part-time job get one—that is, that no firm has *both* involuntary part-time and involuntary full-time workers, and that none of the unemployed want part-time jobs.

All workers in the model thus have an identical, fixed baseline probability of quitting in any given time period. Involuntary part-time employees will also quit if they find a full-time job, which also occurs with a fixed probability per period. Firing does not exist in the model, and firms are always able to fill vacancies immediately.

The firms' problem is how to minimize the labor costs of producing a certain amount of output. The total amount of output is taken to be invariant, since the industries being modeled do not face a cyclical demand. To solve this problem, firms think about the cost of filling a full-time equivalent slot. They have two ways of filling the slot: with one full-time person or two part-time people.

In filling the slots, firms encounter two kinds of costs: compensation and training costs. Training costs are assumed to be incurred during the first period of employment. Compensation costs are lower for part-time employees, as in actual secondary part-time employment. However, amortized per-period training costs of part-timers are greater than those of full-timers for two reasons. First, the employer must train two part-timers to fill a single full-time equivalent slot. Second, part-time workers have a higher average probability of quitting since they include some involuntary part-timers, so their training costs are amortized over a shorter average tenure.

The average probability that part-timers will leave a job depends on what proportion work part-time involuntarily and what chances they have of finding a full-time job outside the firm. Since the number of people who want part-time work is fixed, the proportion who are involuntary part-timers simply depends on how many of the scarce full-time jobs firms make available. The ratio of full-time vacancies to those who want such jobs tells us the probability that someone will land a full-time job in a given time period.

In this model, firms cannot change the relative compensation of full-time and part-time employees. What they can change is the rate of full-time employment. A worker's part-time or full-time status is set for the duration of that worker's employment at the time of hire, so firms can only change the rate of full-time employment by attrition.

Firms choose the rate of full-time employment per head to minimize their total labor costs. Let us suppose that within the given labor market businesses are small enough so that when one firm takes some action that changes the proportion of full-time employment, the firm assumes that others will not react but simply continue to function as they have been. This assumption, generating what economists call a Nash equilibrium, simplifies the mathematics considerably. Solving the minimization problem yields three courses of action for individual businesses: when full-time employment is more expensive, firms hire all part-time workers; when part-time employment is more expensive, firms hire all full-time workers; when the cost is identical, firms make no changes to their workforce.

How does this equilibrium at the firm level translate to the labor market as a whole? Since firms are identical, the rate of full-time employment is the same for the whole labor market as for the firm. But whereas the individual firm took the turnover rate of part-time workers as given, when all firms act together the turnover rate changes. Thus, when looking at the full labor market, the relationship between the turnover rate and the rate of full-time employment must be considered.

What matters to firms is not the part-time turnover rate itself, but the difference in turnover probabilities between part-time and full-time workers. This is the central point of the model. This difference depends on the proportion of part-timers who would prefer a full-time job and on their probability of finding a full-time job; both depend on the number of full-time jobs available but in opposite ways.

In this model, the labor market can reach either of two equilibrium points that are stable in the sense that small economic disturbances will not cause the labor market to make large adjustments. One stable point, although an unrealistic one, is where 100 percent of the workforce works part-time. Although involuntary part-time workers will be unhappy, they will be unable to find full-time jobs, so the part-time turnover rate will equal the full-time rate. Firms will save on compensation costs without having to endure higher turnover. The vagaries of the business cycle would not alter this equilibrium, since the unemployment rate only affects employers' preferred mix of part-time and full-time work by changing the turnover differential, and in this case there is no turnover differential.

A more realistic equilibrium occurs when the added turnover cost of hiring part-timers just cancels out their lower compensation, making the total costs of hiring a part-time or a full-time worker identical. If, based on these equal costs, firms set about to hire more full-time workers, they would find they had unwittingly made part-timers *cheaper*, since creating more full-time jobs leads to fewer dissatisfied part-time workers and thus reduces turnover, and would quickly reverse their actions. If instead firms sought to raise their part-time ratio, they would unwittingly make part-time workers more expensive by boosting the involuntary part-time rate and thus part-time turnover, and again would quickly double back to the equilibrium.

If unemployment rises, part-time turnover decreases since fewer full-time jobs are available, part-time workers become less expensive, and employers will hire a greater proportion of part-timers. Decreasing unemployment has the opposite effect. The unemployment-responsive ups and downs of part-time employment in the model are movements of involuntary part-time employment, matching the movements in the actual retail industry. However, in the simulated world of this model, a *very* large jump in unemployment could potentially induce employers to convert all of their jobs to part-time. As noted, once all firms have shifted to this extreme, even a subsequent drop in unemployment would not induce them to shift back: they would be stuck in an all-part-time equilibrium.

Suppose instead that training costs fall, perhaps due to automation. Then both the training costs associated with turnover and the cost of training two part-timers to fill one full-time slot will drop, once more making part-time workers cheaper. Thus, in this model a drop in training costs leads to heavier use of part-time employment, a connection suggested by Eileen Appelbaum (1987).

Can this model help to explain the rather different pattern of part-time employment in insurance labor markets? Absolutely. If instead of creating more part-time jobs than people want, businesses create too many full-time jobs, the labor market in effect goes "through the looking glass" to a model that is symmetrically opposite to the one just outlined. In this new mirror-image model, there is a shortage of retention part-time jobs, and some people are working full-time involuntarily. Involuntary full-timers have higher turnover based on their probability of finding a part-time job.

A labor market will follow this pattern rather than the other if employing a part-timer is more expensive than employing a full-timer, even when there is no difference in turnover. Recall that while part-timers are cheaper in retail because of reduced compensation, in insurance's salaried labor markets professional-level part-timers can be more expensive due to a substantially complete benefit package being spread over fewer hours and to large training costs (meaning that the costs of training an extra head are prohibitive). It is easy to verify that this mirror-image model acts like an insurance labor market over the business cycle: when unemployment rises, part-time employment falls.

In short, the first version of the model mimics a retail labor market, whereas the mirror-image model mimics an insurance labor market. The two models can coexist in the economy—or even in the same company—as long as the groups of workers involved are noncompeting.

Interestingly, the model replicates two stylized facts discovered by Bednarzik (1975, 1983): changes in involuntary part-time employment lag behind changes in unemployment, and the lag is greater during economic downturns (when unemployment is increasing) than upturns. In the model, the lag occurs as firms convert positions from full-time to part-time and vice versa by attrition, so that any adjustment is paced by turnover. Adjustment is slower when unemployment is rising because firms must wait for the relatively stable full-time employees to turn over before replacing them with part-timers; when unemployment is falling, firms are replacing the rapidly leaving part-timers.[3]

Relaxing Certain Assumptions

Relaxation of certain assumptions changes the look of the model, but it appears that the model can survive at least small changes. For example, suppose that firms can adjust the full-time/part-time compensation differential. A modification within the spirit of the model would be that firms can decrease turnover either by creating more full-time jobs or by raising the pay of part-timers. The question, then, is how firms decide on the proper mix of adjustments to compensation and the rate of full-time employment—price and quantity, if you will—to make. The interviews suggest reasons that compensation adjustments may be costly or difficult. Compensation must be increased for all part-timers, including the fraction (a majority in many firms) that is working part-time voluntarily. If the pay scale is pegged to entry-level part-time wages, then pay increases to part-timers may entail significant ripple effects. Union restrictions may also make it difficult to adjust compensation, although they may also make it hard to adjust the rate of full-time employment. Likewise, incentive considerations may lead to a rigid wage differential. Similar reasons could be posed in reverse for the insurance industry. Thus, even in a model where some wage adjustments are possible, firms are also likely to use the "hidden" wage adjustment of changing the rate of full-time employment.

A second modification is to give workers more choices. In the model, unemployed and involuntary part-time workers search for full-time jobs in every period. A natural modification would be to make the intensity of their search a function of the costs and benefits of searching. The benefits in turn would depend on the rate of unemployment and of full-time employment. The result: when decreasing unemployment increases workers' chances of finding full-time jobs, they will search harder for such jobs. As a consequence, firms have to raise the rate of full-time employment further to reach a new equilibrium. But the basic structure of the model is not affected.

Firm heterogeneity poses bigger problems for the model. In the original model, unless individual employers' cost structures are the same as the labor market average, they will simply sort themselves out into employing either all part-timers or all full-timers. This results from the facts that part-time turnover is determined by a variable external to the firm (the probability of finding a full-time job) and that firms face a knife-edge choice (part-timers either cost less than, more than, or the same as full-timers). Both of these features of the model could be modified. For example, firms could influence part-time turnover by adjusting wages, as suggested above. Part-timers could also be arrayed along a productivity spectrum, with small turnover changes only inducing firms to substitute full-time workers for their lowest-productivity part-time workers (or vice versa)—a truly marginalist model.

Finally, the model could conceivably be enriched by the inclusion of a variety of institutional details, such as the specification of different interests among managers, the role of unions, and so on. But here the usefulness of a formal model breaks down. The model is useful for pointing to a narrowly economic motivation for changing the rate of part-time employment over the business cycle, but the way in which this motivation interacts with other motivations in real actors is something that can be understood better in nonmathematical terms.

Concluding Comments about the Model

The foregoing discussion of the relaxation of assumptions indicates that the formal model is unrealistic in many ways, but that its basic mechanism could well interact with others to determine the overall cyclical pattern of part-time employment. The model provides a way of thinking about some possible reasons for long-term change, such as decreasing training costs. It also raises certain intriguing issues: for example, could temporarily high unemployment cause a labor market to become stuck in an equilibrium with a very high rate of part-time employment?

In any case, beyond the strengths and weaknesses of the model itself, the interview data and aggregate statistics strongly suggest that a hidden wage reduction/increase mechanism is operative in the contracyclical pattern of involuntary part-time employment and that a similar mechanism may drive a contracyclical pattern in involuntary full-time employment.

Breaking the Mold? The Early 1990s Recovery

So far, the rate of involuntary part-time employment during the economic recovery that began in 1991 looks a lot like a roller coaster that does not want to come down. Is this recovery breaking the cyclical pattern we have seen up until now?

As Figure 7.5 shows, the relationship between unemployment and involuntary part-time employment has *not* changed. The involuntary part-

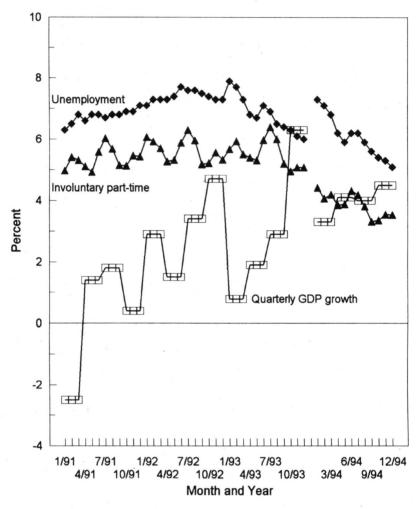

FIGURE 7.5
GDP Growth, Unemployment, and Involuntary Part-Time Employment,
January 1991–December 1994

Note: The U.S. Bureau of Labor Statistics changed the way that unemployment and involuntary part-time employment are measured in January 1994, which explains the jump in those statistics between December 1993 and January 1994. The implications of these changes are discussed at the end of this chapter. GDP is gross domestic product, the total value of goods and services produced.

Source: Growth data from U.S. Bureau of Economic Analysis, *Survey of Current Business,* various months. Unemployment and involuntary part-time employment (not seasonally adjusted) from U.S. Bureau of Labor Statistics, *Employment and Earnings,* various months; supplemented by U.S. Bureau of Labor Statistics, unpublished Current Population Survey data, provided by Thomas Nardone

---

time rate still more or less tracks the unemployment rate. Indeed, regression analysis estimates that between January 1991 and December 1993, on the average, a 1 percentage-point change in the unemployment rate yields a 0.4 point change in involuntary part-time employment, which is well within the range of other estimates over the last 20 years.

What *has* changed is that the link between the economy's output and the labor market has loosened considerably. Although growth went from negative to positive in the second quarter of 1991, signaling the official end of the recession, the rate of unemployment and involuntary part-time work continued to drift upward. Only after a year of growth did these labor market distress signals level off and then start to decline. Other labor market indicators, such as the rate of growth of total employment, behaved similarly. The "jobless recovery" earned its name honestly.

In short, in the early 1990s expansion, output growth has not spelled job growth and labor market tightening to the extent that it has in past recoveries. Some combination of corporate downsizing and caution has led many business to remain "poised for contraction," in Appelbaum's words (1987). The results are ominous in terms of not just the persistence of high involuntary part-time employment but also *all* of the labor market consequences of deficient labor demand.

Back to the Trend

Meanwhile, the rate of part-time employment continues its long-term, gradual rise. Part of this upward trend, as documented in Chapter 2, results from the disproportionate expansion of the industries that rely heavily on secondary part-time workers: retail trade and services. But another part corresponds to increased rates of part-time employment *within* industries. In fact, the part-time proportion has climbed within most major industries in the past 25 years (recall Table 2.5). Employers' demand for part-time labor, not employees' desire for it, has driven this growth.

A number of analysts offer an explanation: structural change within industries has spurred the growth of part-time employment. They point to several kinds of structural change. Some industries have faced heightened competition, which may have led companies to experiment with low-cost contingent work forms (Nine to Five 1986; Bureau of National Affairs 1986). Appelbaum (1987) argued that increased competition combined with rapid automation has forced companies to become "poised for contraction," with a ring of contingent workers including part-timers around the core of full-time permanent workers. Caterpillar Inc.'s chairman, Donald Fites, described the situation bluntly: "The cost structure you put in place in good times is the cost structure you have to live with in hard times" (Rose 1994, B4). And, "what's core today can be considered contingent tomorrow," according to John Thompson, head of Imcor, a firm providing temporary management and professional services (Fierman 1994, 33). Appelbaum also hypothesizes that decreased internal training requirements make part-time employment more feasible and desirable. The decreased training requirements in turn may be due to automation-linked deskilling and/or the growth of higher education (Noyelle 1987a).

These are intriguing hypotheses. So far, those advancing the hypotheses have essentially only noted that the structural changes and the increased utilization of part-time employment are taking place. To establish a causal connection between the two kinds of change requires more careful study of their relationships.

The findings presented in the last several chapters suggest a particular view of part-time growth: if it is largely involuntary part-time employment that is growing, the new jobs must be secondary part-time jobs. Companies can realize economic advantages from secondary part-time employment even when a substantial proportion of the part-time workers are involuntary. And if secondary part-time employment is expanding, this increase must be tied to the spread of secondary labor markets. This appears to hold for the part-time rise linked to trade and service growth, and would be expected to hold as well for the widening part-time employment within industries. Evidence from the retail and insurance interviews supports these views but adds far more detail.

The chapter closes with a glance toward the future, as I offer a forecast of the likely pace of the growth in part-time employment. I also describe how in 1994 the U.S. Bureau of Labor Statistics changed the way it measures part-time employment, making future numbers not entirely comparable with those cited throughout this book.

Structural Change within Industries and the Growth of Part-Time Employment

Once we look within an industry, changes in the rate of part-time employment can again be divided between changing composition and change within subgroups. For example, much of the growth of part-time employment within retail trade has resulted from a compositional change: the disproportionate expansion of eating and drinking places. But what is most interesting is transformations within fairly narrowly defined subindustries. This is where the pressures on employers stand out in sharpest relief, as they choose *not* to act as they always have. Change in employment within these subindustries can occur in one of two ways: either firms adapt or they are supplanted by other firms that do things differently.

The sampled retail and insurance firms offer a microscopic look into the changing utilization of part-time work. The history of such changes in these firms and in the subindustries of which they are part is fraught with industry- and even firm-specific details. Even so, a pattern emerges.

First, the large and long-term changes in the rate of part-time employment consist entirely of increases in the use of secondary part-time employment. The two such changes that are well documented in the interviews are the shifts toward secondary part-time employment in supermarkets and health insurers, respectively.[4] Second, these changes are triggered by changed technology and propelled by price competition. One reason that in these cases the secondary labor markets take the specific form of part-time employment is that scheduling issues accompany the pressures for cost reduction. Third, employers have expanded part-time employment even when it meant hiring more involuntary part-timers. This expansion marks a slow, sometimes decades-long reaction to the initial economic stimuli. Fourth, the gradual nature of the change is explained by a variety of institutional barriers. But, fifth, once a critical mass of employers have expanded secondary part-time employment, the competitive pressures to follow suit are substantial, because such a change can yield cost advantages even when it means a fall in productivity.

In what follows, these five features are examined one by one.

The Expansion of Secondary Part-Time Employment
Among the companies surveyed, supermarket owners and health insurers have both dramatically expanded secondary part-time employment. The rate of part-time employment in supermarkets increased from 35 percent in 1962 to 63 percent in 1992 (*Progressive Grocer* 1993). The grocers created part-time jobs with reduced wages, benefits, and skill levels. According to a Boston union official, the chief motivation for the change was to obtain cheaper labor, and the industry press agrees: "To cut labor costs by switching to lower-paid part-timers with fewer benefits, the industry's percentage of part-timers has continually grown" (Sansolo 1987, 75).

Health insurers started increasing part-time employment much more recently, beginning in the late 1970s. The rate of part-time employment soared from less than 7 percent to over 24 percent at Healthco between 1983 and 1987, and from less than 1 percent to 16 percent at Wellcorp during 1982–87; the third health insurer surveyed had just initiated a part-time job creation program months before the interview took place. The part-time jobs reduced skill levels and fringe benefits. At Healthco, for example, "The benefits package at [the suburban facility] ran at about 25 percent of salaries, while the corresponding figure in Boston was approximately 40 percent," according to a case study of the company.

What Drove the Changes

In both grocery stores and health insurance companies, technological changes led to the initial use of part-timers. These changes—lengthened store hours and the computerization of claims processing, respectively—raised scheduling difficulties that specifically favored part-time employment. Once part-time jobs were introduced, the prospect of reducing labor costs hastened their spread.

The extension of supermarket hours—a change in product technology—initially sparked the growth of part-time jobs in retail food. Said a supermarket chain's personnel director, "The thing that forced the part-time issue was hours." He amplified:

> At that time [the 1950s–60s], we and other stores were basically full-time. Those hours modules could be worked by full-timers. . . . With the flight to the suburbs, and women in the workforce, convenience led to longer hours. . . . As hours started expanding . . . you couldn't efficiently staff without part-timers, unless you wanted to have overlapping schedules and redundancies. . . . [Our company] had to meet the competition. Nonunion companies always had the flexibility to use as many part-timers as they wanted. We were forced to go along for competitive reasons.

Once the issue was forced, other advantages of part-time jobs became apparent to retailers. A retail union official recalled:

> The retail industry woke up one day. The light bulb went on. They got the profit and loss picture, and started to create more part-time for that reason. This started in early to mid's. Since then, it has grown and grown. In the late '40s, early '50s, the key was flexibility. Since then, the key is cost.

Subsequent technological changes have permitted greater boosts in part-time employment. Supermarket operators have moved toward stores that are larger both in floor size and sales volume (Cornell University, *Operating Results of Food Chains*, various years). Since the core of full-time department managers and one or two full-timers per department does not grow proportionally with store employment, larger stores have higher rates of part-time employment (*Progressive Grocer* 1988). Innovation in food processing—such as the introduction of boxed beef—has further shrunk the full-time skilled labor force in supermarkets. A supermarket manager commented:

> The meat cutters in the supermarkets nowadays don't do what they used to . . . because you took out a few steps of processing the cattle. We have automatic wrapping machines. . . . The clerk, the wrapper, only needs to program in pricing to it and make sure all the proper stickers are on it and then stock it in the case.

Given this automation, now stocking the meat case, according to retail analyst William Burns (1982), "is no different from stocking cans in the grocery section of the store" (p. 41).

In health insurance, the key technological change was the development of comprehensive software packages for claims processing. This innovation came in the midst of strong pressures for cost reduction in the health insurance field (Richman 1986). The health insurance case thus supports Appelbaum's (1987) hypothesis that automation and heightened competition lead to the increased use of part-time and other contingent work forms.

For example, Wellcorp used a new, on-line claims system to deskill the benefits approver job and staff many of the functions with part-timers. Because of the routinized nature of the work, a Wellcorp informant reported,

> We get our best production in data entry for four to five hours a day.

The Healthco story is complicated by the addition of suburbanization. At Healthco, the adoption of the computerized claims system led to a tremendous turnover and a search for a new kind of workforce. The executive who initiated the search noted:

> We also wondered whether one of our problems was the eight-hour day. When a keyer sits at a CRT [cathode ray terminal, also called a VDT] all day, you get maybe six hours' worth of productivity before debilitating fatigue sets in. We thought a flexible workday might accommodate our new processing system, but the home office wasn't the right environment for making such a change.

A Healthco task force then selected a suburban location where people needed jobs, and tested the waters by running an advertisement for both full-time and part-time positions. When applicants showed up:

> We had them fill out a survey. So we left it up to the people. We said, "Tell us what hours you want." And they chose six-hour shifts, with one break. And that's how we ended up with what we have in [the suburban facilities].

The manager who headed the task force noted that the applicants' choice of part-time hours had been foreseen:

> INTERVIEWER: Given the VDT productivity issue, if people had expressed a preference for an eight-hour shift, would you have created eight hours?
> MANAGER: It didn't happen that way. The way the questionnaire was designed, they could have answered it that way. It asked when they would like to begin and end work, in half-hour increments from seven in the morning till nine at night. So they could have picked nine to five.

Even though we had a bias for part-time because of the fatigue factor
on the VDTs, it could have come out differently.
INTERVIEWER: So it was fortuitous that it came out the way it did?
MANAGER: I don't know if I'd call it fortuitous. I'd call it: we guessed
right. We were creating jobs close to people's homes, they had other
obligations and life styles.

Once the part-time experiments at Wellcorp and Healthco proved
successful at reducing labor costs, both companies moved to convert
more areas to part-time. At Wellcorp, for example: "Our whole drive is
to go toward more part-time jobs. It's very cost effective."

Why Employers Have Disregarded
Workers' Preferences
Why have employers continued to increase part-time jobs if, at the margin, such increases are involuntary? After all, involuntary part-time employment may come as an acceptable adjunct to secondary part-time jobs
and to rigid compensation differentials, but it surely has costs to employers that rise as the percentage of involuntary jobs rises. The behavior of employers is particularly perplexing if, as postulated in the model
developed earlier in this chapter, they keep a close watch on turnover-re-
lated costs and adjust their use of part-time employment accordingly.

A closer look at what grocers have done offers a solution to this paradox. Although some companies have adjusted the rate of part-time employment up and down as unemployment fluctuated, many other retailers simply set their sights on expanding part-time employment as long as
30 years ago and have only backed off from this goal over the last couple of years, as the labor market became extremely tight. In other words,
it took employers decades to reach an equilibrium.

The testimony of the personnel director at the SuperValu grocery
chain paints precisely this picture:

> Ideally, we would have wanted [the rate of part-time employment in the
> stores] to go up, and it did for a long time. The only reason it stopped
> was because of the labor market. It started going down about one and
> a half years ago. We were as high as 80 percent [part-time] and even
> higher in some stores. . . . I started [working here] 11 years ago. At that
> time, the ratio was about 70:30.

During the 1950s and 1960s, employer expansion of part-time jobs
was ratified by the labor market entry of housewives and youths who
wanted part-time work. But between 1979 and 1987, the rate of voluntary part-time employment *fell* from 24.6 percent to 22.9 percent in retail, even as retail's total rate of part-time work climbed slightly. Retailers were replacing voluntary part-timers with involuntary ones.

By the time food retailers began to reduce part-time employment in the mid-1980s, there was some evidence that the supermarket operators had not been optimizing but overshooting. Recall the SuperValu store manager, quoted at length in Chapter 5, who commented that, "In my produce department, one good full-timer can do as much work [per hour] as any three part-timers." But at the time, SuperValu was paying its full-time employees only twice as much per hour as part-timers. In other words, work performed by a full-timer cost two-thirds as much per unit as that performed by a part-time worker. SuperValu's policy of converting as many jobs as possible to part-time was clearly wrong. Indeed, around this time the trade journal *Progressive Grocer* (1986) was reporting:

> Some retailers are rethinking the pros and cons of part-timers versus full-timers. The high turnover rate and costs of training replacement employees may outweigh the advantages of part-timers. These operators point out that full-timers tend to be more loyal and add stability to a store's staff. Another problem today is the difficulty some retailers experience in locating enough part-timers. (p. 62)

None of the retailers interviewed measure productivity or absenteeism separately for part-timers and full-timers, and some do not even keep separate turnover records. Thus it is quite possible that in their enthusiasm for reducing average wage and benefit costs and matching staffing to demand patterns, quite a few retailers—like SuperValu—overlooked the added costs of part-time employment.

If in the aggregate many retailers found the upper limit of part-time employment during the economic upturn of the late 1980s, in the future more of them would be expected to follow the cyclical pattern outlined in the previous chapter. Cyclical fluctuations would then grow at the expense of the trend.

Like the retail food companies, the health insurers in the sample have been gradually increasing part-time employment after an initial stimulus. Unlike the retailers, however, they have not yet reached a point where they are doubling back or even leveling off toward the use of more full-time employment.

Friction in the System

If the long-term growth of part-time employment in the companies in question is largely a gradual reaction to changes that took place up to 30 years ago, the obvious question is why it took them so long to change. One source of the friction that slowed the change is that both grocers and insurers converted full-time jobs to part-time strictly by attrition. After all, as one Healthco manager said, "It would be punishment to revert [full-timers] to part-time, unless it was their choice, of course." But a variety of other institutional barriers to change have further slowed the spread of secondary part-time jobs.

In the supermarket business, the "light bulb" did not actually just "go on" at a particular point. Instead there has been a learning curve, as over time grocers have become more acutely aware of possible cost savings from the use of part-timers and have implemented management mechanisms to foster this change.

At SuperValu, the personnel director pointed to the impact of "increased knowledge, increased reporting of what full-time pay is actually costing us." A SuperValu store manager offered a more detailed description of the change:

> MANAGER: Before, [the staffing process] was catch-as-catch-can. The manager basically decided. Then there was the development of a specific department [the Targeting Department in Management Information Systems] to give you information. It's a tool. Sometimes you use it, sometimes you don't. . . .
> INTERVIEWER: So that department didn't exist before?
> MANAGER: No, it existed before, but it was pretty loose. It didn't give very precise information.
> INTERVIEWER: Is the improvement because of computers?
> MANAGER: It's partly because of computers.

And a union official added: "At first, store managers were told, 'You have so many man-hours to handle the volume.' But then, it became dollar-man-hours."

Even to the extent that supermarket operators had a clear goal of expanding part-time jobs, a number of other sources of friction slowed them down. The retail unions opposed—and continue to oppose—the growth of part-time employment. This resistance slowed but did not reverse the expansion of the part-time ranks among clerks and cashiers. Retailers are still working to overcome union resistance to part-time jobs among meat cutters, warehouse workers, and truck drivers. At one supermarket chain, the personnel director declared:

> We have problems contractually with working [people] part-time in the warehouses. That's going to have to break down. Next month, the contract with our major warehouse comes up. We can't have stores that never close, and warehouses that run from nine to five. It broke down in the stores, and it must break down in distribution.

The decreasing rate of unionization in supermarkets (from 56 percent of clerks unionized in 1976 to 44 percent in 1992 among chains, and from 25 percent to 12 percent among independents) means that fewer and fewer retailers face this particular barrier to the creation of part-time jobs

(*Progressive Grocer* 1977; 1993). Store managers themselves also sometimes resist the expansion of part-time employment, as described in Chapter 6.

Pittsburgh represents an interesting special case in the evolution of supermarkets toward an overwhelmingly part-time workforce. The retail food industry in Pittsburgh lagged far behind Boston in the rate of part-time employment up to the mid-1970s, but then rapidly overtook Boston in the last 10 to 15 years. In effect, Pittsburgh went through a compressed version of national trends. Whereas in Boston the shift to a low-wage, part-time labor strategy took place somewhat gradually via adaptation by the large chains, in Pittsburgh the shift took place suddenly via the replacement of the large chains by independents. Six food chains left Pittsburgh during the 1970s.

Three factors caused and shaped this speedy transformation of Pittsburgh's retail food sector. First, the rapid decline of heavy manufacturing (particularly steel) in Pittsburgh drove up worker displacement and the unemployment rate, thus weakening labor's bargaining power. Second, the independent supermarkets adopted an aggressive competitive strategy of low wages, high part-time employment, and low prices. Third, union strength in the chains, which accounted for the low rate of part-time employment to begin with, prevented the chains from matching the independents' strategy. The result was that the rate of part-time employment among nonmanagement employees in Pittsburgh stores shot up from a fifty-fifty ratio or less in the early 1970s to 85 or 90 percent in 1987. An independent store manager summarized the change:

> Ten years ago our [Pittsburgh supermarkets'] prices were very high, and our rates of pay were very high. Now, our prices . . . are very low, and our rates of pay are very low, and we're dealing with basically the part-time people.

In the health insurance business, it is not union resistance but management reluctance that explains the uneven spread of secondary part-time employment. For example, Eternal Life, although predominantly a life insurance company, has a group health line as well. The claims processing technology used by Eternal Life appears to be similar to that used by Healthco and Wellcorp: "It's all computerized, and has been for a long time," a manager affirmed. But Eternal Life's culture precludes the secondary part-time option, as the company's personnel director pointed out in an assessment of third-party administrators (TPAs), a term for companies like Healthco:

> They [the TPAs] are paying their workers sweatshop wages and offering them no benefits at all. . . . They also take advantage of workers, particularly of women, because they play into the interests of women to

work on a part-time basis and they have night hours, they pay their claims at night and they get the housewives who can go to work when the husbands come home and that sort of thing. It's a different philosophy of how you treat employees and it's driven by economic realities, and I suppose if things got tough enough it could come to [our company using those methods], but I don't think it will. . . . There are lots of ways to skimp, and those ways [are] inconsistent with our philosophy and culture and approach.

Competition is a harsh judge of corporate strategy. In the Pittsburgh grocery industry, price competition from the independents eventually drove the chains out of the city. In the case of Eternal Life, the company's personnel director admitted:

> One of the difficulties is that we are competing with TPAs . . . and we're offering good benefits, and it can hurt us in terms of a competitive position. . . . It costs us a lot more to process claims than it does the TPAs, and it is a big, big problem. . . . I suppose at some point, if we decided to get out of that line of business and somebody did a post-mortem on what happened and why, . . . one of the answers is expenses overall . . . and that one of the expenses was personnel and benefits expenses.

Just months after this interview, Eternal Life announced plans to get out of the health insurance business "to refocus the company toward its mainline product: life insurance for the upscale market."

The Competitive Context

In both retail and insurance, competition to keep compensation as low as possible is a recipe for at best slow productivity growth. By expanding the secondary labor market, employers accepted low productivity to obtain even lower costs. The spread of part-time work surely contributed to the large fall in productivity in retail over the 1970s and 1980s. But as part of a competitive strategy, the expansion of the secondary labor market worked—at least in the short run. Many of the companies that had tried to steer clear of this strategy, such as the Pittsburgh supermarket chains and Eternal Life, were swept out of the way.

This disjunction between productivity growth and competitive success suggests two things. First, short-term competition may be providing the wrong incentives and thus leading to the sacrifice of the long-term, dynamic advantages of productivity growth for the sake of short-term gains. But second, the companies that fell by the wayside did not succeed in making the opposite trade-off. Instead of pursuing innovations that would make the most of a relatively skilled, committed workforce, they simply persisted in doing things the way they had always been done in a sheltered market. Eternal Life's sense of tradition and propriety was no match for Healthco's benefit-slashing switch to part-time jobs, but the development of specialized health insurance products might have been.

From Case Studies to Industries

To what extent are the supermarket and health insurance cases typical of changes in the retail and insurance industries in general? In retail, the expansion of part-time work in supermarkets appears to be typical of shifts throughout the industry. The rate of part-time employment climbed in every single retail subindustry between 1960 and 1980 (U.S. Census Bureau 1960, 1980). The interviews also documented changes in retail sectors other than food. For example, a union representative for department store workers argued that their stores, too, had increased part-time employment to save on benefit costs. She estimated that, "Since 15 years ago, the stores have probably flip-flopped in terms of ratios [of part-time to full-time]." Two convenience store respondents reported long-term increases in the use of part-time employment that had come to an end in the last several years:

> When I started, and this goes back to '74, they automatically hired full-time. Now, toward the mid to late '70s they changed that and went to hiring part-time only. [This policy was relaxed about a year and a half ago.] [personnel director I]

> The proportion of part-time changed two times in 15 years, since the early 1970s. First, we consciously made a shift from full-time to part-time when I first came in 15 years ago. . . . We probably went to excessive part-time—almost completely part-time. . . . So we made a slight adjustment back about 4 years ago. [personnel director II]

The experience of the health insurers was also not unique. An informant from a life insurance company commented that the firm had been hiring a lot of part-time workers in claims processing, much like the health insurers. But in the insurance industry as a whole, the rate of part-time employment has been on the decline since the early 1970s (see Figures 2.4, 7.4). A likely reason for the decline is that the low-level jobs that can easily be staffed by part-timers are also rapidly being thinned out by automation and consolidation. One Healthco manager said he was replacing full-time data entry clerks with part-timers, but went on to say that overall the fraction of part-timers in his department has declined over time as he has "put in 10 or 12 system enhancements." This decreased employment by almost 40 percent, a cut that disproportionately removed junior and less skilled workers.

An End to the Growth of Part-Time Employment?

Many of the grocers in the research sample seemed to have peaked in their use of part-time jobs and appeared likely to increase part-time employment further only to the extent that the labor market slackens. Is this a sign that the long-term growth of part-time employment is ending?

The answer is that it certainly signals a slowing of the growth of part-time jobs. But an end to the increase is much less certain. For one thing, there may be many more potential "Pittsburghs" out there: geographic areas where the expansion of part-time jobs has been delayed but where competitive pressures will eventually restart that expansion. In addition, the example of Healthco and the other health insurers suggests that there are many industries besides the traditional part-time users that could suddenly discover the benefits of secondary part-time employment, especially given technological changes such as the spread of VDT use.

On the other hand, the health insurance example also raises the prospect of labor-saving automation that will replace the part-timers altogether. For example, scanning technology has made the file clerk (a job typically staffed by part-timers) all but obsolete. Such automation may lie in the future of supermarkets as well:

> Kroger's testing the cash register in Atlanta, Georgia, that basically doesn't need a cashier. And you know, that's almost 40 percent of our workforce, on the front end there. . . . It takes one person to run three [registers], so we can reduce it by one-third. . . . You actually pick up your own merchandise and put it on a belt, and it's electronically, it takes it down a belt, and scans it, and then one cashier will take your money for three different [registers]. [supermarket manager]

Another force offsetting part-time growth is the retail work transfer analyzed by Nona Glazer (1993). As Glazer points out, decades ago the retail industry—in both food and clothing—provided a much higher level of service to customers. Store staffs offered more advice and assistance, even extending to picking out and delivering a week's groceries from a list. But over the years, retailers shifted these tasks to shoppers. They cut costs, but only by transferring work to households. This work transfer has continued in recent years with the growth of warehouse stores offering very low prices, limited selection, and a bare minimum of staffing and service. While the work transfer surely eliminates both part-time and full-time jobs, arguably the largest cuts have fallen on low-skill, customer-oriented jobs, which have been predominantly staffed by part-timers.

Thus, the future of part-time employment takes on the quality of a tug of war between two forces. One force is the spread of secondary part-time jobs, sparked by technological changes, fueled by the prospect of cost cutting, and speeded or slowed by the institutional environment. The other force is the elimination of low-skill jobs by automation and the work transfer.

Even if part-time employment growth slows, other forms of non-standard employment will continue to burgeon. Temporary service employment soared fifteen-fold between 1968 and 1992, exploding from 100,000 to 1.5 million employees. Just between 1982 and 1992, the temporary ranks ballooned 250 percent (Castro 1993). While firms have traditionally taken on temps early in an economic expansion but replaced them with permanent employees as economic growth takes off, during the most recent recovery businesses bucked tradition by continuing to add temporary employees. "More companies are turning to flexible staffing to maneuver through the ups and downs of the business cycle, avoid layoffs, and transform fixed costs into variable costs," explained Stuart Olsten, president of the Olsten Corporation, along with Manpower Inc. and Kelly Services one of the "big three" temporary help services (quoted in Schellhardt 1992, B4).

U.S. government statistics do not regularly count other types of short-term employment in addition to temporary agency employment, but one-time surveys show growth across the board. Economist Katharine Abraham (1990), now the U.S. Commissioner of Labor Statistics, found expansion in companies' use of in-house short-term hires and on-call workers from 1980 to 1985. A 1986 U.S. Bureau of Labor Statistics special survey of four manufacturing industries found that employers in all four sectors reported higher rates of contracting-out compared to 1980. For example, in the textile industry the proportion of employers using contracting grew by 7 percentage points for accounting services, and 3 points for building and grounds maintenance. Contracting in other industries and of other services (engineering and design, computer, production equipment maintenance, and protective services) typically showed modest rises of 1 to 6 points (Murphey 1989). Financially strapped state and local governments have also expanded their subcontracting of social services and public works in an effort to cut costs (duRivage 1992). Finally, private firms have hired increasing numbers of workers as independent contractors. The U.S. General Accounting Office (1991) estimated that the number of workers reporting only nonemployee compensation on tax returns grew by over 50 percent from 1985 to 1988, reaching 9.5 million persons.

In short, if part-time employment's future growth prospects mimic a tug of war, other forms of contingent work are surging forward like a game of crack-the-whip, with the very real possibility of workers being flung off the end. But rather than simply sitting back and watching these games progress, we as a society can bring another force to bear: public policy. Such policy could be used not only to reduce the spread of secondary part-time jobs but also to create more retention part-time jobs. The concluding chapter addresses a policy agenda for part-time work.

Statistics on Part-Time Work: A Moving Target

An abrupt change in U.S. government statistics beginning in 1994 muddies the picture of part-time employment growth. If one just looked at the official numbers, one would conclude that a dramatic shift in part-time employment took place in January 1994. Official statistics showed a sharp drop in involuntary part-time employment, and a large bounce in voluntary part-time employment between December and January. However, this seesaw did not reflect a change in the labor market but rather in how data are collected. Beginning in January 1994, the U.S. Bureau of Labor Statistics implemented major changes in the Current Population Survey, the key source for information on part-time employment. Not surprisingly, the changes—which include computerizing the survey's execution, modifying and adding questions, and altering some definitions—greatly affect measurements of part-time work.

The Bureau conducted two parallel surveys during 1993, one using the old method and the other using the new one, allowing comparison of the two (Table 7.1). The reasons for the differences are straightforward. The new survey classifies more people—particularly women—as "at

TABLE 7.1
Old Versus New Measurements of Part-Time Employment, 1993 (in Thousands) *

	Old Survey		New Survey		Difference	
	Number	Percent of Total	Number	Percent of Total	Number	Percent of Total
Total at work	113,438	100.0	114,201	100.0	763	—
Total part-time	21,496	18.9	21,917	19.3	421	0.4
Involuntary part-time	6,325	5.6	5,028	4.4	−1,297	−1.2
Voluntary part-time	15,171	13.4	16,889	14.8	1,718	1.4

*This table compares part-time employment in 1993 as measured by the old Current Population Survey and the new Survey that went into effect in January 1994. Consistent with the treatment of part-time numbers elsewhere in the book, the figures exclude people who usually work full-time but who worked part-time during the survey week for noneconomic reasons such as illness or vacation.
Source: Data from Cohany, Polivka, and Rothgeb (1994), Table 4.

work" because it employs a more expansive definition of work, including forms of self-employment and sporadic employment that were previously overlooked or excluded. Fewer people also show up as involuntary part-time workers, because two new questions inquire directly whether a part-time worker *wants* and *is available for* full-time work, whereas the previous questionnaire simply asked why the person was working part-time. The two new questions—particularly the former—screen out people who otherwise would have been enumerated as involuntary part-time workers. Finally, the voluntary part-time tally rises because of the other two changes: people who would have been classified as nonworkers or as involuntary part-timers now show up as voluntary part-time workers.

One drawback of these changes is that if involuntary part-time workers show any tendency to convince themselves that they actually prefer part-time employment (see Chapter 1), the new instrument will increase the underreporting of involuntary part-time work. Even so, on the whole, the new survey marks an improvement over the old. Unfortunately, it also represents a discontinuity in the data over time. Suddenly, there are 1 million fewer involuntary part-time workers! Nonetheless, it is probably safe to say that the 20-year growth trend in involuntary part-time employment is a durable fact, one that would have shown up on the new survey as well.

The Case for New Policies

8

■ IN APRIL 1994, SEVENTY THOUSAND TEAMSTERS WENT ON strike against Trucking Management, Inc. The key issue—part-time work. "They want to shift to part-time workers with low wages and little or no benefits," declared Teamster President Ron Carey, who had led reformers to win the union's top leadership posts three years earlier. "This is wrong for workers and their families, and it is wrong for America." But Arthur H. Bunte, Trucking Management's president, fired back, "They would rather risk the livelihood of their members than negotiate a settlement that would have provided increased wages . . . and the job security that can only come from working for competitive companies." Management needed the added flexibility to survive "in a highly competitive market," Bunte insisted (quoted in Vaillancourt 1994). I visited a number of Teamster picket lines that April, and defiant Teamsters told me, "We're doing this for the next generation."

After several tense weeks during which almost all of their trucks remained idle, Trucking Management relented. They agreed to a new contract without the part-time work provision. The Teamsters compromised on other issues, but declared victory because they had held the line on part-time employment.

Part-time employment has become a flash point for class struggle in the United States. However, most public policy remains curiously indifferent to the issue, either ignoring it outright, or addressing it only incidentally and in many cases accidentally. As Labor Secretary Robert Reich put it, "The contingent workforce is outside the system of worker-management relationships and expectations we've created over the years" (quoted in Castro 1993). Current policies are still built around that old system. Most laws regulating working conditions, wages, hours,

158

benefits, and labor representation implicitly reflect an increasingly outdated model of employment: full-time, long-term—even lifetime—employment with a single employer. Social welfare policy also remains largely predicated on this model. Such policy has taken for granted that the "normal" family configuration features a husband holding a long-term job that pays a "family wage"; the safety net serves to sustain those unfortunate few who deviate from this configuration.

Of course, not all jobs and not all families *ever* matched these idealized images. But undeniably, the last 30 years have seen a fundamental transformation in the relationships between work and family, and between worker and employer. On the one side, women's labor force participation has climbed steadily, while men's has declined slightly. In 1947, a woman was only 38 percent as likely to be working or looking for work as a man. By 1993, that percentage had more than doubled to 77 percent (U.S. Council of Economic Advisors 1994). And on the other side, the flexibility and volatility of job attachment have grown decade by decade, with part-time and contingent work posting one major indicator of the change. "We're really breaking those assumptions about the relationship between the worker and the enterprise," commented Karen Nussbaum, director of the U.S. Labor Department's Women's Bureau. "It puts an incredible strain on working people" (quoted in Shao 1994, 18).

What could be done to ease this strain? This chapter proposes a policy agenda on part-time work. To start, I try to identify as clearly as possible the problems with part-time work, thus closing the circle begun in the first chapter, in which I first argued that we need to worry about part-time employment's growth. Next, I review the patchwork of existing policies, including union bargaining approaches, which have in general been more proactive than government initiatives on this issue, although unions' shrinking base sharply limits the reach of these strategies. Where relevant, I contrast U.S. policies with those in other countries, highlighting alternatives from which we can learn. I close by posing a policy strategy for reducing the economic pain associated with part-time employment, while preserving the flexibility and opportunity that it brings.

The Case for Policy Changes
Four interlocking issues make out the case for new policies toward part-time employment: (1) the low wages and benefits paid to part-timers contribute to polarization in the distribution of earnings and income; (2) skimping on part-timers' compensation also contributes, less directly, to slow productivity growth; (3) the large number of people who work part-time or full-time involuntarily raises equity and efficiency problems; and

(4) part-time employment creates obstacles to worker voice and representation through unions.

Low Wages and Benefits
The most clear and urgent policy concerns involving part-time employment are distributional. For too many workers in the United States, schedule flexibility breeds social and economic insecurity. Many part-time jobs fail to provide employment security, fringe benefits, or a living wage. Indeed, the expansion of part-time employment—as well as contingent forms of work such as temporary employment—heralds the renewed growth of a secondary labor market. Employers have shifted more responsibility for health-care insurance and adequate wages onto workers themselves. It is this unilateral employer abdication of responsibility that has turned flexibility from a positive into a negative in many cases.

The growth of low-compensation part-time jobs has definitely contributed to disequalization in the distribution of individual earnings. This polarizing effect is straightforwardly documented by the finding of Chris Tilly, Barry Bluestone, and Bennett Harrison (1986) that the growth of part-time employment and the widening difference between part-time and full-time earnings accounts for 42 percent of the increase in inequality in annual wages and salaries between 1978 and 1984.

But what about the effects on the distribution of family income? The seriousness of the problems posed by the growth of low-compensation jobs depends on the nature and family context of the changes involved. Certainly few would object to teen-agers baby-sitting or shoveling snow for low wages and no benefits in order to accumulate spending money for discretionary purchases. Nor would many object if a stiffening of the work ethic led more teen-agers to take such jobs. Low-wage job growth thus could, in theory, result from just this sort of change in work ethic.

Low-compensation jobs do, on the other hand, pose a problem when the opportunity to work more productive, better compensated jobs is lacking for those who are willing and able to hold such jobs, and when the growth of low-compensation jobs leads to the stagnation and fall of the standard of living of a significant fraction of the population, either in absolute or relative terms. In other words, the growth of low-compensation jobs such as secondary part-time jobs is a problem when in some sense they replace high-compensation jobs. In this case the growth of low-wage jobs leads to regressive redistribution. Families who end up with low-compensation jobs—and thus with lower family income or higher levels of effort expended—lose. Families who hold onto high-compensation jobs or enjoy property income (from profits, rent, or interest) gain—at least in the short run from the lower prices for the goods and services produced by low-compensation workers.[1]

There is evidence that the growth of secondary part-time employment does pose these problems. Low-compensation secondary part-time
jobs are in fact replacing full-time jobs in two ways: the industries with
high rates of secondary part-time employment are growing, and individual industries are converting full-time, primary labor market jobs to part-
time, secondary labor market jobs. A gross indication of this trend is that
between 1969 and 1993, part-timers in service and trade surged from
11.1 percent to 14.7 percent of all nonagricultural wage and salary workers; part-timers in clerical, sales, and service occupations climbed from
9.5 percent to 11.7 percent of all nonfarm workers.

Furthermore, only one-sixth of this replacement trend can be accounted for by the growth of workforce groups with high rates of part-
time employment. Roughly five-sixths of the growth in the rate of part-
time employment is due to the spread of involuntary part-time work. This
replacement does indeed represent a decline in the opportunity to work
in more productive, more highly compensated jobs—because the desire
and capacity to work those jobs remain.

The compensation penalty endured by part-timers goes beyond what
can be measured in dollars and cents. The combination of private and
public benefits for workers constitutes a system—and that system does
not work well for part-time employees. A large proportion of part-timers
lack health insurance from any source, a larger proportion do not par-
ticipate in a pension plan, and many lack job security. Ironically, publicly
provided benefits, instead of filling the gap, in some instances widen it.
Programs such as unemployment insurance and social security pay back
less to those who have earned less.

Furthermore, while low wages and minimal benefits clearly pose a
problem for part-time workers and their families, they also impose costs
on others. Taxpayers pay part of the price: in 1985, persons experiencing involuntary part-time employment were almost twice as likely to receive public assistance as the average person in the labor force (U.S. Bureau of Labor Statistics 1987). And to the extent that those without
health insurance provided by an employer or family member still received
health care, the costs were shifted onto taxpayers (through Medicaid) or
those who do carry health insurance (through increased premiums). Full-
time workers lose out as well. According to research by Massachusetts
Institute of Technology economist James Rebitzer (1987; see also Rebitzer and Taylor 1991), the greater the number of part-time workers in a
given industry, the lower the wages of full-timers, and the less likely full-
time workers are to receive health insurance or pension benefits. For example, full-time workers employed in a sector where one-third of the
workforce is part-time earn $1.21 less an hour, on average, than identi-
cal full-timers in an industry with no part-timers.

Two final notes of caution are needed. The existence of retention part-time jobs indicates that it is not part-time employment in general but low-compensation secondary part-time employment in particular that has negative distributional consequences. And the fact that the growth of secondary part-time employment appears to have hurt earnings opportunity and living standards on the margin does not imply that all or even most secondary part-time employment has negative effects. Much secondary part-time employment is surely benign in the same sense that baby-sitting and snow-shoveling jobs are.

Lagging Productivity
The proliferation of low-compensation part-time jobs also raises the specter of slower productivity growth and dynamic inefficiency—the failure of businesses to adapt and innovate. It is abundantly clear that secondary part-time jobs have low productivity, as evidenced both by the consensus of interviewed managers and by the low compensation attached to such jobs.

Although in conventional economic theory low productivity leads to low compensation, the causality can also run in the opposite direction for a couple of reasons. First, as Harvard Business School professors Leonard Schlesinger and James Heskett (1991) have explained, paying employees poorly can trigger and perpetuate a vicious circle for businesses in service industries. Minimal pay and limited training bring low-skill, low-commitment employees and drive up turnover. All of this erodes the level of service, reducing the business's attractiveness to customers. As a result, the business must cut prices or suffer low volumes, both of which push the employer to keep compensation low.

Second, simply having access to labor at low compensation makes productivity increases unnecessary for employers. Because many service employers have used secondary part-time employment to go the route of low compensation and low productivity, they may have failed to search for or utilize possibilities to increase productivity that would involve full-time work and higher compensation. In short, rather than leading to greater efficiency, as some business spokespeople have claimed, the growth of part-time employment may have led to decreased efficiency.

The retail industry, and particularly retail food, is a case in point. Retail productivity plummeted by about 1 percentage point per year over the last 20 years, and grocery store output per person-hour fell even faster. The main reaction of grocers to falling productivity was to slash compensation further (primarily that of part-timers) via two-tier compensation schemes and other cutbacks, rather than to increase skills or adopt new technology (although there have been some attempts to innovate, such as the—slow—adoption and utilization of bar code scanners and the multi-customer cash register described in Chapter 7).

The particular form of productivity differences will, of course, vary by industry. In retail, a part-time produce clerk may stock vegetables slowly or sloppily. In higher education, political scientist Lawrence Flood (1987) points out that a second-class status for part-time faculty can lead to poor education and the corrosion of academic freedom.

Arguably a high-wage/high-productivity strategy can be a viable competitive strategy for many—perhaps all—industries, at least when coupled with an appropriate product market strategy. But to explore higher productivity options requires more than a marginal adjustment. The qualitative changes necessary for this exploration exceed the range of vision of retailers, and the strategy built around secondary part-time employment becomes self-reinforcing in this and related industries. This set of choices drags against any substantial improvement in service sector productivity, which advocates as diverse as liberal economist Lester Thurow and management guru Peter Drucker have identified as a key economic objective.

Of course, some of the sluggish productivity performance of the service industries simply reflects consumer preferences for low price and convenience over higher quality. Again, retail food illustrates the point. For example, a major contributor to falling grocery store productivity is the extension of store hours, which undoes economies of scale (and not incidentally involves the hiring of many more part-timers). But retailers see 24-hour operations as a necessary competitive device. Even in the acute labor shortage in the Boston area in the late 1980s, SuperValu's personnel director declared that "nobody wants to be the first one to cut back store hours." She added, "No chain wants to be first to raise the prices to compensate for labor costs." As *Progressive Grocer* commented in their "Annual Report of the Grocery Industry" (1988), "Consumers want services, but they don't want to pay the cost of providing them" (p. 5).

To the extent that retailers and other service employers have accurately determined the lowest-cost way of satisfying consumer preferences, charges of economic inefficiency—in the narrow sense—can be deflected. But at the risk of violating the precept of *de gustibus non est disputandum,* (there is no disputing taste), a case can still be made for overriding consumer preferences to achieve distributional goals. After all, we don't leave issues such as child labor or occupational safety and health to consumer choice. Rather than expecting consumers to take a company's child labor practices or injury rates into account when buying goods and services, we have adopted laws to enforce basic protections for workers. Part-time employment also calls out for protection.

Involuntary Part-Time and Full-Time Work
Only a minority of part-time workers (about one-third in 1993) would prefer a full-time job; only a minority of full-time workers (about one-tenth in 1985) would prefer a part-time job. But the discontented minority represents quite a large group: 6 million involuntary part-time workers and another 6 million involuntary full-time workers.[2] And the rate of involuntary part-time employment is growing over the long run–by about 0.12 percentage points per year between 1969 and 1993, of which 0.11 percent is due to the growing number of involuntary part-timers who report that they usually work part-time. Furthermore, workers are constrained not only by the job market but also by the child-care market: one-third of women working part-time would work more hours if they could get good child care (Presser and Baldwin 1980).

Most fundamentally, involuntary part-time and full-time jobs raise the issue of choice. Involuntary part-time and full-time workers clearly possess the requisite skills and talents for a job; why shouldn't they have access to their preferred work schedule? These two forms of involuntary hours also raise issues of both equity and efficiency.

Involuntary part-time employment most clearly raises equity concerns. The loss of potential income by involuntary part-timers is disequalizing: the median family income of involuntary part-timers in 1991 was only 56 percent of that of full-time workers. Involuntary full-time work, while it does not imply heightened income inequality, does involve inequality of opportunity. Women with young children, people near retirement age, and others for whom working full-time entails personal sacrifice are forced either to make that sacrifice or to leave their jobs.

Involuntary part-time and full-time jobs also hamper macroeconomic and microeconomic efficiency. At a macroeconomic level, the forgone output represented by 6 million people who are underemployed and working part-time against their wishes is comparable to losses from unemployment. At a microeconomic level, both involuntary part-time and full-time employment represent—at least in theory—opportunities for trade-offs that could help everybody. For example, if full-time/part-time wage differentials are based on incentive considerations, then government funding to help create more of the "overcompensated" jobs (full-time jobs in the secondary context, part-time jobs in the salaried context) could actually lead to an improvement in standard of living and well-being worth more than the dollar amount of the subsidy, as Jeremy Bulow and Lawrence Summers (1986) have demonstrated.

What kinds of changes would be necessary to reduce or eliminate involuntary part-time and full-time employment? There are several reasons for such employment in the service industries, where three-quarters of involuntary part-timers and full-timers[3] work. Consider in order the impacts of macroeconomic slack, compensation differentials, managerial tradition, and frictional forces in the labor market.

Insufficient aggregate demand and the resulting unemployment cannot be the major source of either the problem or the solution, at least in terms of involuntary part-time employment. Ninety percent of the rise in the rate of involuntary part-time employment remains after controlling for unemployment rate changes. Even had there been a zero percent unemployment rate in 1993, involuntary part-time employment would still have afflicted 3 percent of the workforce.

Rigid compensation differentials probably play a more crucial role in involuntary part-time and full-time employment: if part-timers earned more relative to full-timers, employers would create fewer part-time jobs. One indication of the importance of these differentials follows from a look at how responsive the supply and demand of part-time work are to changes in compensation. Economists John Owen (1979) and Ronald Ehrenberg and colleagues (1988) offer estimates for this responsiveness. Based on these estimates, the 1993 level of involuntary part-time employment could have been wiped out by a 3.5 percentage point decrease in Owen's estimated 29 percent adjusted hourly wage differential, or a drop of as little as 0.3 percentage points in Ehrenberg et al.'s adjusted differential of 12.6 percent (which controls for additional worker and job characteristics).[4] In other words, small changes in the wage differential would have large effects on involuntary part-time employment, at least at the margin. Of course, for these changes in the wage differential to take place, rigidities in the differential would have to be overcome. If, for instance, the pay difference is partly a wage premium designed to elicit greater effort from full-time workers, narrowing the gap may not be a simple matter.

The interviews cited in this book also point to the role of tradition and managers' conservative beliefs in limiting retention part-time employment and thus maintaining involuntary full-time employment. There is no way, of course, to estimate the size of this effect.

Finally, some residual amount of involuntariness can be attributed to labor market frictions. Because it takes time to find a job even when one is available, some job-seekers may temporarily take a part-time job while looking for a full-time one. This can be considered frictional involuntary part-time employment to the extent that the full-time jobs are actually available. The frictional component in involuntary part-time and full-time employment is probably quite small. Persons experiencing from one to four weeks of involuntary part-time employment—amounts that could plausibly be considered frictional—totaled 29 percent of the persons working part-time involuntarily, but only 5 percent of the total weeks spent in involuntary part-time employment.

Obstacles to Worker Representation
Part-time workers are far less likely than full-timers to have union representation. In 1993, 7.2 percent of part-timers were union members compared with 17.8 percent of full-time workers. Even after controlling for gender, race, age, and education, over two-thirds of the gap in union membership rates between part-time and full-time members remains (Tilly 1991b). This low rate of unionization results from the tremendous obstacles unions face in bargaining for part-time workers as well as for contingent workers such as temporary or on-call workers. Much of this difficulty stems from the complex employee classification schemes associated with the diversification of employee work schedules. The National Labor Relations Board has issued inconsistent rulings on whether part-time and contingent workers should vote along with full-time employees in representation elections (Bronfenbrenner 1988b), and often has inappropriately split full-time workers apart from other groups. In addition, of course, part-time workers may feel they have a limited stake in gaining benefits and representation in a particular workplace.

In some cases, employers have expanded part-time or contingent jobs to undercut union organizing drives or exact concessions during contract negotiations. For example, the Wisconsin Physicians Insurance Corporation, following bitter negotiations with the United Food and Commercial Workers, brought in hundreds of part-time, temporary, and home-based workers (Costello 1989). During a recent organizing drive by the United Auto Workers, Hudson Department Stores in Detroit increased its hiring of part-time workers and began phasing out full-time workers (Colatosti 1990).

Despite their dwindling strength, unions are a positive force in the American labor market. They raise pay and productivity, although this means cutting into profits in industries that wield market power. Unions, on balance, equalize the distribution of income (Freeman and Medoff 1984). And most fundamentally, they offer a representative voice for workers in an otherwise undemocratic workplace. Given these benefits, the difficulty of incorporating part-timers into unions is indeed a problem.

Unanswered Questions About the Part-Time Problem
The picture of part-time employment—and its problems—painted by this book remains incomplete. Several additional pieces of information would clarify the case for new policy action considerably.

To start, it would be valuable to know more about the nature of part-time jobs in industries other than retail and insurance. To what extent is the secondary part-time employment that I found typical of part-time work in other industries? Both case studies and statistical research could help fill out this knowledge.

Next, to what extent have employers created secondary part-time jobs simply to reduce compensation costs in the absence of schedule-related stimuli? In the cases reviewed in Chapter 7, businesses created a secondary labor market in the form of part-time employment at least in part because short-hour workers proved more productive on video display terminals (in the health insurance companies) and better able to staff extended store hours (in retail food). If in general employers do not institute part-time employment except where such scheduling advantages arise, then there are natural limits on the spread of secondary part-time employment, although secondary labor markets may continue to expand in other forms.

Finally, a definitive assessment of the distributional impacts of growing part-time employment depends on tracing the effects of this employment shift on family incomes. The growth of part-time work appears to be part of a more general movement away from the traditional model of a family supported by one breadwinner. Given this, we need to know more about three channels whereby the proliferation of secondary part-time jobs might erode family living standards. First, is the displacement of high-compensation full-time jobs by low-compensation part-time jobs compelling families to work more total hours to maintain the same living standard? For example, does the growth of multi-earner families in part reflect the fact that multiple family members must now work part-time jobs to earn what a single worker used to obtain (via the "family wage") in a full-time job? Second, does the low average income of the growing number of female-headed families in part reflect the fact that female heads are particularly likely to be trapped in part-time jobs with wages and benefit packages designed for "supplementary" earners? And third, is the unavailability of full-time jobs artificially binding families together—for example, preventing young adults from leaving home or wives from leaving husbands—with emotional rather than directly economic costs? Firm conclusions about the distributional effects of growing secondary part-time employment await this research.

Current Policy Approaches

To obtain an accurate sense of current policies, it is necessary to disentangle rhetoric from reality. At the level of ideological pronouncements, representatives of business and labor—much like the Teamsters and Trucking Management—have proposed sharply divergent approaches to part-time employment. Business spokespeople have claimed that the growth of part-time employment and other flexible work forms is essential to restoring efficiency and competitiveness to U.S. industries. In the words of Audrey Freedman, at that time chief economist of the Conference Board, a corporate lobbying group,

> I don't think we're going back to any fixed arrangement [between employers and workers]. I think that this time of fluidity is not momentary. We needed it in order to have an adaptive economy. If we don't have an adaptive economy, we are really going to be behind the eight ball. (quoted in Worsnop 1987, 293)

Many labor leaders, on the other hand, have opposed part-time employment as a threat to full-time jobs and compensation levels. The AFL-CIO's John Zalusky, the labor federation's main spokesperson on part-time work, exemplifies this hositility:

> This nation sorely needs more jobs, not different ways of pulling people into the labor market, or repackaging the 40-hour work week, or redefining the relationships of employee/employer and work. What is being created is a new sub-class of workers. (quoted in Bureau of National Affairs 1986, 98)

But at the level of practice, the policies and collective bargaining agreements that affect part-time employment exhibit quite a bit more subtlety. Within the labor movement, for instance, unions have pursued a wide range of strategies, as illustrated by a verbal exchange at a symposium on part-time work at the 1986 Industrial Relations Research Association meetings. Three union representatives got up to make statements about part-time jobs. The first representative stated: "We believe that part-time jobs undermine the full-time workforce and threaten its wages and benefits. We oppose the introduction of part-time jobs under any circumstances." The second union rep, on the other hand, said: "A large fraction of our members are part-time, and we can't change that fact. Our goal is to get parity of benefits for our part-timers." Finally, the third representative spoke up: "Many of our members—particularly women with babies—*want* to switch from full-time to part-time. We're trying to win the right to job-share, plus protections for part-timers."

In practice, public policy and collective bargaining have pursued four general approaches to meet the challenges posed by part-time employment: (1) to limit or prevent the growth of part-time and contingent work (as the first union is attempting); (2) to control compensation and working conditions (like the second union); (3) to exploit new possibilities for flexibility (like the third union); or to supplement employer-provided benefits with public or universal protections (Carré, duRivage, and Tilly 1995). I shall discuss each approach in turn, emphasizing union actions, since the labor movement has taken a lead on these issues that—so far—government has been slow to follow.

Limiting or Preventing Growth

Historically, many unions have attempted to hold the line, through collective bargaining, on the growth of part-time work. As a United Food and Commercial Workers (UFCW) official told me, the union has long been "trying to increase and enlarge the full-time workforce" in retail stores through bargaining over the permissible proportions of full-time and part-time employment. "But," the official acknowledged, "the tide has been running the other way." A wide variety of unions in retail, manufacturing, food processing, transportation, and the public sector have negotiated full-time percentages (Bronfenbrenner 1988a). To date, federal, state, and local governments in the United States have made no efforts to help unions contain the growth of part-time employment.

In Western Europe, a similar tug of war between unions and employers prevails. Researcher Robert Hart (1984) comments that unions in most European countries are "somewhat hostile" to the use of part-time employment (p. 56). The International Labour Office ([ILO] 1989) concurs that "most trade unions view with concern the steady increase in part-time work, particularly in commerce, banking, and insurance" (p. 24), while in contrast "employers' organizations are largely in favor of part-time work" (p. 26). But unlike the United States, some European countries—such as France and Belgium—restrict the conversion of full-time to part-time jobs, or require consultation with unions or works councils before undertaking such conversion (ILO 1986).

Controlling Conditions of Employment

For unions representing a workforce with substantial numbers of part-timers—especially in services, retail, and government—regulating the use of these workers has become a central goal. The first step is the inclusion of part-time workers in the bargaining unit, if sometimes with a separate status. Existing labor agreements do typically include part-timers, at least above some minimum number of hours (Bronfenbrenner 1988a).

The next step is to bargain for parity in wages and benefits. For example, since the UFCW has been unable to prevent the growth of the part-time workforce in most retail settings, it has targeted equal wages and prorated benefits for part-time workers, with some success. According to John Reilly, president of the American Federation of Teachers' United University Professions Division, "The best strategy is to fully integrate part-timers into the union and academic life with pro-rated benefits and equivalent participation" (United University Professions 1992; see also Service Employees International Union 1993). In addition, many contracts mandate the upgrading of part-time workers, who under such agreements typically accumulate seniority and the right to bid for full-time jobs, although the formula for calculating seniority can be controversial (Bronfenbrenner 1988a).

A comparison of the United States and Canada suggests that union pressure can in fact significantly reduce the pay differential between part-time and full-time workers. Canada's part-timers *and* full-timers are far more likely to be unionized than their counterparts in the United States. In the early 1980s, 18 percent of Canadian part-time workers and 40 percent of the full-timers were union members, well above the U.S. levels of 7 percent and 20 percent, respectively (Commission of Inquiry into Part-Time Work 1983; Appelbaum and Gregory 1988). The part-time/full-time hourly wage differential is also much smaller in Canada. Canadian full-timers earned only 21 percent more on average than part-timers in 1981, compared to 39 percent more in the United States in the same year, even though in most respects the profile of part-time employment is quite similar in the two countries. In fact, there is only a 2 percent part-time/full-time wage differential among unionized jobs in Canada (Commission of Inquiry 1983).[5]

Existing government policies assist only in limited ways union attempts to control the levels of compensation and benefits for part-time and contingent workers. The Employee Retirement and Income Security Act of 1981 (ERISA) requires employers who have a pension plan to extend it to all employees working over 1,000 hours per year (about 20 hours per week). However, loopholes often allow employers to exclude part-time workers who average more than 1,000 hours per year. At the state level, Hawaii's universal health-care plan requires employers to provide health benefits to all employees working more than a certain number of hours. In 1987 New Hampshire passed a law preventing insurers from barring part-timers from group health plans. The *Wall Street Journal* (1987) termed that legislation "apparently the first of its kind."

Additional federal measures requiring part-time/full-time benefit parity have been proposed but, so far, not enacted. For example, Section 89 of the Tax Reform Act of 1986, which would have made health insurance and some other benefits liable to taxation unless extended to all employees working over 17.5 hours per week (Mason 1988), was killed before implementation.

President Clinton's original (September 1993) health plan, building on a number of state plans including Hawaii's, would have mandated employer contributions to health coverage costs for all employees working over 10 hours a week. Employer contributions to part-timers working 30 hours per week or less would have been prorated, with workers responsible for paying the remainder unless they qualified for low-income subsidies. However, Congress failed to pass a health plan in 1994, and the new, Republican-dominated Congress appears unlikely to act on any health plan at all—let alone one featuring universal coverage or employer mandates.

Congresswoman Patricia Schroeder of Colorado has proposed alternative legislation, the Part-Time and Temporary Workers Protection Act of 1993. Among other things, this act would extend health and pension benefits available to full-timers to any employee working 500 or more hours per year (an average of 10 hours per week), on a pro-rated basis. Parallel state legislation has been introduced in Massachusetts.

Such guarantees of equal benefit coverage would, of course, make part-timers more expensive—at least to employers who currently offer a curtailed fringe package to their part-time staff. So it is not surprising that one restaurant chain told the *Wall Street Journal* (1993) that if Clinton's employer mandates became law, "we would definitely be looking at moving those part-time positions into full-time positions." Similarly, retailers quizzed about an earlier version of Schroeder's bill stated that they would respond by "shifting from part-time to full-time staffing" *(Wall Street Journal* 1992). These laws designed to *control* part-time employment thus would also have the effect of *limiting* its growth.

Industrialized countries other than the United States tend to have more interventionist policies toward part-time employment, and more coordination between government and unions on the issue. The ILO (1986, 1989) surveyed legislation and collective bargaining agreements on work schedules, including part-time work, in Western and Eastern Europe, North America, Japan, Australia, and New Zealand, and noted that

> a basic principle explicitly included in the legislation in most countries is that terms and conditions of employment should be no less favourable than those of full-time workers, account being taken as appropriate of the shorter hours of work. This principle covers a range of extremely important conditions: hourly wages, holiday entitlements, security of employment, the right to join trade unions and hold trade union office, etc. Protection varies, however. (1986, 16)

Specifically, France, the Federal Republic of Germany, and Spain statutorily affirmed nondiscrimination between part-time and full-time workers, and several other countries (including Belgium, Italy, Luxembourg, Portugal, Sweden, and Switzerland) implicitly embraced this principle through laws that made no distinction between part-time and full-time (ILO 1989, 10). All of the socialist bloc countries fell into the latter category prior to 1989, although their labor market policies have subsequently been in flux for obvious reasons. A majority of the 15 countries surveyed by the ILO required—via either law or collective bargaining agreements—proportional pay for part-timers, and many also mandated proportional sick pay and holidays. But the ILO acknowledges that the principle of parity in the law books does not necessarily translate into equal treatment on the shop floor.

Exploiting the Opportunity for Flexibility

Although unions have typically opposed part-time and contingent employment, a growing number have concluded that flexibility is actually a *benefit* for part of their workforce and accordingly have bargained to make that flexibility available. Over a decade ago, Service Employees International Union (SEIU) Locals 6 (representing private mental health clinics in Seattle), 535, and 715 (both representing Santa Clara County workers in California) won full-time employees the right to request job sharing or a permanent part-time arrangement. Local 6's agreement protects part-timers from overtime demands by requiring that overtime be offset by compensatory time. The contract for Local 535 and 715 even sets a minimum number of part-time positions in the bargaining unit (Nollen 1982). In Locals 535 and 715, part-time workers are also free to return to full-time status, since Santa Clara County maintains an excess of vacant full-time job slots (Lewis-Munroe 1994).

Other unions have followed the SEIU's lead. For example, the Portland, Oregon, Council of the American Federation of State, County, and Municipal Employees (AFSCME) has also secured the right to set up job-shares when both workers who would share the job come forward (Martinez 1994). The Boston Globe Employees Association, an independent newspaper union, bargained for employees' right to bid for reduced hours and then subsequently to bid for increased hours, an arrangement particularly attractive to parents of young children. Essentially, these unions are creating retention part-time jobs.

Federal and state governments have also, in some cases, adopted policies to broaden access to part-time jobs with favorable terms and conditions of employment. The Federal Career Part-Time Employees Act of 1978 encourages the creation of permanent part-time positions at all levels, offering the same hourly wage as full-time jobs and prorated fringe benefits. The act instructs federal agencies to specify goals and timetables for part-time job creation. Twenty-five states have similar programs to create better part-time employment options, often at the urging of public sector unions. Unfortunately, a 1984 evaluation of the federal program found that managers were dragging their feet in making high-level part-time positions available to federal workers (Kahne 1985).

Some other countries—particularly the Western European countries that were plagued by high unemployment through much of the 1980s—actively promote the creation of part-time jobs, especially within government agencies or government-owned industries (Hart 1984; ILO 1989). Such jobs are particularly targeted to mothers, older and retired workers, and students. The governments of France, the Federal Republic of Germany, and the Netherlands, among others, have taken steps to encourage private employers to hire part-timers, ranging from prorating employer social security payments for part-timers (so employers do not end up paying a fixed amount regardless of the employee's hours) to subsidizing part-time job creation outright. Many countries also subsidize part-time hours on the worker's side through schemes such as old-age benefits that are made available upon partial retirement or unemployment compensation that is payable to part-time workers. The Belgian government subsidizes "partial career breaks," reductions of work hours for up to five years, by paying the worker in question cash benefits, as long as the firm hires an unemployed person to make up the remaining hours (ILO 1989, 148–149).

A number of European countries have even established an entitlement to part-time work for certain demographic groups—older workers and the parents of young children. "In practice, however," the ILO notes, "nearly all part-time work takes place independently of legislated access" (ibid., 20).

Few European unions have promoted part-time employment since in general they view it as "precarious" and undesirable. But the ILO does cite an unnamed "professional women's organization at the international level" and a "national organization of managerial staff" that favor the creation of part-time jobs (ibid., 25).

Supplementing Employer-Provided Benefits
Unions historically have sought to obtain benefits from the individual employer. They have begun, however, to explore benefits provided directly by the union itself, such as credit cards or special insurance rates (AFL-CIO, Committee on the Evolution of Work, 1985). These benefits are particularly important for workers who move frequently from job to job, shift in and out of the labor force, and/or are employed in nonstandard arrangements.

Federal and state governments have long supplemented employer-provided benefits through programs such as Social Security, Medicare, and Medicaid. Universal health coverage, if adopted, would form another link in this chain. At the state level, Hawaii's universal health-care plan provides for a public pool for persons not covered by their employers and requires employers to "play or pay"—that is, to cover their workers or to pay into the pool.

President Carter's 1981 Commission on Pension Policy recommended that Congress establish an employer-funded minimum universal pension scheme to supplement Social Security, with a mandated minimum contribution and assured pension portability from one employer to another. Although other countries, including France, Finland, Denmark, Sweden, and Switzerland, have universal employer-funded pensions in parallel with publicly funded retirement benefits, the United States has yet to act on such a plan.

The U.S. unemployment insurance system offers specific provisions for part-time workers—for better or worse. For better, short-time compensation (STC) offers partial unemployment benefits to workers whose hours are temporarily reduced for economic reasons. As of 1992, 16 states offered STC programs, all created since 1978 (U.S. Congressional Research Service 1992, Kahne 1985). However, many states bar unemployed people who seek part-time jobs from receiving unemployment insurance benefits, ruling them "not available for work"! A recent survey of unemployment insurance programs in large industrial states plus the New England states (a total of 16 states) by the Massachusetts Division of Employment and Training found that about one-third of these states require unemployed workers to be available for full-time work, one-third allow them to collect while seeking part-time work only if they can show good cause for needing part-time hours *and* have a history of part-time employment, and one-third allow part-time availability as long as the worker can show good cause (King and McElligott 1994; see also Pearce 1985). Congresswoman Schroeder's Part-Time and Temporary Workers Protection Act would require states to provide benefits as long as the worker is available for as many hours of work as he or she had before being unemployed.

Backhanded Policies

In addition to laws and contract language expressly related to part-time employment, numerous policies exert an indirect—and often uncontemplated—effect on part-time work. In the arena of collective bargaining, for example, two-tier plans that confer lower wages and benefits on new hires than on incumbents widen the breach between part-timers (who tend to be newer hires) and full-time workers. Seniority-based promotion rules may also discourage managers from creating full-time jobs because they feel they have inadequate control over who will end up in them.

Over a decade ago, I saw firsthand a small example of how union attempts to protect workers can backfire. In the early 1980s, I worked as an on-call file clerk in the outpatient medical records department of a large hospital, and was a member of a Service Employees International Union local. I soon discovered that "on-call" only meant that I got called daily for the first week or so; after that the supervisor just told me to come in Monday through Friday, 8:30 to 5:00. The regular hours were great, but my on-call status meant that I received no benefits. I heard that there had been precedents for reclassification: on-call workers who had worked 30 days or more on a regular schedule without being called had successfully filed grievances to be reclassified as regular employees. So an on-call co-worker and I filed grievances. The better part of a year and three levels of the grievance procedure later, we won. But management had the last laugh. "Congratulations," the department head told us, clearly displeased at our victory but smiling nonetheless. "You are now both regular workers—scheduled for 16 hours a week, on the Saturday and Sunday evening shifts!"

In addition to union provisions, government statutes can generate unintended consequences for part-time employment. Laws with an indirect impact on part-time employment are in fact quite a varied lot. Laws mandating a wage premium for overtime (the Fair Labor Standards Act of 1938 and related subsequent legislation) encourage employers with variable work loads to use part-timers to take up the slack. Social Security places earning ceilings on benefit eligibility, creating an incentive for older workers to work part-time so that they can collect benefits as well. On the other hand, ceilings on the payroll taxes that fund Social Security and Unemployment Insurance mean that employers (sometimes) pay higher average tax rates on part-timers. The minimum wage places a limit on the part-time/full-time wage differential in low-wage industries such as retail.

Thresholds and exemptions written into laws can create a variety of perverse incentives. The various versions of health-care reform legislation proposed during 1993 and 1994 incorporated a number of such exemptions:

> Consider, for instance, a company with 48 low-wage workers. Under the back-up employer mandate in the Senate Democrats' plan, the company would eventually have to pay 50 percent of the cost of its employees' care. But if it breaks into two companies with 24 employees each, both would be exempt from the mandate. Moreover, the workers could collect hefty federal subsidies. The inevitable result: more small businesses. . . . The Congressional Budget Office estimates that as many as 1.8 million additional workers will find their way to businesses with fewer than 25 employees if that provision takes hold. (Murray 1994)

Since smaller businesses on average employ more part-timers, a growing number of small businesses would most likely further swell the part-time ranks. Another example: Clinton's original health-care bill exempted employers from contributions for workers with less than 10 hours per week. Such a provision could induce employers to reduce hours for employees working just over 10 hours (currently, more than 5 million Americans work 5 to 14 hours per week), or in some cases even replace full-time workers with several minimum-hour part-timers.

In less direct ways, many types of legislation—such as college financial aid, truancy laws, and restrictions on teen-age labor—affect the supply of potential part-time workers, while still other laws, such as equal employment opportunity and affirmative action provisions, affect the demand. Even more broadly, a variety of policies—both macroeconomic and microeconomic—that are not directed primarily at the labor market affect part-time employment. For example, aggregate demand management helps to determine the level of involuntary part-time employment. And policies involving trade, monetary policy, and military procurement shape the industry mix of employment and thus the share of jobs located in industries with high rates of part-time employment.

What Will Work?

How can we best choose among or combine strategies of prevention, control, exploitation, or supplementation used to meet the challenges of part-time employment? It is important to keep in mind where the problems lie: not with part-time employment in itself, but in a series of problems predominantly associated with secondary part-time jobs—income inequality, lagging productivity, involuntary part-time and involuntary full-time status, and weakened union representation. The key policy instruments include not just federal legislation but also union bargaining, which has proven quite effective in shaping employers' use of part-timers. We must also recognize that the world has changed—the world of work, the world of families, and particularly the interaction between the two—so that restoration of some golden *status quo ante* simply is not on the agenda.

The Limits on Limiting Part-Time Employment

The goal of placing some absolute limit on the number of part-time jobs may be misguided as well as unattainable in the current era, given the large number of workers who want these schedules. The French government's attempt to limit the creation of temporary and fixed-duration jobs is instructive. In 1982, early in François Mitterand's Socialist government, France directly restricted the creation of such jobs. By 1986, however, the government had dropped these restrictions. French labor market inflexibility was widely believed responsible for the country's persistently high unemployment. In addition, the sharp distinctions between temporary and permanent positions had become blurred by the "flexibilization" of permanent jobs (Carré 1993).

Nonetheless, the spread of involuntary part-time employment justifies some policy intervention to contain the creation of lousy part-time jobs. At a macroeconomic level, federal government attempts to regulate the nation's overall level of economic activity should take involuntariness into account. Current macroeconomic policies setting spending and taxing policies (fiscal policy), and determining interest rates and money supply (monetary policy) focus only on the unemployment rate, to the extent that they target labor market variables at all. Macroeconomic targeting should be modified to explicitly include goals for involuntary part-time and involuntary full-time employment as well as unemployment.[6]

Historical data on involuntary part-time employment indicate that taking involuntariness into account can in fact markedly change the apparent state of the macroeconomy. For example, the unemployment rate in the "boom" year of 1987 was 6.2 percent, not much higher than the 5.8 percent in the previous economic peak year of 1979. But the underemployment rate—calculated as the unemployment rate plus one-half of the involuntary part-time employment rate—was 8.4 percent in 1987, closer to the 9.1 percent in the recession year of 1980 than to the 7.5 percent of 1979.[7]

Macroeconomic intervention alone is insufficient to eliminate involuntary part-time and full-time employment. Involuntariness results not just from macroeconomic slack but also from structural causes, in particular rigid compensation differentials between part-time and full-time jobs. Steps to narrow these compensation differentials represent efforts to control part-time employment. Such steps would lessen involuntary part-time employment both by decreasing employer demand for secondary part-timers vis-à-vis full-time workers and by increasing the supply of people who would willingly work part-time. In other words, policies to control part-time employment will in many cases end up limiting that employment as well. Indeed, control policies designed to prevent employer abuses and build basic protections for part-time workers may be the most effective measures for limiting part-time job growth.

Asserting Control
The control strategy attempts to enhance the quality of part-time jobs by transforming them into primary labor market jobs without necessarily changing their scheduling attributes. The state has at its disposal a variety of microeconomic employment policy instruments that could be applied to this goal. In many cases, the use of broad-gauge instruments would lead to a general contraction of secondary labor markets and expansion of primary labor markets, including the more specific effect of curtailing the growth of secondary part-time employment. It makes sense to use such broad policies in addition to singling out part-time employment for attention in some selected cases. Low-paid full-time workers need help as much as low-paid part-time workers.

There are two ways to redirect employment toward higher compensation jobs. First, industrial policies could be used to encourage the relative growth of industries such as heavy manufacturing that are characterized by primary labor markets, thereby undoing some of the compositional shifts that have led to the expansion of secondary part-time employment. Second, other policies could be used to spur the growth of primary labor markets within a wide range of industries. While industrial policy must be part of the solution, I will leave that set of prescriptions to others, such as economists Bennett Harrison and Barry Bluestone (1988) and Michael Best (1990). This discussion instead examines possible policy changes designed to act within industries, which have been less thoroughly explored in other work.

The goal is to push employers within each industry in the direction of primary labor markets. Probably the single most effective policy to achieve this end is to support unionization. Overall, the two most common union bargaining agendas with respect to part-time employment are to limit the spread of secondary part-time jobs and to obtain equal compensation for part-timers. Union efforts to lessen the part-time/full-time compensation differential extend the notion of taking wages out of competition. These efforts form part of a more general union objective of minimizing employer use of secondary labor markets. Unions have had some success in meeting this objective. In fact, the nonunionized supermarket manager who was quoted in Chapter 6 as describing the cycle of "the less skill, the less money, the higher turnover," went on to say, "Now, the only way to get around that is if there's a union, you know. Then you're obligated to pay a higher wage."

Of course, unionization in the United States is currently experiencing a long-term steep decline. Federal policies could, however, help reverse this decline. For example, the National Labor Relations Act of 1935 could be amended to a Canadian-style union certification system, in which a union is certified as the bargaining agent for workers once a majority have signed certification cards. This would eliminate the current prolonged election campaign that has become an opportunity for employers to engage in a one-sided barrage of information and disinformation, intimidation, and outright firing of union supporters. Such heightened employer resistance to unionization—often involving illegal tactics—has contributed significantly to the decline of union representation (Freeman and Medoff 1984). Stiffer penalties could also be levied on unfair labor practices such as firings in retaliation for organizing activity. Congress could ban the hiring of permanent replacements for strikers, a practice that has largely negated the strike, historically the union's main weapon. But in the current political discourse that categorizes unions as a "special interest" rather than a necessary part of a democratic society and economy, such measures seem unlikely to garner sufficient political support.

Alternatively or additionally, unions themselves can explore new models of worker organization particularly suited to workers who move in and out of part-time and temporary employment or who simply do not stay with the same employer for the major part of their work career (Carré, duRivage, and Tilly 1994). As sociologist Dorothy Sue Cobble (1990) points out, the most natural place to look for these models is in the rich history of craft unionism.

For example, unions representing part-time and contingent workers could borrow certain aspects from the construction trades unions, which were designed for workers with fleeting attachments to contracting firms. In this model, the union, not the firm, provides stability and equity in terms of wages, health benefits, and pensions. Unions actively control training and, in many instances, the hiring process itself. Construction unionism demonstrates the possibility of stable worker representation in a highly fluctuating sector.

Cobble (1990, 1991) cites examples in a variety of other trades, including waitress unions that successfully ran hiring halls in Butte, Montana, and Los Angeles for over half a century. She draws out a model of "occupational unionism" based on strong occupational (skill-based) identity, union control over labor supply in the industry, definition of rights and benefits as functions of occupational membership rather than work-site affiliation, peer control over occupational performance standards, and emphasis on employment security rather than rights to a particular job.

Economist Howard Wial (1993, 1994) spells out in greater detail the institutional changes required to implement the multi-employer bargaining structures inherent in occupational unionism. Generalizing from the "Justice for Janitors" campaign undertaken by the Service Employees International Union, Wial elaborates "geographical/occupational" union institutions entailing a uniform wage and benefit structure covering loosely defined occupational groupings within a localized geographical area. Unlike Cobble's model, geographical unionism departs from craft-based forms of organization in requiring neither strong occupational identity, nor union enforcement of job performance standards, nor union control over labor supply.

Arts and entertainment unions, which also represent workers with short-term, project-based jobs, incorporate many elements of both the Cobble and Wial models (Kleingartner and Paul 1992). These unions provide a variety of services to ease job transitions, including referral, placement, and transitional loan funds. They have bargained for pension portability and for health coverage that can be self-paid during spells of unemployment. As with the construction unions, the arts and entertainment unions are directly involved in a number of areas traditionally left to management, such as hiring and the administration of compensation. These unions also index dues to income, so that those who find little work owe little in dues, and accommodate worker membership in multiple unions.

Some of these elements also resemble components of the model for associational unionism proposed by sociologist Charles Heckscher (1988) to enable unions as a whole to coordinate and effectively represent the growing diversity of claims and concerns in the workforce, be it in full-time or part-time, permanent or contingent, employment. Heckscher advocates that unions provide multiple forms of representation and services in addition to traditional collective bargaining. Unions and worker associations, he argues, can perform other functions such as providing direct services and extra insurance and benefits to those within, as well as those outside, the collective bargaining unit. They can also help establish training funds for new jobs, even if these fall outside the bargaining unit or the industry. In this way, "workers who cannot be protected by a contract nevertheless can get help from their representative organization" (p. 189).[8]

How readily can these models be extended more generally to part-time or other contingent employment? The construction model clearly depends on the bargaining power of the skilled building trades, with their control of apprenticeships and threat of strikes, and the government regulation of the construction industry. On the other hand, Archie Kleingartner and Alan Paul (1992) of the University of California at Los Angeles note that "unions in arts and entertainment are effective, relevant, and valued by workers in the industry without being powerful in the sense of being able to impose their will on employers through strikes" (p. 3). Unions can replicate parts of these models, even in the absence of traditional sources of bargaining power, if they take on a role in maintaining continuity and communication that makes them essential to management and workers alike. This role would include ensuring continuity of benefits (possibly through direct union sponsorship of health or pension plans, which is not a new idea). It could also encompass participation in recruitment and placement, and in training and certification of skill within a particular occupation. Successful implementation would require modifications of union structures, such as associate membership (available even to workers not currently working in a unionized shop), broadened bargaining units, and representation organized primarily by occupation and geographic area rather than work site and industry.

But amidst all this attention to unions, let's not forget the federal government's power to push employers from secondary to primary employment. Supporting unionization is a rather indirect way of restricting the within-industry growth of secondary part-time employment. A more direct approach is to use public policy to do one of the things that unions do—narrow the compensation differential between part-time and full-time workers.

Narrowing the compensation differential could have a number of positive effects in settings where secondary part-time employment is used. It would lead to some combination of increased part-time compensation and decreased full-time compensation, resulting in downward redistribution. It would also lead to the replacement of some secondary part-time jobs with full-time jobs, thus decreasing involuntary part-time employment. Whereas the option of employing part-timers at rock-bottom compensation encourages complacency about stagnating productivity, a limit on the differential would induce employer attempts to increase productivity.

Narrowing the compensation differential is also likely to have negative effects. It may lead to disemployment, as firms react to higher required compensation levels for part-time workers by shedding workers. And it may have destructive incentive effects within the workforce, to the extent that the part-time/full-time wage differential serves incentive purposes.

However, the negative effects are likely to be relatively small. Studies of the most recent minimum wage increase, which would be expected to have an employment effect similar to that of a law enforcing benefit parity, found that the employment effect of the increase was zero or even slightly positive (Card and Krueger 1995). This may be due to its effects on aggregate demand: raising the compensation of the lowest paid workers does destroy lousy jobs, but the greater purchasing power created by a higher wage floor generates roughly the same number of better jobs. Or it may be that low-wage employers mistakenly set wages too low, and that a forced wage increase brings benefits in reduced turnover and heightened productivity that offset the higher wage costs. While employers currently use the prospect of promotion from part-time to full-time work (or, in a retention part-time environment, the fear of losing a well-compensated part-time job) to motivate workers, they can certainly design other promotion and compensation incentives that do not depend on this invidious distinction.

The main policy instruments needed to narrow the part-time/full-time compensation differential already exist or have been designed: the minimum wage, mandates for employer-provided health coverage, Congresswoman Schroeder's Part-Time and Temporary Workers Protection Act, ERISA, and Section 89 of the 1986 Tax Reform Act. The minimum wage has never regained its late 1970s purchasing power peak, but it still forms an important floor for part-time wages. In 1985, 28 percent of part-time workers earned the minimum wage or less, and 65 percent of workers earning the minimum wage or below worked part-time (Mellor and Haugen 1986). The minimum wage hike enacted in 1989 raised the wage to $4.25 effective in 1991, but after adjusting for inflation this is still roughly equivalent to 1985's $3.35 minimum. Thus, raising the minimum wage—at least back to its real 1978–79 value—and indexing it to inflation would effectively compress the part-time/full-time differential. Extension of the coverage of minimum wage laws, particularly to smaller businesses, would assist in this effort.

As for the gap in fringe benefits, Schroeder's legislation mandating health insurance and benefit parity would be the most straightforward solution. Universal health coverage based on employer-provided mandates would also do the trick for health benefits, which represent the most significant fringe disparity between part-time and full-time workers. Failing either of these, ERISA (which covers pension benefits) and Section 89 (which would have covered health benefits and a number of other fringes had it not been rescinded) provide a framework for policy intervention. A number of loopholes in these laws should be closed: for example, additional legislation should be adopted to discourage firms from subcontracting their low-compensation jobs to avoid paying fringe benefits. In addition, insurers should be required to extend group coverage to part-time workers, as New Hampshire now mandates. Once these changes are incorporated, serious enforcement of ERISA and Section 89 would go a long way toward narrowing the fringe benefit differential between full-time and part-time workers.

Of course, creating a law does not automatically translate into universal employer compliance. A recent study of employers' responses to the Family and Medical Leave Act of 1992, for instance, found that 40 percent of employers were failing to offer 12 weeks of such leave, to guarantee jobs after the leave, or to continue benefits during the leave. Almost two-thirds of surveyed workers who took leaves reported problems with their employers. Only "a very small minority of companies are really trying to implement the law," commented University of California professor Andrew Scharlach, co-author of the study (Shellenbarger 1994, B1).

Thus, even if government regulations mandating wage and benefits parity are adopted, unions will play a crucial role in monitoring and enforcing these regulations, just as they do for current wage and hour laws that in principle apply to all nonexempt workers. Monitoring wage parity in nonunion settings is problematic at best. Harvard University's Paul Weiler (1990), among others, has argued for universal works councils of the type in place in Northern European countries, and some expect John Dunlop's U.S. Labor Department Commission on the Future of Labor-

Management Relations to propose representative institutions of this sort. The Occupational Safety and Health Reform Act, introduced in several congressional sessions during the early 1990s (but not yet passed), has already called for the formation of labor-management safety committees in all workplaces with over 10 employees, union and nonunion, with workers electing their own safety representatives. Kindred or overlapping structures might be established to oversee wages and benefits parity.

Discussion of ways to narrow the part-time/full-time earnings gap would be incomplete without mention of the Earned Income Tax Credit (EITC). The EITC, which reduces taxes for those with low earnings, and pays a cash subsidy to those with the very lowest earnings has been the Clinton administration's preferred instrument of redistribution. While it does provide important relief for the working poor, it has two important shortcomings. One, it offers little assistance to the lowest earners—who are in the main part-time, part-year workers—because they owe so little in taxes in the first place. For instance, among those welfare recipients who combine work and welfare, the EITC yields a pittance of $1,200 per year, on average (Hartmann and Spalter-Roth 1993). Second, the tax credit gives employers no incentive to change their compensation policies. In fact, the EITC in effect subsidizes low-wage employers by supplementing the pay they offer, thus making it easier for them to attract and retain employees at no extra cost. So while the EITC is a lifesaver for many low income families, it only makes sense in combination with other policies.

Workers Exploiting Part-Time Jobs
Measures to expand and exploit flexibility for the employee, such as parental leave, flextime, or the right to move between full-time and part-time status, are likely to become increasingly important as women of child-bearing age become more entrenched in the workforce, and as men take on growing responsibility for child care and involvement with their families. Already, a 1993 survey by the Families and Work Institute found that among the factors workers rated "very important" in deciding to take their current job, the effect on family/personal life (cited by 60 percent of workers surveyed) and the company's family-supportive policies (46 percent) ranked higher than fringe benefits (42 percent) or salary (35 percent) (Shellenbarger 1993). Ensuring that a wide range of jobs allow flexibility in response to changing worker preferences is the other side of making sure that flexible jobs bring decent wages, benefits, and security.

In fact, a strong case can be made for reducing work time for all (Schor 1992). Shorter working hours could be implemented through laws such as a lower hours threshold for overtime pay and a minimum vacation leave requirement. For many families, shorter hours would only be a practical option if accompanied by no drop in total wages. In many European countries, both unions and governments have made reductions in work time without reductions in pay a priority, in large part as a job-creation measure.[9]

Closer to home, although employees do now have the right to unpaid family or medical leave, many cannot afford to take time off. Paid leave would, of course, solve this problem, greatly expanding workers' options. Alternatively, temporary disability insurance (TDI), funded by a payroll tax, could help meet the need. Five states (California, New York, New Jersey, Rhode Island, and Hawaii) currently run a TDI system, Roberta Spalter-Roth (1994) of the Institute for Women's Policy Research points out, "and it runs in the black." TDI would be most effective if extended to a wide range of family needs, not just illness and pregnancy.

In order to win flexibility for workers, it will be important to promote the equal participation of women and older workers in unions and management. Women in particular have been the most active constituency working for more retention part-time employment. Increasing women's representation in unions and management provides one of the bases for mobilization in support of other parts of this program. In the labor movement, a variety of voluntary steps can be taken to foster women's activity: support for the Coalition of Labor Union Women, leadership training aimed specifically at women, even provision of child care at union meetings. In management, federal and state governments can play a role by enforcing affirmative action and equal employment opportunity policies has well as age discrimination laws. A stronger voice for women and older workers would increase advocacy for the part-time option within businesses and unions.

Sensible Supplements

Universal, government-guaranteed benefits have reappeared on the national policy agenda, after a decade or more in eclipse. Union support for universal benefits supplementing or replacing employer-provided benefits also offers a particularly important strategy for the labor movement, given the declining rate of unionization and the corresponding diminution of unions' bargaining power. Advocating for universal benefits, such as health care, facilitates the formation of coalitions linking union federations with community groups and public policy reform groups. Together, all three types of organizations can argue for the design of a mechanism of social protection that is more rational than the current one, which is better suited to a fading form of production organization. By "more rational" I mean a mechanism that prevents large segments of the workforce from falling outside the protection of either employer-provided benefits or the public welfare system.

"Rationalizing" employee benefits extends beyond a universal health-care plan. For starters, public policy reforms are needed to allow for the conversion and portability of worker pensions. One possible model for this reform is the national collective bargaining agreement governing the French temporary-help industry. The agreement includes rules for industrywide seniority and pension portability that allow workers to build seniority and protection not only across temporary assignments but also as they shift across temporary-help service agencies over the course of their career (Carré 1993).[10]

Federal laws should standardize eligibility for unemployment insurance and for workers' compensation so that part-time workers, as well as sporadic or contingent workers, are not left out in the cold (see duRivage 1992). One starting point is Congresswoman Schroeder's proposed rule that people seeking part-time jobs can be eligible for unemployment insurance (UI) as long as they were working part-time before becoming unemployed. But this is only a starting point. In Massachusetts, the Greater Boston Legal Services is currently pursuing a case to extend UI eligibility to all who seek part-time work for legitimate reasons. In this particular case, a single mother's child-care arrangements collapsed, requiring her to limit her work to school hours. She requested a reduction to part-time hours from her employer, but was forced to leave her job instead. The state of Massachusetts then denied this woman unemployment benefits, since she had been working full-time prior to her termination.

On a related issue, there is also a crying need for a universal system of child and dependent care so that job options will not be so dramatically narrowed by unavailability of such care. The only comprehensive child-care program in the United States today is the child-care tax deduction in the federal tax code. It is inadequate: it covers only a small portion of costs and only benefits families who make enough income to pay income taxes. Most importantly, it does not increase the supply of child care (Albelda and Tilly 1994).

The Need to Know

To guide intelligent policy-making about part-time work, we also need policies to increase our knowledge about part-time employment. Important gaps loom in existing data series about part-time employment. For example, even the newly expanded Current Population Survey asks a relatively narrow set of questions about involuntary part-time employment. It would be useful to know how many part-timers would want a full-time job if they could get adequate dependent care, and how many would still want a full-time job if they could get prorated benefits on their part-time job. Also, no statistics are currently kept on involuntary full-time employment. Questions added to the Current Population Survey for particular months could deepen our knowledge about part-time work considerably, guiding further action.

An even larger data lacuna looms for contingent workers, such as temporary, leased, on-call, or subcontracted workers. Congresswoman Schroeder's Part-Time and Temporary Workers Protection Act calls for the Bureau of Labor Statistics to carry out an annual survey of temporary workers, presumably as part of the Current Population Survey. Pilot surveys probing other forms of contingent work are also needed. The U.S. Bureau of Labor Statistics has taken an important first step with a February 1995 special survey on contingent work.

In addition, further support should be provided for research on part-time employment as well as other "flexible" work forms. Even as such types of work have become a hot topic for the media, research in these areas remains thin. The same facts and statistics are discussed over and over in policy debates, and many of the most important questions remain unanswered. Much of the scholarly literature on employment overlooks part-time employment altogether. Given that almost one-fifth of the workforce works part-time, and that this share (as well as the share of other flexible work forms) has been increasing over the long run, these subjects deserve more attention.

Time for a Change

Taken together, this combination of new and existing policy tools could substantially reshape the way that companies use part-time employment. Both government regulation *and* union representation are needed to head off the problems of part-time work, and the two can strengthen each other. On the one hand, union presence in the workplace plays a critical role in enforcing new policy measures. On the other hand, new forms of worker representation oriented toward a workforce peppered with part-time and contingent workers would work best given a set of enabling policies, just as the industrial union model was complemented by a set of government policies regulating employment.

Fixing the part-time problem requires that labor, management, and government let go of outdated definitions of workplace and worker protection in favor of reforms that ensure that flexibility benefits employees as well as employers. As part-time employment grows, we can no longer use a full-time job as the standard to which policies are pegged. We can neither assume that part-time jobs are simply employers' response to workers' needs, nor that these jobs are an undesirable last resort: they are both, in different settings. Understanding the distinction between secondary and retention, and good and bad, part-time jobs is essential to formulating policy responses.

Responding appropriately to increasing part-time employment also means reconceiving the family. Never was it true that most women just worked for "pin money," but as women's labor force participation rate converges with men's, that notion becomes more of an anachronism than ever. Unwise, also, to assume that a teen-ager works only to save money for luxuries and recreation. For many families, part-time jobs have become part of a carefully pieced-together package to keep their finances afloat. And, given the growing numbers of those lacking health insurance *and* rising numbers of single mothers, we cannot count on some "other" family member to earn the benefits to cover part-timers.

At bottom, the four major policy approaches—limit, control, exploit, and supplement—translate into four somewhat different fundamental goals, all of which need attention. The first goal is to transform or replace bad, secondary labor market jobs with good, primary labor market jobs. Carrying out this shift from bad to good jobs is the core objective behind limiting or controlling part-time employment. I repeat that this does *not* necessarily mean replacing part-time with full-time jobs, although it certainly does mean curtailing the current proliferation of bad part-time jobs. It also means looking for ways to transform the lousy full-time jobs that have likewise grown rapidly.

Second, broadening the notion of exploiting part-time employment, workers need greater schedule flexibility in all dimensions. This applies with particular force to the millions of workers trapped in 40-plus-hour jobs who would prefer to be working fewer hours. It speaks also to women with young children who need to temporarily drop out of the labor force or reduce hours, older workers who seek phased retirement, people of all ages who need to deal with illness or other family crises, and those who seek to add to their education. Availability of part-time work in a wider range of occupations, and easier mobility back and forth between part-time and full-time hours, offer parts of a solution to ease the conflicts between the demands of work and the rest of life.

The third objective is to build a system of security and supports that protects all workers. The list of elements of such a system includes health coverage, retirement income, unemployment assistance, and child care. Some workers will obtain these benefits at work, some through unions, some from the government (as I have emphasized in discussing ways to supplement what employers offer), and some can afford to fend for themselves in the private sector, but the goal is to construct a sufficiently broad and sturdy umbrella so that no one will get drenched.

Finally, threading through this entire discussion is the notion that part-time workers need and deserve citizenship in the workplace. Citizenship means equal rights, a voice and a vote on wages and working conditions, and, as businesses are increasingly recognizing, say on how best to provide the goods and services that the business sells. It may seem a bit utopian to call for workplace citizenship for part-timers when so few full-time workers enjoy citizenship of this sort. But I state the aim both to press all workers' claim on citizenship and to inveigh against the destructive distinctions that mete out different amounts of rights to different types of workers.

A part-time job does not have to be half a job. It can be a full job, despite its reduced hours. Today it is the half-jobs that are spreading across the economic landscape. But take heart: the character of jobs does not spring mysteriously from some "natural" market process free of conscious intervention. That character is decisively shaped by institutions that we as a society are constantly building and rebuilding. We have the power to turn half a job into a full job.

APPENDIX

A Formal Model of the Cyclical Adjustment of Part-Time Employment in Noncyclical Industries

■ THIS MODEL OFFERS AN EXPLANATION FOR WHY THE level of part-time employment fluctuates over the business cycle in industries that undergo little cyclical fluctuation in total employment. The model is based on two assumptions. First, as unemployment falls, people who are working a schedule other than the one they prefer become more likely to find a job with their preferred schedule and quit. Second, since turnover entails costs for firms, they adjust their mix of part-time and full-time jobs to try to satisfy more workers. The reverse mechanism operates when unemployment rises. Both mechanisms operate within a particular institutional structure, and since retail and insurance have different institutional structures, the outcome of the model is different in the two industries.

Chapter 7 provides additional descriptive details. This appendix presents the model's algebraic equations as well as a discussion of some of the more technical aspects of the model.

In this model, involuntary part-timers have a total quit probability of $m + f$ per period, where

m = workers' underlying quit probability per period
f = involuntary part-time workers' probability of finding a full-time job per period

The labor cost to the firm of employing a full-timer is given by

$$C_F = w_F + T(r + m) \tag{A.1}$$

and the cost of employing two part-timers by

$$C_P = w_P + 2T(r + m + p_F f) \tag{A.2}$$

where

C_F = labor cost of employing a full-time worker
C_P = labor cost of employing two part-time workers (one full-time equivalent)
w_F = per-period compensation to a full-time worker
w_P = per-period compensation to a part-time worker
T = training costs per new hire (assumed incurred in first period)
r = the interest rate
p_F = fraction of part-timers who want full-time work

Note that $T(r + m)$ and $T(r + m + p_F f)$ represent amortized, per-period training costs. Although this model shows no productivity difference between part-time and full-time workers, such a variable could easily be accommodated by adding a constant to the cost of employing part-timers. Unless the productivity difference is itself a function of the rate of full-time employment, this modification does not change the workings of the model at all.

Worker preferences and behavior are summarized in m, p_F, and f. The underlying quit probability, m, is simply exogenous, but more can be said about the other two parameters. The fraction of part-timers (PT) who want full-time work, p_F, is determined by the rate of full-time employment and the (constant) number of people who prefer part-time work:

$$p_F = \frac{\text{total PT} - \text{voluntary PT}}{\text{total PT}} = \frac{n_P N - K}{n_P N} = \frac{n_P - k}{n_P} \tag{A.3}$$

where

n_P = rate of part-time employment
N = total number employed
K = number of workers who want part-time work
k = rate of voluntary part-time employment (K/N)

The probability of finding a full-time job, f, depends on the number of vacancies and the number of people searching for a full-time job:

$$f = \frac{\text{full-time vacancies}}{\text{searchers}} = \frac{mF}{mF + p_F P + U} \tag{A.4}$$

$$= \frac{mn_F}{mn_F + p_F n_P + [u/(1-u)]}$$

where

F = total number of full-time employees (so mF is the number of full-timers leaving their jobs each period)

P = total number of part-time employees

U = total number of unemployed workers

n_F = rate of full-time employment per head, (F/N)

n_P = rate of part-time employment (P/N)

u = unemployment rate $U/(N+U)$

Note that all unemployed workers want full-time jobs, since people who want part-time work are all employed in the part-time jobs.

Firms choose the rate of full-time employment per head to minimize total labor costs. Take the resulting equilibrium to be a Nash equilibrium, meaning that each firm takes the position of all other firms as given. To state the optimization problem, all quantities must be converted to either a per-head basis or a per-full-time-equivalent (FTE) basis. Converting to a per-FTE basis simply involves using the rate of full-time employment per FTE, which is $2n_F /(n_F + 1)$. Expressed in per-FTE form, the minimization problem is

$$\min_{n_F} C = \frac{2n_F [w_F + T(r + m)]}{1 + n_F} + \frac{1 - n_F [w_P + 2T(r + m + p_F f)]}{1 + n_F} \quad (A.5)$$

subject to

$$n_F > 0$$

$$n_F < 1-k$$

(The last inequality means there are no more full-time jobs than people who want them). The first order conditions are:

(i) $n_F = 0$ for $C_F > C_P$

(ii) $n_F = 1 - k$ for $C_F < C_P$ (A-6)

(iii) $n_F = n_F$ for $C_F = C_P$

In other words, when full-time employment is more expensive, firms hire all part-time workers; when part-time employment is more expensive, firms hire all full-time workers; when the cost is identical, firms make no changes.

To move from the firm's solution to the market equilibrium, it is helpful to use a graphic representation of the possible equilibria. Firms care about the difference in turnover between part-time and full-time employees. This difference depends on two things: p_F, the fraction of part-time workers that want full-time work (or alternatively put, the probability of wanting a full-time job given that one is employed part-time), and f, the probability of finding a full-time job. In fact, the part-time/full-time difference in quit probabilities is simply the product of these two, $p_F f$. Both of these variables in turn depend on the rate of full-time employment, n_F. Thus, the product can be plotted as a function of the rate of full-time employment. Call this function the turnover difference schedule, or $D(n_F)$. This schedule summarizes the relevant aspects of worker behavior.

While the algebraic expression for the turnover difference schedule is somewhat unwieldy, a number of facts about the schedule's shape can be readily ascertained. When the rate of full-time employment is zero, the probability of finding a full-time job is zero, and D is equal to zero. On the other hand, when the rate of full-time employment reaches the level where all part-time workers are voluntary ($n_F = 1 - k$, where k is the rate of voluntary part-time employment), the probability of wanting a full-time job given that one is a part-time worker is equal to zero, and D is once more equal to zero (as long as $k > 0$). In between these two extremes, both probabilities are positive. Since D rises from zero to a positive number and then falls to zero again over the domain $[0, 1 - k]$, there must be an odd number of critical points in the function—in effect, what goes up must come down. But the first derivative $D'(n_F)$ is quadratic, so there are at most two roots (see proof beginning with next paragraph). Thus $D(n_F)$ has precisely one critical point—a maximum—in the domain we are considering. The turnover difference schedule can be drawn as in Figure A.1.[1]

Here is the proof that the turnover difference schedule has at most two critical points within the relevant range. Start with definitions:

Turnover difference schedule, $D(n_F) = p_F f_F$ (A.7)

$p_F = 1 - k/(1 - n_F)$ (A.8)

$f_F = mn_F / [mn_F + (1 - n_F - k) + (u/\{1-u\})]$

    $= n_F /(b - cn_F)$ (A.9)

where

    f_F = probability of finding a full-time job
    $b = (1/m)(1 - k) + (1/m)(u/[1 - u]) > 0$
    $c = (1/m) - 1 > 0$

The relevant range of n_F is given by

$0 < n_F < (1 - k)$ (A.10)

since for the rate of full-time employment above $(1 - k)$, there is no involuntary part-time employment (indeed, there is involuntary full-time employment).

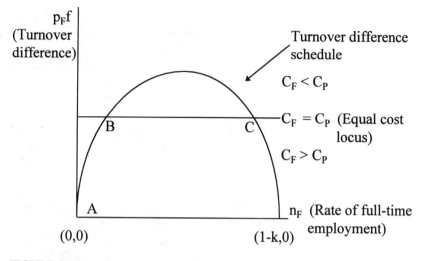

FIGURE A.1
Labor Market Equilibria

Then solve for critical points, where the first derivative of D is equal to 0:

$$0 = dD/dn_F$$
$$= [-k/(1 - n_F)^2][n_F/(b - cn_F)]$$
$$+ [1 - (k/\{1 - n_F\})][b/(b - cn_F)^2] \tag{A.11}$$

Multiplying through by the relevant denominators and gathering terms, we have

$$0 = (kc + b)n_F^2 + (-2b)n_F + (b - kb) \tag{A.12}$$

This is a quadratic expression and has at most two solutions, proving the proposition. Applying the quadratic formula gives two possible roots for n_F:

$$n_F = [2b \pm (4b^2 - 4\{kbc - k^2bc + b^2 - kb^2\})^{1/2}]/2(kc + b)$$
$$= [b \pm (k^2bc + kb^2 - kbc)^{1/2}]/(kc + b) \tag{A.13}$$

Having established that Figure A.1 represents the turnover difference schedule accurately, let us now return to its implications. When the difference in turnover between part-time and full-time employees $(p_F f)$ is zero, part-timers are less costly to employ than full-timers, since they receive less compensation per hour. As the turnover difference grows, the cost gap narrows, until at some point the cost of filling a full-time equivalent slot with one full-timer or two part-timers is identical, $C_F = C_P$.[2] Call the locus of points where this equality holds the equal cost locus, as shown in Figure A.1. The equal cost locus summarizes firm objectives. In the interesting case, the equal cost locus intersects the turnover difference schedule at two points. Below the equal cost locus (i.e., at lower values of turnover difference), full-timers are more costly than part-timers; above the locus, part-timers are more costly.

Referring back to the firm's first-order conditions in Equation A.6, it is clear that three points solve the firm's optimization problem (Figure A.1). At point A, the origin, part-time employment is cheaper, and firms use all part-time employment. At points B and C, where the equal cost locus crosses the turnover difference schedule, costs are equal, and firms do not wish to adjust.

A look at dynamics reveals that only two of the three equilibria are stable. Consider small perturbations from each of the equilibria. If there is a small increase in full-time employment from A, firms, aware that part-time employment is less costly, will replace the full-timers with part-timers, moving back toward A. If there is a small increase in full-time employment from the third equilibrium, C, firms will respond in the same way, replacing full-timers with part-timers until they return to C. Given a small *decrease* in full-time employment from C, firms will temporarily find full-time employment less expensive than part-time and will once more move back toward C. However, a small perturbation in either direction from the second equilibrium, B, will lead firms to adjust away from B, toward either A or C. Thus, there are two stable equilibria: the corner solution of all part-time employment and an interior solution. The interior solution is more economically plausible, since in fact retailers employ both part-time and full-time workers, often in the same jobs. But in general the model implies that two subregimes exist: to the right of the maximum is a regime of stable interior equilibria, whereas to the left of the maximum is a regime in which firms come to rest only when they have eliminated all full-time employment.

The graphic representation of the labor market is ideal for looking at the comparative statics and dynamics of change. Consider the effects of an increase in the unemployment rate on the interior equilibrium (Figure A.2). Higher unemployment shifts the entire turnover difference curve downward, since it decreases the probability of finding a full-time job at every rate of full-time employment. Employers formerly at rest at C find themselves on the new turnover difference schedule at point D. Since they are below the equal cost locus, part-time employment is less expensive, and they replace full-time with part-time workers, moving along the turnover difference schedule until they reach a new equilibrium at E. A higher unemployment rate leads to a higher rate of part-time employment, as is observed in actual retail labor markets. A decrease in unemployment has the opposite effect.

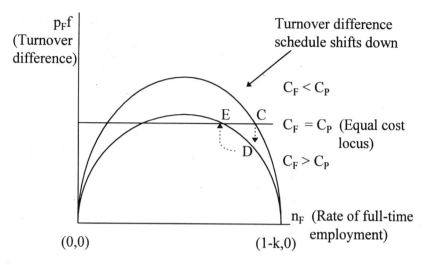

$p_F f$ (Turnover difference)

Turnover difference schedule shifts down

$C_F < C_P$

$C_F = C_P$ (Equal cost locus)

$C_F > C_P$

n_F (Rate of full-time employment)

(0,0)   (1-k,0)

FIGURE A.2
Static and Dynamic Effects of an Increase in Unemployment

Note that a sufficiently large, positive unemployment shock (large enough that the maximum of the turnover difference schedule falls below the equal cost locus) will drive firms to zero full-time employment. Then, even if unemployment falls, firms will stay at the corner solution, since they optimize locally. The only ways to get out of the corner would be through a dramatic increase in compensation of part-timers (to above full-time levels) or some sort of coordinated effort by firms. Firms become trapped in the part-time-only regime.

This framework can also be used to examine the effects of other kinds of changes. For example, suppose training costs fall, perhaps due to de-skilling automation. This is reflected in an upward shift in the equal cost locus (Figure A.3), since it decreases the cost of training two heads as well as the cost of turnover. Then firms will move from C to a new equilibrium at D. Thus, a drop in training costs leads to heavier use of part-time employment in this model, a connection suggested by Eileen Appelbaum (1987).

A variant of this model can describe a situation like the insurance industry. In this variant, part-time jobs are in short supply, and some people are working full-time involuntarily. Involuntary full-timers have a higher probability of quitting, based on their chance of finding a part-time job.

A convenient way of representing this variant in combination with the original model is to add a new turnover difference axis extending downward from the origin (Figure A.4). This new axis measures $e_p f_p$, the

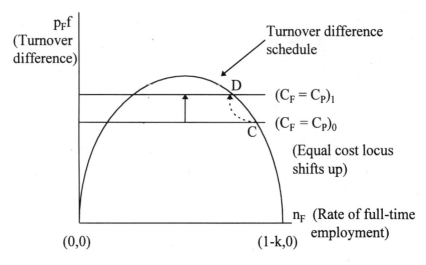

FIGURE A.3
Effects of a Decrease in Training Costs

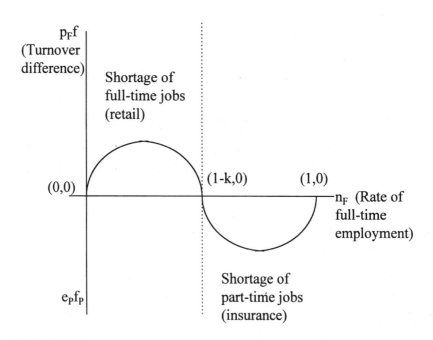

FIGURE A.4
Turnover Difference Schedules in Retail and Insurance Labor Markets

product of the fraction of full-timers who want a part-time job times the probability of finding a part-time job. Then a new turnover difference schedule can be drawn between $n_F = 1$ (where there are no part-time jobs to be had) and $n_F = 1 - k$ (where everybody who wants a part-time job has one).

A given labor market will fall on one or the other of the two turnover difference schedules. A labor market will fall on the second schedule if even when there is no difference in turnover, it is more expensive to employ part-timers than full-timers, so that the equal cost locus falls below the zero-turnover-difference axis. This will be true when per-hour compensation costs are greater for part-time employees than full-time, and/or when training costs are high (so that the costs of training an extra head are prohibitive)—both features of the salaried labor markets in insurance. It is easy to verify that this variant model acts like an insurance labor market over the business cycle: when unemployment rises, part-time employment falls.

NOTES

1. In this book, two definitions of part-time employment are used. Throughout discussions of economic theory and the interview data, the term is used to refer to jobs that in the short run usually involve fewer than the standard number of hours per week considered full-time by a given employer. This job-centered definition is chosen because the book primarily examines why and to what extent employers use part-time work. Thirty-five hours turns out to work well as a general cutoff point, although each company has its own definition of full-time work. Part-time employment is taken to include involuntary part-time positions and temporary reductions in hours, since both situations involve a firm's decision to create a part-time job—if only temporarily.

In addition to jobs that fall below the hours cutoff, jobs that involve full-time hours but are classified as part-time are considered to be part-time. For example, a grocery store manager reported that about 15 percent of his part-time employees were working 40 hours a week in order to deal with a severe labor shortage. Yet they are still classified as part-time since they have not been promoted to full-time positions and therefore receive lower hourly pay, fewer benefits, and a smaller number of guaranteed hours than full-timers. It seems appropriate to view these workers as part-time.

Virtually all statistical results cited in the book draw on household data that use a second, person-based definition of part-time employment: the U.S. Bureau of Labor Statistics (BLS) definition of persons working "part-time schedules" as those working less than 35 hours a week, except for the usually full-time workers who are working part-time for noneconomic reasons (including a legal or religious holiday, vacation, temporary illness, bad weather, industrial dispute, or a job for which regular full-time hours are less than 35 hours per week). In particular, all results based on the BLS's Current Population Survey or *Employment and Earnings* use this person-based definition.

Until 1994, the BLS classified part-timers as voluntary or involuntary according to how they answer the question, "Why are you working less than 35 hours a week?" Persons reporting the reason as slack work, material shortages or repairs, a job that started or ended during the survey week, or inability to find full-time work were considered involuntary, or "part-time for economic reasons"; all others were considered voluntary. In 1994, the BLS also began to count as voluntary anyone who said he or she did not want, or was not available for full-time work (these questions were not asked in earlier years).

Of course, the BLS counts as involuntary part-time workers only those who would prefer a full-time job in their present circumstances. For example, a woman who can only work part-time because she is unable to find day care is a voluntary part-timer by this criterion. Presser and Baldwin (1980), who surveyed mothers with children under five, discovered that one-quarter of those employed part-time felt they were blocked from working more hours by the unavailability of day care.

On the other hand, because the BLS definition does not ask part-time workers whether they would prefer a full-time job at the same rate of pay and benefits, many involuntary part-time workers are presumably expressing a desire for greater hourly compensation as well as for more hours.

In my interviews, involuntary part-time employment and involuntary full-time employment were gauged by asking whether part-time workers would prefer having full-time jobs and asking whether full-time workers would prefer having part-time jobs. This concept is somewhat different from the BLS definition. However, it is simple and readily understood by the managers and workers interviewed.

2. Note that involuntary part-time employment may be understated because it includes only workers who are unable to work full-time for narrowly economic reasons and not, for example, people unable to find care for their dependents.

3. The rate of involuntary part-time employment is given here as a proportion of those at work, rather than those employed, because persons employed but temporarily away from work are excluded from the total of involuntary part-time workers according to BLS definitions.

4. U. S. Bureau of Labor Statistics, *Employment and Earnings,* January 1994. Throughout the book, where the source for statistics such as this one are not otherwise given, it is the BLS's *Employment and Earnings.*

5. The figure of 42 percent results from a univariate analysis. The effects of other variables correlated with part-time status may contribute to the size of this estimate.

6. Another useful European source on this debate is Standing (1988).

7. Bluestone and Harrison (1986) define low-wage jobs as those with total annual wages and salaries below half of the 1973 median, inflated by the Consumer Price Index. The fact that these and other researchers define a job as a person's total complement of paid work, regardless of how many jobs are involved, is one of the peculiarities of this literature, induced by data limitations. See Loveman and Tilly (1988).

8. These two types do not exhaust the kinds of part-time employment. For example, work-sharing in manufacturing and construction represents a third

type. However, secondary and retention part-time jobs are the major species of part-time work in retail and insurance, and probably in the service industries as a whole.

9. The terms "good" and "bad" are used as shorthand for high-wage, high-productivity jobs and low-wage, low productivity jobs, respectively.

CHAPTER 2

1. Beginning in January 1994, the U.S. Bureau of Labor Statistics added new questions to the Current Population Survey in order to redefine involuntary part-time employment. The redefinition reduces the measured level of involuntary part-time work. This revised survey yielded an estimate of 5 million involuntary part-time workers for 1993. In this book, I use the old definition of involuntary part-time work, since only it is comparable with the last several decades of data. The change in the Current Population Survey is further discussed in Chapter 7.

2. I regressed the rate of part-time employment on independent variables constructed from the unemployment rate, the part-time/full-time hourly wage gap, the size of fringe benefit costs compared to wage costs, and a time trend. In ordinary least squares and two-stage least squares models, the estimated coefficients on the compensation (wage and fringe) variables are negative, indicating that larger gaps in wages and fringes are associated with lower utilization of part-time employment. Coefficients were negative and significant at the .01 level in ordinary least squares regression; they remained negative but lost significance in two-stage least squares. Furthermore, the time trend in part-time employment increases slightly after accounting for changes in compensation. These are puzzling findings, but certainly provide no evidence that growing full-time wage or benefit costs are pushing employers to switch to part-time workers. For a more detailed and technical description of the analysis, see Tilly (1991a).

3. The size of this change may be affected by the change in the Current Population Survey's occupational classification in 1983. Examination of changes from 1982 to 1983 suggests that the growth in importance of these occupational groups is likely to be understated.

4. Retail figures from unpublished data were provided by Thomas Nardone of the U.S. Bureau of Labor Statistics. Percentages include wage and salary workers only.

5. Computed from Current Population Survey computer tapes.

6. See Chapter 4 of Tilly (1989) for a shift-share analysis examining the contribution of eating and drinking places to the growth of part-time employment in retail.

7. Computed with data from U.S. Bureau of Economic Analysis, *Survey of Current Business,* December 1974 and February 1994. The consumer price index was used to adjust output value for inflation.

8. Computed with data from *Progressive Grocer*'s "Annual Report of the Grocery Industry," April 1976 and April 1993. The consumer price index for foods and beverages was used to adjust for inflation.

9. Insurance percentage was computed from Current Population Survey computer tapes.

10. Percentage growth is a geometric mean computed from U.S. Bureau of Economic Analysis, *Survey of Current Business,* July 1970 and July 1987, using U.S. Commerce Department deflators. Only combined figures for finance and insurance are published for 1969. Output figures for insurance have not been published since 1987.

11. Companies were selected from the Boston and Pittsburgh Yellow Pages and from referrals by other informants. In addition to the 31 companies where I conducted interviews, representatives of 3 companies (1 insurance company, 1 supermarket chain, and 1 convenience store chain) declined to be interviewed, yielding a response rate of 91 percent.

CHAPTER 4

1. From unpublished U.S. Bureau of Labor Statistics data provided by Thomas Nardone.

2. Unfortunately, because of the open-ended character of the interviews and because the concepts of secondary and retention part-time work emerged only from analysis subsequent to the interviews, there are substantial amounts of missing data. For the tabulations referred to here, see Tilly (1992).

3. "Statistically significant" is used as shorthand for "statistically significant at the 5% level."

4. The models control for numerous personal characteristics, including gender, position in family, age, race, Hispanic origin, education, and region of residence. Results are not shown here but are available from the author upon request.

5. In F-tests of differences in regression coefficients, the hypothesis that the overall set of coefficients is identical in the two samples was rejected at the 1 percent level in both cases.

CHAPTER 5

1. The latter type of involuntary part-time employment is much more typical of construction and manufacturing.

2. For a more detailed and technical discussion of these results, including tables, see Tilly (1992).

3. These results were also confirmed with probit analysis, a special method of regression. See Tilly (1992).

4. Technically, this variable is the individual's standardized residual from an ordinary least squares regression of the natural log of hourly wages on years of education and experience, and the square of years of experience. I computed two versions of this variable, one based on pooling part-time and full-time workers, and one based on residuals from separate regressions on the two groups. Results were qualitatively identical for both versions.

5. All estimated coefficients are significant at the 1 percent level, except for full-time men.

6. These reasons apply to workers' inability to find a full-time job, not to temporary hours reductions. As noted above, the involuntary part-time em-

ployment observed in the sampled companies invariably had the former character.

7. Calculated from Table 7 of U.S. Bureau of Labor Statistics (1987), based on the assumption that the average spell length in each interval is given by the midpoint of the interval. "Spells" actually refers to total weeks of involuntary part-time employment, not to continuous periods of involuntariness.

CHAPTER 6

1. Computed from Current Population Survey computer tape.

2. The personnel director who offered this description added that these practices are "beginning to change," for reasons that need not concern us here.

3. The net impact of other costs is ambiguous. Part-timers have the additional cost of high turnover, whereas full-timers bring the cost of diminished schedule flexibility.

CHAPTER 7

1. That is, the coefficient on the unemployment remains statistically significant at the 5 percent level. Regressions are on annual data, 1956–93. The models include a constant and time trend. To correct for serial correlation, models either incorporate a one-period lag term for the dependent variable, or use the Cochrane-Orcutt correction. Results are similar with either correction. The independent variable is the proportion of the at-work population employed part-time. The hypothesis is rejected even more resoundingly for involuntary part-time employment in particular.

2. An F-test on the significance of the set of coefficients on industry dummy variables rejects the second hypothesis at the 1 percent level. Models are as described in n. 1.

3. Bednarzik (1975) explains these facts by temporary work-hour reductions. His explanation surely has some truth but is less satisfactory today than it was in 1975, given the decreasing proportion of part-time employment accounted for by such hours reductions.

4. To be sure, the interviews revealed plenty of other changes, such as the broadening of retention part-time employment at Eternal Life (a long-term but small change), and the reduction of secondary part-time employment by retailers in response to the tightening labor market (in some cases a large adjustment but presumably not long-term).

CHAPTER 8

1. Taking imperfect competition into account would modify this outcome quantitatively but not qualitatively. More importantly, different macroeconomic models lead to different predictions of the effects of these changes in general equilibrium—that is, after all the ripples have worked their way through the economy. Macroeconomic adjustment certainly will not rectify the maldistributive effects. It is reasonable, although far from incontestable, to suppose that one likely

outcome is that upward redistribution will also lead to slower growth or even economic contraction, *ceteris paribus.*

2. These figures include agricultural workers. Thus, they differ from figures cited elsewhere in the book. For policy purposes, the most complete measure of part-time employment is appropriate.

3. The estimate for full-timers (77 percent) is calculated from Shank (1986, Table 3) and May 1985 Current Population Survey data reported in *Employment and Earnings,* June 1986. It is assumed that the fraction of workers stating a preference for less hours and less money is proportional to the fraction who are involuntary full-timers, with the constant of proportionality common across industries.

4. The estimated responsiveness measures (elasticities) relate the ratio of part-time to full-time employment (Ehrenberg et al. 1988) or the logarithm of that ratio (Owen 1979) to the logarithm of the ratio of hourly wages. The elasticities are assumed constant in the relevant ranges. Ehrenberg et al. actually estimate a separate wage differential for each of 46 industries. The 12.6% differential cited here is an employment-weighted average of the industry differentials. Note that Owen's estimation uses 1973 data; Ehrenberg et al's is based on 1984 data. Since the raw wage differential has changed little since 1973 (see Figure 2.2), there is no particular reason to think that estimates based on more current data would differ greatly.

5. The earnings differential figures for the two countries are not strictly comparable, because the Canadian figure is based on mean wages, while the U.S. figure is based on median wages. This discrepancy probably means that the difference between the two countries is understated, since wage distributions are right-skewed. Part of the reason for the very small Canadian part-time/full-time differential for unionized jobs is that these jobs tend to be concentrated in particular industries and occupations. However, the part-time/full-time wage differential can be large even within industries. For example, the unweighted average of the wage differentials within 8 selected service industries in Ontario in 1975 was 19 percent (Commission of Inquiry 1983, 164). For evidence on the similarity of the profiles of part-timers in the two countries, consider the following: in 1981, 78 percent of Canadian part-timers worked in trade and services, compared to 79 percent in the United States; 72 percent of part-time workers in Canada were women and 44 percent were less than 25 years of age, compared to 66 percent and 47 percent, respectively, in the United States.

6. Setting goals for involuntary full-time employment requires the measurement of such employment over time, as proposed below.

7. This approximation is apt, since involuntary part-timers work an average of 22 hours per week. A full underemployment rate would also count discouraged workers.

8. In addition to multiple forms of representation, Heckscher (1988) describes the other key elements of associational unionism as: (1) a focus on principles and general goals that are negotiated with the membership; (2) increased internal education and participation; (3) a wider choice of tactics other than the strike; and (4) the formation of extended alliances with interests within and outside the union movement.

9. One example is the 1987 agreement between German unions and manufacturing employers to reduce the work week to 37 hours in metalworking.

10. This agreement was attained partly under government threats of strict regulation of the industry if no national collective bargaining agreement was reached.

APPENDIX

1. The second derivative of D is not necessarily negative throughout the interval, so the schedule is not necessarily concave to the origin as shown (even though it only has a single maximum). However, the static and dynamic properties of the model to be addressed below depend only on the first derivative, so no generality is lost in drawing the schedule this way.

2. This point will not exist if part-timers are less costly even with 100 percent turnover. This possibility is unrealistic and not terribly interesting.

REFERENCES

Abraham, Katharine G. 1990. "Restructuring the Employment Relationship: The Growth of Market-Mediated Work Arrangements." In Katharine G. Abraham and Robert B. McKersie, eds., *New Developments in the Labor Market: Toward a New Institutional Paradigm* (Cambridge, MA, and London: MIT Press), pp. 85–119.

AFL-CIO, Committee on the Evolution of Work. 1985. *The Changing Situation of Workers and Their Unions*. Washington, DC: AFL-CIO.

AFL-CIO, Industrial Union Department. 1986. *The Polarization of America: The Loss of Good Jobs, Falling Incomes, and Rising Inequality*. Washington, DC: AFL-CIO.

Akerlof, George A., and William T. Dickens. 1982. "The Economic Consequences of Cognitive Dissonance." *American Economic Review*, Vol. 72, No. 3, 307–19.

Albelda, Randy, and Chris Tilly. 1994. *Glass Ceilings and Bottomless Pits: Women, Income, and Poverty in Massachusetts*. Boston: Women's Statewide Legislative Network.

American Council of Life Insurance. 1992. *Life Insurance Fact Book Update, 1992*. Washington, DC: ACOLI.

———. 1985. *Life Insurance Fact Book Update, 1985*. Washington, DC: ACOLI.

Appelbaum, Eileen. 1987. "Restructuring Work: Temporary, Part-Time, and At-Home Employment." In Heidi Hartmann, Robert Kraut, and Louise Tilly, eds., *Computer Chips and Paper Clips: Technology and Women's Employment*, Vol. 2 (Washington, DC: National Academy of Sciences), pp. 269–310.

Appelbaum, Eileen and Judith Gregory. 1988. "Union Responses to Contingent Work: Are Win-Win Outcomes Possible?" in Kathleen Christensen and Mary Murphree, eds., *Flexible Workstyles: A Look at Contingent Labor,*

Conference Summary, U.S. Department of Labor Women's Bureau (Washington, DC: U.S. Government Printing Office), pp. 69–75.

Barrett, Michelle, and Mary McIntosh. 1980. "The 'Family Wage': Some Problems for Socialists and Feminists." *Capital and Class,* No. 11, pp. 51–72.

Bednarzik, Robert. 1983. "Short Workweeks during Economic Downturns." *Monthly Labor Review,* June, pp. 3–11.

———. 1975. "Involuntary Part-Time Work: A Cyclical Analysis." *Monthly Labor Review,* September, pp. 12–18.

Berger, Suzanne, and Michael Piore. 1980. *Dualism and Discontinuity in Industrial Society.* Cambridge, England: Cambridge University Press.

Best, Michael. 1990. *The New Competition: Institutions of Industrial Restructuring.* Cambridge, MA: Harvard University Press.

Blank, Rebecca. 1990. "Are Part-Time Jobs Bad Jobs?" in Gary Burtless, ed., *A Future of Lousy Jobs? The Changing Structure of U.S. Wages* (Washington, DC: Brookings Institution).

Blank, Rebecca. 1986. "Part-Time Work and Wages Among Adult Women." *Proceedings of the 39th Annual Meeting of the Industrial Relations Research Association* (Madison, WI: IRRA), pp. 479–86.

Bluestone, Barry, and Bennett Harrison. 1986. *The Great American Jobs Machine: The Proliferation of Low-Wage Employment in the U.S. Economy.* Washington, DC: U.S. Congress, Joint Economic Committee, December.

Bronfenbrenner, Kate. 1988a. "Bargaining for Part-Time and Temporary Workers." *Labor Notes,* August, pp. 11–12.

———. 1988b. "Organizing the Contingent Workforce." New York State School of Industrial and Labor Relations, Cornell University. Prepared for presentation to the AFL-CIO Organizing Department, September 14.

Buhle, Mary Jo. 1981. *Women and American Socialism, 1870–1920.* Urbana, IL: University of Illinois Press.

Bulow, Jeremy I., and Lawrence H. Summers. 1986. "A Theory of Dual Labor Markets with Application to Industrial Policy, Discrimination, and Keynesian Unemployment" *Journal of Labor Economics,* Vol. 4, No. 3, pp. 376–414.

Bureau of National Affairs. 1986. *The Changing Workplace: New Directions in Staffing and Scheduling.* Washington, DC: BNA.

Burns, William. 1982. "Changing Corporate Structure and Technology in Retail Food," In Donald Kennedy, Charles Craypo, and Mary Lehman, eds., *Labor and Technology: Union Response to Changing Environments* (State College, PA: Department of Labor Studies, Pennsylvania State University) pp. 27–53.

Burtless, Gary, ed. 1990. *A Future of Lousy Jobs? The Changing Structure of U.S. Wages.* Washington, DC: The Brookings Institution.

Card, David E. and Alan B. Krueger. 1995. *Myth and Measurement: The New Economics of the Minimum Wage.* Princeton, NJ: Princeton University Press.

Carré, Françoise. 1993. "Temporary, Short-Term, and Part-Time Employment in French Banks and Insurance Companies During the 1980s: An Institutionalist Approach." Ph.D. dissertation, Department of Urban Studies and Planning, Massachusetts Institute of Technology.

Carré, Françoise, Virginia duRivage, and Chris Tilly. 1995. "Piecing Together the Fragmented Workplace: Unions and Public Policy on Part-Time and Temporary Employment." In Lawrence G. Flood, ed., *Unions and Public Policy*. (Westport, CT: Greenwood Press).

————. 1994. "Representing the Part-Time and Contingent Workforce: Challenges for Unions and Public Policy." In Sheldon Friedman et al., eds., *Restoring the Promise of American Labor Law* (Ithaca, NY: Industrial and Labor Relations Press), pp. 314–23.

Castro, Janice. 1993. "Disposable Workers." *Time,* March 29, pp. 43–47.

Christopherson, Susan. 1988. "Production Organization and Worktime: The Emergence of a Contingent Labor Market." In Kathleen Christensen and Mary Murphree, eds., *Flexible Workstyles: A Look at Contingent Labor* (*Conference Summary*) (Washington, DC: U.S. Department of Labor, Women's Bureau), pp. 34–38.

Cobble, Dorothy Sue. 1991. "Organizing the Postindustrial Workforce: Lessons from the History of Waitress Unionism." *Industrial and Labor Relations Review,* Vol. 44, No. 3, pp. 419–36.

————. 1990. "Union Strategies for Organizing and Representing the New Service Workforce." Paper presented at the 43rd annual conference of the Industrial Relations Research Association, Washington, DC, December 28.

Cohany, Sharon R., Anne E. Polivka, and Jennifer M. Rothgeb. 1994. "Revisions in the Current Population Survey Effective January 1994." *Employment and Earnings,* February, pp. 13–37.

Colatosti, Camille. 1990. "Department Store Clerks Organize Against Sales Quotas; Vote UAW." *Labor Notes,* June, pp. 4 and 10.

Commission of Inquiry into Part-Time Work. 1983. *Part-Time Work in Canada.* Ottawa, Ontario: Minister of Labour, Canada.

Cornell University. Annual. *Operating Results of Food Chains.* Ithaca, NY: New York State College of Agriculture, Cornell University.

Costello, Cynthia B. 1989. "The Clerical Homework Program at the Wisconsin Physicians Service Insurance Corporation." In Eileen Boris and Cynthia R. Daniels, eds., *Homework: Historical and Contemporary Perspectives on Paid Labor at Home* (Champaign-Urbana, IL: University of Illinois Press), pp. 198–214.

Dente, Leonard A. 1977. *Veblen's Theory of Social Change.* New York: Arno Press.

Deutermann, William V., Jr., and Scott Campbell Brown. 1978. "Voluntary Part-Time Workers: A Growing Part of the Labor Force." *Monthly Labor Review,* June, pp. 3–10.

Doeringer, Peter, and Michael Piore. 1971. *Internal Labor Markets and Manpower Analysis.* Armonk, NY: M. E. Sharpe.

Drucker, Peter. 1991. "The New Productivity Challenge." *Harvard Business Review,* Vol. 69, No. 6, pp. 69–78.

Dugger, William M. 1988. "Radical Institutionalism: Basic Concepts." *Review of Radical Political Economics,* Vol. 20, No. 1, pp. 1–20.

duRivage, Virginia L. 1992. "Social Policy and the Contingent Workforce." In

Virginia L. duRivage, ed., *New Policies for the Part-Time and Contingent Workforce* (Armonk, NY: M. E. Sharpe), pp. 89–121.

Ehrenberg, Ronald, Pamela Rosenberg, and Jeanne Li. 1988. "Part-time Employment in the United States." In Robert A. Hart, ed., *Employment, Unemployment, and Labor Utilization* (Boston: Unwin Hyman), pp. 256–87.

Employee Benefits Research Institute. 1994. *Characteristics of the Part-Time Workforce.* Special Report and Issue Brief, No. 149. May.

Fierman, Jaclyn. 1994. "The Contingency Work Force." *Fortune,* January 24, pp. 30–36.

Flood, Lawrence G. 1987. "Part-Time Faculty and Staff: A Union Perspective." Paper presented at the 41st annual conference of the New York Political Science Association, New York, April 3–4.

Freeman, Richard, and James Medoff. 1984. *What Do Unions Do?* New York: Basic Books.

Glazer, Nona Y. 1993. *Women's Paid and Unpaid Labor: The Work Transfer in Health Care and Retailing.* Philadelphia: Temple University Press.

Harrison, Bennett, and Barry Bluestone. 1988. *The Great U-Turn: Corporate Restructuring and the Polarizing of America.* New York: Basic Books.

Hart, Robert A. 1984. *The Economics of Non-Wage Labour Costs.* London: George Allen and Unwin.

Hartmann, Heidi and Roberta Spalter-Roth. 1993. "The Real Employment Opportunities of Women Participating in AFDC: What the Market Can Provide," paper presented at Women and Welfare Reform: Women's Poverty, Women's Opportunities, and Women's Welfare—A Policy Conference to Break Myths and Create Solutions, Institute for Women's Policy Research, Washington, DC, October 23.

Heckscher, Charles. 1988. *The New Unionism.* New York: Basic Books.

Hochschild, Arlie Russell. 1983. *The Managed Heart: Commercialization of Human Feeling.* Berkeley: University of California.

Ichniowski, Bernard, and Anne E. Preston. 1985. "New Trends in Part-Time Employment." *Proceedings of the 38th Annual Meeting of the Industrial Relations Research Association* (Madison, WI: IRRA), pp. 60–71.

International Labour Office. 1989. "Part-Time Work." *Conditions of Work Digest,* Vol. 8, No. 1.

———. 1986. "Flexibility in Working Time." *Conditions of Work Digest,* Vol. 5, No. 2.

Kahn, Shulamit, and Kevin Lang. 1992. "Constraints on the Choice of Work Hours: Agency vs. Specific Capital." *Journal of Human Resources,* Vol. 27, No. 4, pp. 661–78.

Kahne, Hilda. 1985. *Reconceiving Part-Time Work.* Totowa, NJ: Rowman and Allanheld.

King, Jack, and Sue McElligott. 1994. Testimony at Massachusetts Department of Employment and Training, Board of Review Hearing, Boston, MA, July 27.

Kleingartner, Archie, and Alan Paul. 1992. "Member Attachment and Union Effectiveness in Arts and Entertainment." Paper presented at the 44th annual meeting of the Industrial Relations Research Association, New Orleans, January 3.

Kochan, Thomas A., Harry C. Katz, and Robert B. McKersie. 1986. *The Transformation of American Industrial Relations.* New York: Basic Books.

Krugman, Paul. 1990. *The Age of Diminished Expectations: U.S. Economic Policy in the 1990s.* Washington, DC: Washington Post.

Levine, Hermine Zagat. 1987. "Alternative Work Schedules: Do They Meet Workforce Needs? Part 1." *Personnel,* February, pp. 57–62.

Levitan, Sar A., and Elizabeth Conway. 1988. "Part-Timers: Living on Half Rations." *Challenge,* May–June, pp. 9–16.

Lewis-Munroe, Frances. 1994. President, Service Employees International Union Local 535. Conversation with author, Cambridge, MA, February 23.

Lindbeck, Assar, and Dennis J. Snower. 1985. "Explanations of Unemployment." *Oxford Review of Economic Policy,* Vol. 1, No. 2, pp.34–59.

Loveman, Gary, and Chris Tilly. 1988. "Good Jobs or Bad Jobs: What Does the Evidence Say?" *New England Economic Review,* January–February, pp. 46–65.

March, James G., and Herbert A. Simon. 1993. "Organizations Revisited." *Industrial and Corporate Change,* Vol. 2, No. 3, pp. 299–316.

Martinez, Yvonne. 1994. Council Representative, American Federation of State, County, and Municipal Employees, Portland, Oregon. Conversation with author, Cambridge, MA, February 23.

Mason, Kent. 1988. "Closing the Gap," *Business and Health,* April, pp. 8–12.

Mellor, Earl, and Steven Haugen. 1986. "Hourly Paid Workers: Who They Are and What They Earn." *Monthly Labor Review,* February, pp. 20–26.

Meredith, Jane. 1963. "Persons Seeking Part-Time Jobs." *Employment and Earnings,* June, pp. iii–v.

Milkman, Ruth. 1980. "Organizing the Sexual Division of Labor." *Socialist Review,* No. 49 (January–February), pp. 95–150.

Mishel, Lawrence, and Jared Bernstein. 1993. "The Joyless Recovery: Deteriorating Wages and Job Quality in the 1990s." Briefing paper, Economic Policy Institute, Washington, DC, September.

Moffitt, Robert. 1984. "The Estimation of a Joint Wage-Hours Labor Supply Model." *Journal of Labor Economics,* Vol. 2 (October), pp. 550–66.

Montgomery, Mark. 1988. "On the Determinants of Employer Demand for Part-Time Workers." *Review of Economics and Statistics,* Vol. 70, No. 1 (February), pp. 112–16.

Morrow, Lance. 1993. "The Temping of America." *Time,* March 29, pp. 40–41.

Murphey, Janice D. 1989. "Business Contracting-out Practices: Evidence from a BLS Survey." Paper presented at the Eastern Economic Association Meetings, Baltimore, March 3–5.

Murray, Alan. 1994. "Mom, Apple Pie, and Small Business." *Wall Street Journal,* August 15, p. 1.

National Association of Convenience Stores. 1986. *Employee Turnover and Productivity in the Convenience Store Industry.* Alexandria, VA: NACS.

Nine to Five, National Association of Working Women. 1986. *Working at the*

Margins: Part-Time and Temporary Workers in the United States. Cleveland: Nine to Five.

Nollen, Stanley. 1982. *New Work Schedules in Practice: Managing Time in a Changing Society.* New York: Van Nostrand Reinhold.

Nollen, Stanley D., Brenda Broz Eddy, and Virginia Hider Martin. 1978. *Permanent Part-Time Employment: The Manager's Perspective.* New York: Praeger.

Nollen, Stanley D., and Virginia H. Martin. 1978. *Alternative Work Schedules, Part II: Part-Time Employment and Compressed Work Weeks.* New York: AMACOM Division of American Management Association.

Norwood, Janet L. 1987. "The Job Machine Has Not Broken Down." *The New York Times,* February 22.

Noyelle, Thierry. 1987a. *Beyond Industrial Dualism: Market and Job Segmentation in the New Economy.* Boulder, CO: Westview.

————. 1987b. "The New Technology and the New Economy: Some Implications for Equal Employment Opportunity." In Heidi Hartmann, Robert Kraut, and Louise Tilly, eds., *Computer Chips and Paper Clips: Technology and Women's Employment,* Vol. 2 (Washington, DC: National Academy of Sciences), pp. 373–94.

OECD Observer. 1988. "The Great American Jobs Machine," No. 152 (June–July), pp. 9–12.

Osterman, Paul. 1988. *Employment Futures: Reorganization, Dislocation, and Public Policy.* New York: Oxford University Press.

————. 1985. "Technology and White-Collar Employment: A Research Strategy." *Proceedings of the 38th Annual Meeting of the Industrial Relations Research Association* (Madison, WI: IRRA), pp. 52–59.

————. 1982. "Employment Structures Within Firms." *British Journal of Industrial Relations,* November, pp. 349–61.

————. 1975. "An Empirical Study of Labor Market Segmentation." *Industrial and Labor Relations Review,* Vol. 28, No. 4, pp. 508–23.

Owen, John D. 1979. *Working Hours: An Economic Analysis.* Lexington, MA: Lexington Books.

————. 1978. "Why Part-Timers Tend to Be in Low-Wage Jobs." *Monthly Labor Review,* June, pp. 11–14.

Pearce, Diana. 1985. "Toil and Trouble: Women Workers and Unemployment Compensation." *Signs: Journal of Women in Culture and Society,* Vol. 10, No. 3, pp. 439–59.

Phillips, Kevin. 1990. *The Politics of Rich and Poor: Wealth and the American Electorate in the Reagan Aftermath.* New York: Random House.

Piacentini, Joseph S., and Timothy J. Cerino. 1990. *EBRI Databook on Employee Benefits.* Washington, DC: Employee Benefits Research Institute.

Plewes, Thomas J. 1988. "Understanding the Data on Temporary Employment." In Kathleen Christensen and Mary Murphree, eds., *Flexible Workstyles: A Look at Contingent Labor (Conference Summary)* (Washington, DC: U.S. Department of Labor, Women's Bureau), pp. 9–13.

Presser, Harriet B., and Wendy Baldwin. 1980. "Child Care as a Constraint on

Employment: Prevalence, Correlates, and Bearing on the Work and Fertility Nexus." *American Journal of Sociology,* Vol. 85, No. 5, pp. 1202–13.

Progressive Grocer. 1993. "Annual Report of the Grocery Industry," April, pp. 43–107.

———. 1990. "Annual Report of the Grocery Industry," April, special supplement.

———. 1988. "Annual Report of the Grocery Industry," April, special supplement.

———. 1986. "The Changing Product Mix: Labor–Growing Pains," October, pp. 62–64.

———. 1977. "Annual Report of the Grocery Industry," April, pp. 34–216.

Rebitzer, James B. 1987. "The Demand for Part-Time Workers: Theory, Evidence, and Policy Implications." Mimeographed. University of Texas, Department of Economics, December.

Rebitzer, James B., and Lowell Taylor. 1991. "A Model of Dual Labor Markets When Product Demand is Uncertain." *Quarterly Journal of Economics,* Vol. 106, No. 4 (November), pp. 1373–83.

Repko, David V., and Joseph J. Martingale. 1988. "What the Future May Bring: A Retailer's Perspective." *Business and Health,* April, p. 18.

Richman, Dan. 1986. "Blues' Cooperation, Innovation Key to Retaining Industry Position." *Modern Healthcare,* January 31, pp. 40–46.

Rose, Robert L. 1994. "As Economy Grows, Cyclicals Keep Wary Eye on Costs." *Wall Street Journal,* April 18, p. B4.

Rosen, Sherwin. 1986. "The Theory of Equalizing Differences." In Orley Ashenfelter and Richard Layard, eds., *The Handbook of Labor Economics,* Vol. 1 (Amsterdam: North-Holland), pp. 641–92.

Rumberger, Russell, and Martin Carnoy. 1980. "Segmentation in the U.S. Labour Market—Its Effect on the Mobility and Earnings of Blacks and Whites." *Cambridge Journal of Economics,* Vol. 4, No. 2, pp. 117–32.

Samuelson, Paul. 1983. *Foundations of Economic Analysis.* Cambridge, MA: Harvard University Press. First published, 1945.

———. 1957. "Wages and Interest: A Modern Dissection of Marxian Economic Models." *American Economic Review,* Vol. 47, No. 6, 884–912.

Sansolo, Michael. 1987. "Take This Job . . . Please." *Progressive Grocer,* January, pp. 75–78.

Schellhardt, Timothy D. 1992. "Temporary Help Rebound May Prove to be Permanent." *Wall Street Journal,* July 28, pp. B4.

Schlesinger, Leonard, and James Heskett. 1991. "The Service-Driven Service Company." *Harvard Business Review,* Vol. 69, No. 5, pp. 71–81.

Schor, Juliet. 1992. *The Overworked American.* New York: Basic Books.

Service Employees International Union, Research Department. 1993. *Part-Time, Temporary, and Contracted Work: Coping with the Growing "Contingent" Workforce—A Guide to Organizing and Bargaining for Contingent Workers.* Washington, DC: SEIU.

Shank, Susan. 1986. "Preferred Hours of Work and Corresponding Earnings." *Monthly Labor Review,* November, pp. 40–44.

Shao, Maria. 1994. "New U.S. Workers: Flexible, Disposable." *Boston Globe,* April 3, pp. 1, 18.

Shellenbarger, Sue. 1994. "Many Employers Flout Family and Medical Leave Law." *Wall Street Journal,* July 26, pp. B1, B5.

———. 1993. "Work-Force Study Finds Loyalty is Weak, Divisions of Race and Gender are Deep." *Wall Street Journal,* September 3, pp. B1, B8.

Spalter-Roth, Roberta. 1994. Telephone interview with author, August 17.

Standing, Guy. 1988. *European Unemployment, Insecurity, and Flexibility: A Social Dividend Solution.* World Employment Program Working Paper, no. 23. Geneva: International Labor Office.

Steuernagel, Bruce, and Don Hilber. 1984. "Part-Time Workers." *Review of Labor and Economic Conditions* (now *Labor Market Review* of the Minnesota Department of Economic Security), Vol. 11, No. 3 (November).

Stinson, John F., Jr. 1986. "Moonlighting by Women Jumped to Record Highs." *Monthly Labor Review,* November, pp. 22–25.

Supermarket News. 1987. "Entry-Level Hiring Woes Spread." July 21.

———. 1985. "Part-Time Workers Scarce, Some Say." February 11.

Terry, Sylvia Lazos. 1981. "Involuntary Part-Time Work: New Information from the Current Population Survey." *Monthly Labor Review,* February, pp. 70–74.

Thurow, Lester. 1989. *Toward a High-Wage, High-Productivity Service Sector.* Washington, DC: Economic Policy Institute.

Tilly, Chris. 1992. "Dualism in Part-Time Employment." *Industrial Relations,* Vol. 31, No. 2 (Spring), pp. 330–47.

———. 1991a. "Reasons for the Continuing Growth of Part-Time Employment." *Monthly Labor Review,* Vol. 114, No. 3 (March), pp. 10–19.

———. 1991b. "Testimony on Part-Time and Temporary Work." Arbitration proceedings, U.S. Postal Service, National Association of Letter Carriers, and American Postal Workers Union, Washington, DC, May 7.

———. 1991c. "Understanding Income Inequality." *Sociological Forum,* Vol. 6, No.4 (December), pp. 739–56.

———. 1989. "Half a Job: How U.S. Firms Use Part-Time Employment." Ph.D. dissertation. Departments of Economics and Urban Studies and Planning, Massachusetts Institute of Technology.

Tilly, Chris, Barry Bluestone, and Bennett Harrison. 1986. "What Is Making American Wages More Unequal?" *Proceedings of the 39th Annual Meeting of the Industrial Relations Research Association.* (Madison, WI: IRRA), pp. 328–48.

U.S. Bureau of Economic Analysis. Monthly. *Survey of Current Business.*

U.S. Bureau of Labor Statistics. Monthly. *Employment and Earnings.*

———. 1994. "The Employment Situation: May 1994." *Bureau of Labor Statistics News,* June 3.

———. 1993. *Geographic Profile of Employment and Unemployment, 1992.* Bulletin 2428, July. Washington, DC: U.S. Government Printing Office.

———. 1991. *Employee Benefits in Small Private Establishments, 1990.* Bulletin 2388, August. Washington DC: U.S. Government Printing Office.

———. 1989. "Multiple Job Holding Reached Record High in May 1989." *Bureau of Labor Statistics News,* November 6.

———. 1988a. *Geographic Profile of Employment and Unemployment, 1987.* Bulletin 2305, April. Washington, DC: U.S. Government Printing Office.

———. 1988b. *Labor Force Statistics Derived from the Current Population Survey, 1948–87.* Bulletin 2307, August. Washington, DC: U.S. Government Printing Office.

———. 1987. *Linking Economic Problems to Economic Status.* Bulletin 2282, August. Washington, DC: U.S. Government Printing Office.

U.S. Census Bureau. 1993. *Money Income of Households, Families, and Persons in the United States: 1992.* Current Population Reports, Consumer Income, Series P60–184. Washington, DC: U.S. Department of Commerce, Economics and Statistics Administration, Bureau of the Census.

———. 1992. *Statistical Abstract of the United States, 1992.* Washington, DC: U.S. Government Printing Office.

———. 1980. *Census of Population, 1980,* "Detailed Population Characteristics," RC80-1-D1-A.

———. 1970. *Census of Population, 1970,* "Industrial Characteristics," PC(2)-7F.

———. 1960. *Census of Population, 1960,* "Industrial Characteristics," PC(2)-7F.

U.S. Chamber of Commerce. Annual. *Employee Benefits* (earlier titled *Fringe Benefits*).

U.S. Congressional Research Service. 1992. "Unemployment Compensation in the Group of Seven Nations: An International Comparison." Joint Committee Print. U.S. Senate, Committee on Finance (Print 102–88); U.S. House of Representatives, Committee on Ways and Means (Print 102–41). April.

U.S. Council of Economic Advisors. 1994. *Economic Report of the President.* Washington, DC: U.S. Government Printing Office.

U.S. Department of Commerce. 1994. *County Business Patterns, 1991.* Washington, DC: U.S. Government Printing Office

U.S. General Accounting Office. 1991. *Workers at Risk.* Washington, DC: U.S. Government Printing Office.

U.S. House of Representatives, Select Committee on Children, Youths, and Families. 1989. *U.S. Children and Their Families: Current Conditions and Recent Trends, 1989.* Washington, DC: U.S. Government Printing Office.

United University Professions. 1992. "Part-Time Concerns Are a Full-Time Issue," *UUP Voice,* May, p. 3.

Vaillancourt, Meg. 1994. "Part-Timers—The Teamsters Main Issue." *Boston Globe,* April 18, pp. 49–50.

Waldstein, Louise. 1989. "Service Sector Wages, Productivity, and Job Creation in the U.S. and Other Countries." Background paper. Washington, DC: Economic Policy Institute.

Wallace, Phyllis. 1989. *MBAs on the Fast Track: The Career Mobility of Young Managers.* Cambridge, MA: Ballinger.

Wall Street Journal. 1993. "Health Care Reform Means Change for Part-Timers." In "Labor Letter," September 28, p. 1.

————. 1992. "Mandating Part-Timers' Benefits: Discord Reigns over the Effects" In "Labor Letter," July 28, p. 1.

————. 1987. "Part-Time Workers Could Get Better Benefits under a New Hampshire Law." In "Labor Letter," March 24, p. 1.

Weiler, Paul C. 1990. *Governing the Workplace: The Future of Labor and Employment Law.* Cambridge MA: Harvard University Press.

Wial, Howard. 1994. "New Bargaining Structures for New Forms of Business Organization." In Sheldon Friedman, Richard W. Hurd, Rudolph A. Oswald, and Ronald L. Seeber, eds., *Restoring the Promise of American Labor Law* (Ithaca, NY: ILR Press), pp. 303–13.

————. 1993. "The Emerging Organizational Structure of Unionism in Low-Wage Services." *Rutgers Law Review,* Vol. 45, No. 3 (Spring), pp. 671–738.

Worsnop, Richard L. 1987. "Part-Time Work." *Editorial Research Reports,* Vol. 1, No. 22 (June 12), pp. 290–99.

INDEX

217